"For anyone who's ever struggled to find their place in the world, Bill Fellenberg's coming-of-age memoir offers the literary equivalent of a warm hug. Pulled between two cultures, two countries and two parents, he navigates his childhood with wry self-deprecation and gentle insight. *Sayonara Cowboy* is, at its heart, about the wars we fight—across oceans, in our own homes, within ourselves—and the love that is the only path to peace.

— BIZZY COY, *The New Yorker, Vulture*

In Sayonara Cowboy, Bill Fellenberg looks back in rueful amusement at his troubled youth as a boy with a complicated ethnic background and no parents in sight. After stumbles ranging from the embarrassing to the hilarious, Bill finds his equilibrium as a writer, a lover, and an adult. Written with skill and wit, Sayonara Cowboy is an enjoyable lesson for us all in how to forgive.

— RAYMOND P. SCHEINDLIN,
professor emeritus of Hebrew literature,
author of *The Book of Job* and other works of literary translation

Sayonara Cowboy explores the wild frontier of time and geography, of youth and love, of destiny and freedom. Fellenberg's recollections are spun into a personal tale stretched between a war-torn Japan and 20th century Americana, cross-stitched with the colorful fibers of finding identity, purpose, and artistic voice, a voice that is in turns innocent, honest and searching, and always humorous and poetic.

— TOBY POSER, film maker,
Where the Devil Roams, Hellbender, The Deeper You Dig

SAYONARA COWBOY

A MEMOIR

REDHAWK
PUBLICATIONS

SAYONARA COWBOY

A MEMOIR

BY WILLIAM YUKIKAZU FELLENBERG

Copyright © 2024 by William Yukikazu Fellenberg

All rights reserved. This book or parts thereof may not be reproduced in any form, stored in any retrieval system, or transmitted in any form by any means—electronic, mechanical, photocopy, recording, or otherwise—without prior written permission of the publisher, except as provided by United States of America copyright law. For permission requests, write to the publisher,

Redhawk Publications
The Catawba Valley Community College Press
2550 US Hwy 70 SE
Hickory NC 28602

ISBN: 978-1-959346-47-0

Library of Congress Number: 2024934675

Printed in the United States of America

Layout and Cover Design by Melanie Johnson Zimmermann

redhawkpublications.com

To Donna,
who's shown me how it's done, my first time around

William Yukikazu Fellenberg
with his mother, Sachiko

William K. Fellenberg

AUTHOR'S NOTE

When you invoke memory, it may offer you a soft shoulder to lean on, as you reminisce about those times you were kind, funny, or maybe even heroic. This is memory as your personal sidekick. It panders to you, screens your past through a soft lens. But when it's memory that summons you, it may not be so sweet. It might remind you of things you'd prefer to forget. This is memory as your personal prosecutor, lining up old shames for their perp walk in front of your pride. Whether or not you invoke memory, or it's memory that beckons you, there's usually more to it than what first meets your eye. That's why I can't help myself from looking again. In re-remembering, what comes to mind is a memory of a memory. Depending on your point of view, the original memory is either illuminated by, or contaminated by, imagination. My story is a memoir, not a deposition, and the facts of its circumstances are subject to matters of the heart. I've done my best to tell it as it was.

The author with his parents

The full moon, waxing,

invokes the sixth sense that makes

the first five worthwhile

-W.Y.F.-

Table of Contents

Part One
1. Encounter in a Distant Souvenir Shop 17
2. Japan 21
3. No Fighting 25
4. Children of the In Between 31
5. Sachiko Feels Tears Before Writing 37
6. Of Cowboys and Whales 41
7. America 45
8. Language Makes Us 51
9. Northbound and Back 57
10. Fugitives and Punishment 65
11. Arson, Martians, and Bankers 73
12. The Goodness of Mrs. Thurlur 83
13. A Boy Chooses 87
14. Sayonara 91

Part Two
15. Bachelor Life 101
16. Specks of Dust 107
17. Of Fish and Fisherman 111
18. A Stone Porch in an Old House 119
19. My Crooked Path 123
20. Foreigner Go Home 131
21. Adventures with the Ancient Ones 137
22. What I Took for Granted 145
23. Conga 151
24. Boom 159
25. Mortuary Rumors, Dream Girls, and Games of Chance ... 169
26. Things are Tough All Over 175
27. Artful Friendship 181
28. Mail Call From Yokohama 187
29. Dad's Girlfriends 195

30. Broadway Legend in my Own Mind 199

Part Three
31. Jungle Intrigues. 207
32. On the Farm 213
33. A Manasquan Kind of Day. 217
34. Legion of the Lonely and the Bitter. 221
35. Driving Ambitions. 227
36. Work Ethnic 231
37. When You Have It Made 237
38. Heart on Fire 241
39. Leaving the Nest. 251
40. Carpe Diem 255
41. Some Creatures Shed Their Skin 265
42. A Hatchling Pounds Inside My Head. 273
43. A Bounce off the Bottom 281
44. College Redux. 287

Part Four
45. When We Were Beautiful. 295
46. Nothing Lasts Forever, Much Less Love 301
47. Walking Wounded 309
48. Marriage Proposal, The Hard Way 313
49. Souls Old and New 315

Epilogue 321

Acknowledgments 323

About William Yukikazu Fellenberg 324

Part One
The Way to the Ocean

Show me the way to the ocean!
Break through half measures,
These small containers.

— *Rumi*

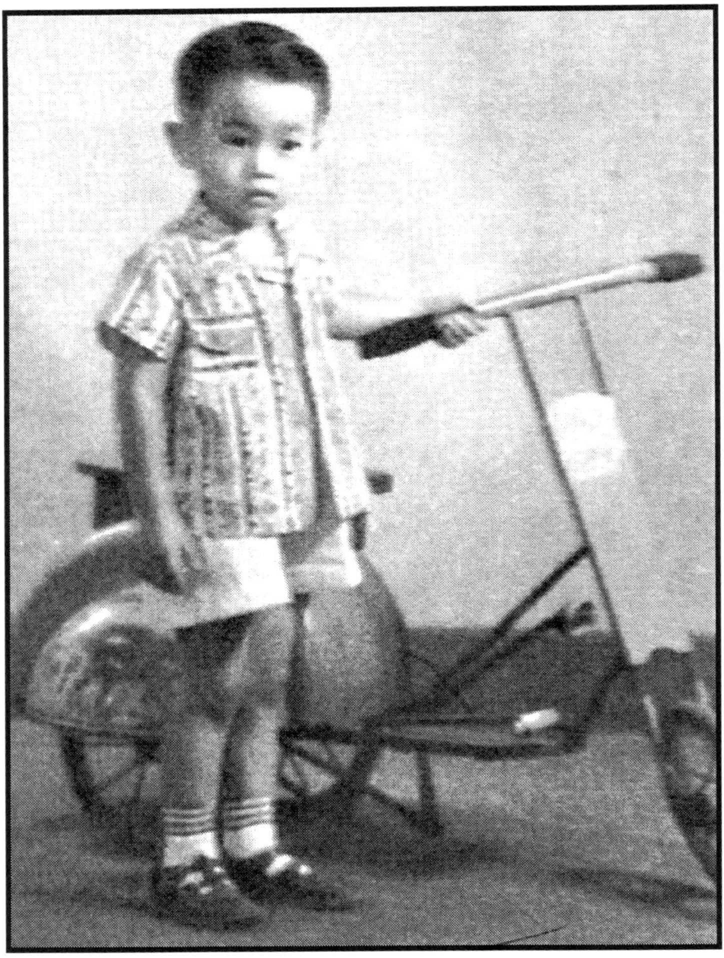

Chapter 1
ENCOUNTER IN A DISTANT SOUVENIR SHOP

I didn't wonder about how my parents met until they were both beyond my reach. When my father reminisced about Japan, he'd chatter freely about hikes up Mount Fuji or exploits with his army buddies. He would not, however, talk about my mother, Sachiko. I wanted to know how things were with them before I was born. It was too painful, he said. I could sympathize. She had sailed back to Yokohama when I was eight. Dad was the only witness who could say how it was before I was born. He'd deflect my questions as if I was prying. All I could wheedle out of him was that everything was great, then went bad when they came here. Details? He'd scowl and say he couldn't recall. His reluctance waned as he got older, but so did his memory. Sometimes, even when I didn't ask, he might blurt scenes from that world long gone—like the way one might find a misplaced shoe, by stumbling over it in the dark.

When Dad told me how he met Mom, he was ancient, a resident in Bethany Village, an assisted living facility. He recalled the long overdue story, sitting on the edge of his bed, while intermittently examining specimens from his collection of American buffalo nickels.

They met in 1947, a year before I was born, the beginning of my father's tour as a GI in Occupation Japan. Both barely understood or spoke the other's language. "But we managed to communicate," my father said, getting a little choked up.

He had poked into a Yokohama shop where Sachiko sold mementos—crude woodcuts of Mount Fuji and ceramic mugs bearing General Douglas MacArthur's likeness, replete with his signature sunglasses and corncob pipe. There were items in the shop of greater worth—bespoke silk kimonos and elegant art objects—a family's priceless keepsakes, now demeaned on consignment and sold to American soldiers. Those keepsakes were probably salvaged from the rubble after B-29 bombers incinerated the city in 1945.

That's when Hirohito stopped being a god, lost his empire that had enslaved half the world. The Japanese, once the occupiers, were now the occupied. Regardless, the soldier and the shop girl were unconcerned about such circumstances. At any moment, I expected Dad to say, "That's enough," and shut down, like he often did. Instead, he gathered himself and resumed talking, mostly repeating what he had just told me. "It was nice, in that shop, just us in the quiet."

◈ ◆ ◈

I imagine their conversation as a pleasant labor of halting utterances, hand signals, and body language—a dance that animated the underlying grace of their first encounter. Each must have felt the possibilities beyond the moment.

"What are you looking for, soldier?" Sachiko says, moving from behind her counter to the side where Bill examines souvenirs.

"I want to buy a gift for my parents."

"To give them a remembrance of your time here. Yes?"

"Not just a souvenir, but something that has ... heart," he says, then taps his chest. His attention hovers over a miniature tableau in which a peasant leads an ox. The tired beast tows a cart full of barrels. The tawny pieces in the set are at once finely detailed and delicate, yet muscular and earthy. "What's this?" he asks. "I think they'd like it."

She compliments him on his taste. "You have a good eye. It is hand carved in ivory. An old piece from long ago. Beautifully done."

Bill considers telling her that he thinks she is also beautifully done. But since he is only 19 years old and 8,000 miles away from the world he knows, he lacks the confidence to flirt. Instead, he points to the tiny barrels in the oxcart and shrugs. Again, he asks, "What's this?"

It takes a long time of meaningful gibberish and gesturing to convey that the peasant is a night-soil collector. The barrels—euphemistically called "honey buckets"—are laden with human waste. When that's understood, they share a burst of nervous laughter. But the soldier composes himself. He's been in Japan long enough to know that this practice isn't considered disgusting or vulgar. The waste will be transformed, endowed with purpose to fertilize rice paddies. Rice, and anything to do with it, presides at the top of a poetic arc that speaks to the identity, spirit, and meaning of being Japanese.

"I'll take the old man and his oxcart," the soldier says, and turns to another vitrine that displays enameled chopsticks, ceramic teacups, and the like. "I think my mother would like these, too."

Sachiko smiles, but not in an arch way. "Perfect," she says.

But perfection rarely lasts forever, much less love. Years later, the ivory carving of the night-soil collector and his oxcart will be sold in an antique shop in New Jersey, owned by Bill's mother, my grandmother. When, as an adolescent, I notice that the artifact is for sale, I won't resent my grandmother for it. It's different in America—the letting go. For example, there's no poetic arc that holds human waste as something precious. However, it does have a ubiquitous and mighty presence in American experience—as in *shit storms* or *shit shows*. Such events recur in my life, often of my own making.

Imagine memories inside old scrapbooks, warped and collecting dust in an old woman's attic. I want to save them from being gnawed by insects and time. When you peel back memory's skin, you must claim all of it while you can, even when it hurts. This is how you reconcile your shames and remember what was good, beautiful, and loving. This is how you find out who you are, and who you intend to become. This is the story I want to tell you.

Chapter 2
JAPAN

1952

If the wind blew a certain way, I might feel an unsettling presence as I stepped out of my family's house of bamboo and earth. I didn't know what it was, but it made me imagine ghosts, even in broad daylight. I was four years old, and much was beyond my knowing.

This was my Yokohama, where a self-proclaimed master race once launched a great navy to lord over the sea and to send armies abroad to rape and plunder. They were my mother's people.

To thwart them, the American airplanes dropped napalm bombs on the city, and burned it to the ground. They were my father's people.

Vanquished, the master race scrounged through dunes of waste for useful scraps. They no longer answered to Emperor Hirohito, the god who was forced to resign his position as a deity by a greater power—namely, General MacArthur, Supreme Commander of the Allied Forces. Now, seven years after crushing the Japanese Empire, the Allied Forces—mostly American GIs, along with a smattering of Aussie, British, and Indian troops—began their withdrawal. As Japan transitioned to self-government, the degree of misery felt by its people improved to a survivable state of scarcity. They recovered enough strength to quietly nurse their resentments. Perhaps that was the source of the lingering presence I sensed outside my family's home—the redolence of spent napalm and repressed humiliation.

Slivers of green began to break through what had been an unrelenting landscape of char and slag. Stunted trees groped upward, barely high enough to cast shadows. In neighborhoods that had been long silent, breezes again carried voices of everyday life. Decrepit buses groaned along a pocked road and kicked up dust. In the distance, iron wheels clacked and screeched on mended tracks. Rusty trains returned from the edge of extinction.

In government and military offices, in backrooms of brothels and bars, money increased its velocity. Commerce, once left for dead, was resuscitated by the black market of Occupation Japan. Crude shelters sprouted one after the other as homes for hundreds of thousands of the recently homeless. The structures were hardly more than wooden shacks huddled shoulder-to-shoulder as far as the eye could see.

My memories of a small family in Japan begin here.

◇ ◆ ◇

I lived with Mother and my grandfather, my *Sofu*. My grandmother died before I was born, left us for the Pure Land. When and how was a mystery to me. Sofu never said anything about her. Mother still grieved and calmed herself by kneeling before her *butsudan*, the home-made altar where she placed incense, tea, and other offerings in front of a small ceramic Buddha.

My father was stationed at an army base nearby and visited often. I understood that one day we would live together but not yet. Our house was crowded among others, all jostling for space along the city's dirt streets and footpaths. Father visited when his superiors allowed it and left when they demanded his return. I regarded his moustache and uniform as emblems of importance. I enjoyed a notion that he led armies, because he was a sergeant. During some visits he'd lift me on his back, and we'd go for a walk in the neighborhood. The men and women who circulated around their shacks or in the street stepped aside as we approached. They pretended to ignore us, holding their tongues until we passed them, and clucked insults from behind. Father said nothing and walked on. Children stared at us, gossiping among themselves. "The *gaijin* and his offspring smell like wet animals!"

The nastiest among them was a runt. Astride my father's shoulders, I towered over the lowly mouse of a boy. I gave him a threatening look as we passed. I fantasized what I would do if Father and I ruled over all of them. They should pay for their insults. I'd see the runt again another time when I was alone. I pedaled my scooter on a dirt path by an idle section of railroad tracks obscured by weeds. I sensed an opportunity for revenge. I stopped at a calculated distance from him, just in case I decided to retreat.

"Get out of my way or I'll run you over," I said.

"This is *my* path," he said. "Go away, or you'll have trouble."

"No, it's *my* path." Although I stood my ground, I was coiled to flee if he challenged me. Instead, Mouse turned and skittered away—my first victory.

When I returned home, I told Mother I had overcome a bully. She put down a spoon that she was preparing soup with and glared at me.

"No fighting," she said.

"But he picks on me," I said.

"I said no fighting."

Sofu had been listening and congratulated me, "Good for you, standing up for yourself."

"Your grandfather is making jokes. Stay away from them."

A few days later I pedaled to the railroad tracks to check on my path. The boy was there again! I intended to teach him a lesson until I saw two bigger boys approaching him. From a distance I watched them laugh, tousle each other's hair, and pat each other on the back. That's when the runt glanced in my direction, pointed at me, and shouted, "He's the one who says he owns this path!" The boys hesitated momentarily, then sprang toward me, shouting that they would kill me.

I turned my scooter and fled in the opposite direction, zigzagging across dirt streets and footpaths among the huddled homes. I thought I escaped the boys. When I stopped to catch my breath, the boys rushed through an alley and blocked my way. Again, they screeched and raised their fists, threatening to beat me. They called me an Amekoh, a dirty American, an ainoko, a mongrel, and a hafu, meaning only half of me was human. The runt hurled insults as he hopped around me. I trembled because of his two dark-eyed friends who loomed over me like giants.

I insisted I had nothing to do with Americans. "I'm just like you." I lied.

Mouse snapped at me. "You think we're stupid! We saw you perched on the shoulders of your Amekoh father!"

Laughing, they tossed road dust and more insults at me. I clung to the handlebars of my scooter and bowed my head, wishing I could disappear. If they had extended friendship to me, I would have eagerly accepted it. They let me slink away and guffawed when I tripped over my scooter and skinned my knee. When I was far enough away, I turned around and shouted, "Shinjimae!" It was the only curse I knew. It meant Die! Drop dead!

I slunk away and felt shame collect in me like sludge. Who but the lowest of the low would deny who his father was? I stomped on the ground, wishing it were the runt's face. When I returned home, Mother tended to my knee, dabbing the scrape with iodine. I boasted about the gang I had beaten up because they insulted our family. Sofu, always the eavesdropper, smirked, to let me know he didn't believe me.

Again, Mother said, "I told you, no fighting."

Chapter 3
NO FIGHTING

No fighting. Yet Imperial Japan had suckled itself on war. For longer than a generation and across an entire hemisphere, Japan built an empire by dancing in an orgy of plunder, rape, and murder of millions. On the other side of the ocean, the Americans settled an argument among themselves about the measures required to end the war—that the only way to overcome extreme brutality was to render more powerful and efficient brutality.

My father would say that such thinking made perfect sense for a world that had lost its mind. When he visited us, he and my grandfather would litigate the same argument, which bound them in a comfortable ritual. The two men knelt on opposite sides of the *chabudai*, the low table between them where they drank sake and bickered about politics and the war. It was a haphazard conversation because they too, barely understood each other. They kept their chattering friendly. The more they drank, the more garbled their positions. When their ritual argument ran its course, Father shrugged his shoulders. Sofu grimaced as if his sake had turned bitter. Perhaps he remembered too vividly how the Empire ended.

I watched them bottoms-up their cups of sake and toast *"Kanpai!"* to each another. Before long, the old one would list like a sinking ship and topple, his fall softened by the *tatami* on the floor. When they drank and argued, Mother embroidered a doily. Once finished, she would place it on her butsudan and kneel before it, praying to the *kami* – the spirits of the Pure Land, where our ancestors resided, a place where there is no fighting.

❧ ◆ ☙

I picture my mother when she was a teenager in early 1945, on a day when Japan's sky was welded shut, a canopy of hundreds of B-29 bombers, wing-to-wing, pledged to incinerate all below. Perhaps she, like other girls and boys, gazed up at the sky as planes thundered overhead and for now, passed Yokohama to bomb other cities targeted for the kill. She might have been among many of the naïve and curious who stood on Yokohama's streets, riverbanks, and bridges, laughing, shouting curses, and shaking their silly fists at the sky—the graveyard humor of the mindless young. In time, the bombers would torch sixty-four cities—neighborhood after neighborhood, house after house, body after body, nightmare upon nightmare.

⋄◆⋄

No fighting.

When it came Yokohama's turn to burn, there was no time to point at the sky or curse. Bombs swollen with jelled oil and gasoline tumbled onto the city's houses and buildings, tinderboxes of paper and wood. Then, in staccato sequence, one structure after the next burst into flames. Wild winds ranted through the streets and incited rogue flames to unite as one massive tsunami of fire and terror, engulfing the city and much of the Kanagawa prefecture beyond. Feckless fire departments reported for duty, only to be cremated in narrow streets and alleys. The burning surrounded nearly everyone. Families fled from their homes, carried babies, children, and whatever valuables they could grab from the flames.

Even before the firebombs, the Japanese war machine had shriveled, reduced to a humiliating cottage industry in which Hirohito's worshipers made weapons in their homes, no matter how primitive. The emperor commanded them to do so. They carved spears, sharpened knives, and fashioned table legs into clubs. Civilian defenders assembled at the beachheads to practice their resistance. Would-be warriors, rabbles of old men and women, gathered by the harbor to yell, spit, and rattle their bamboo spears and crude swords to repulse an invasion. Perhaps Sofu was one of the silly old men who joined the imaginary resistance by the ocean's edge. But those scoundrel Americans never arrived by sea or by land to take the Motherland. They attacked from the sky.

Stubbornly, Japan remained a red demon that would not die. Even after the atomic blast above Hiroshima in August '45, the fanatics among Japan's military leaders and ministers of state persuaded the hapless emperor to resist surrender. When another B-29 dropped the second bomb on Nagasaki three days later, the emperor reluctantly conceded.

What bells tolled in Hirohito's head when he heard his empire was undone by devices named "Little Boy" and "Fat Man?" Those monikers seemed better suited for characters in a children's story, not weapons that vaporized humans in an instant. The flash points in Hiroshima and Nagasaki became tombs filled with more of the dead and dying than seemed possible, all in two blinking blinks. Worse, those who survived the blast lived long enough to suffer a lolling death, their skins cooked and peeling from the poisoned flesh underneath.

While some leaders committed hara-kiri, Hirohito had no stomach for it. After all, can a god kill himself? Instead, the little man was obliged only to step down from his high horse, renounce his claim as a living god, and retire in tranquil splendor at the Imperial Palace. What bells tolled in the American President's head? His name—True Man—might evince a notion that he epitomized good in humanity. True Man—a lofty surname for a shopkeeper whose career before politics was selling men's hats and trousers. True Man—who turned deaf ears to generals and admirals who told him that the Empire was already on its knees and that unleashing Little Boy and Fat Man was unnecessary.

> *Imagine True Man sitting on the knee of absurdity, high in the sky, looking down at what he had wrought; godlike, far above the mushroom cloud, far above conscience.*

❧ ◆ ☙

Mother knelt before her *butsudan* and prayed each day next to the ladder that went up to the loft where we slept. I'd watch her strike a match, then light incense, wisps of its sweet smoke drifting through our home. She wondered out loud about the *butsudans* of the rich, which were probably magnificent, as one would expect to honor their type of ancestors.

"Imagine the one in the emperor's palace!"

I didn't care about the emperor or his fancy house, so I couldn't picture it. However, my grandfather took exception and stopped in the middle of his slow climb up the ladder to bed. He turned and spoke to me, but just loud enough so Mother could hear. He said that the emperor was a fraud— said it quietly but so intensely that his mop of white hair shook. She ignored him and poured tea into a cup and offered it to the *kami*.

When Sofu reached the top of the ladder, he looked down at me and told me that my mother prayed to our dead ancestors, including her own dead mother. He said that the war was good for making more dead ancestors to pray to and also good for the religion business. I said goodnight to Sofu. I watched the dim loft absorb him. It was full of shadows. Probably ghosts, I thought, maybe relatives. Despite him, Mother continued to pray to the spirits and ancestors for grace and protection. As far as I could tell, her prayers did no harm; perhaps they shielded me from the neighborhood punks. Although I understood little about my grandfather's anger, he talked often about how the fools destroyed the world.

While other children may have heard bedtime stories from their mothers or grandmothers, I sat by Sofu as he complained about the Americans—that the liberators were here not out of pity, but to make us in their image, so that we would not become communists.

After the war, the Reds swarmed over China and Korea and poked their heads into the tent of the Philippines. What Japan feared most was an invasion by Russia, which had conveniently declared war on Japan two days after Hiroshima and one day before Nagasaki. Sofu reserved his harshest rants for the emperor and his henchmen. He scoffed and struck a pose, clasping a teacup with his pinky fully extended, mimicking how the emperor and his family daintily sipped tea in the Imperial Garden, surrounded by pink chrysanthemums that the little man himself famously tended to. Grandfather mumbled something about the emperor caring more about his gardens than about his own people.

⋄ ♦ ⋄

The shames of the empire plunged further downward. The Japanese had plundered, murdered, and raped their way across Asia. After surrender to the Allies, they expected to be on the receiving end of similar brutality. The Japanese elite feared that the wives, sisters, and daughters of the Empire would serve as comfort women at the whim and pleasure of the gaijin invaders. Japan became a snake eating its tail. To avert wholesale rape, Japan coerced thousands of girls and women from its lesser classes to become sex workers. The logic was that these girls would serve as low-hanging fruit—they'd satisfy the conquering beasts before they began sniffing and pawing at the doors of the wives and daughters of Japan's upper class.

⋄ ♦ ⋄

When the first contingent of GIs arrived in the early autumn of 1945, they reveled in drunken sprees of rape, mayhem, and violence. One day the question will gurgle upward from my throat: *Was my father involved?* My mother was silent about the war, not that I ever asked her. Sachiko, having survived fire and chaos, never spoke of it.

Chapter 4
CHILDREN OF THE IN BETWEEN

When I searched for my place and my kind, the measures of this world seemed vast and distant, as if seen through the wrong end of a telescope. Every distance in space and each moment in time are not so much too far or too close, but like us, somewhere in the In Between.

My memories of Japan are empty of children at play and the childish things that speak to their existence. No swings or seesaws come to mind. I remember no bicycles carelessly abandoned on the ground for a game of tag nor did I watch any errant balls sail over a fence. Where were children's voices, their yelps and calls over nothing of importance?

When I saw children in public, they were *pure* Japanese. Mother told me to ignore their smirks. Hafus—half breeds like me—were shunned in public, their existence wasn't officially acknowledged. At best, they were complications, assigned to the purgatory of being unseen—neither here nor there. How many of them were there? Some claimed 200,000. The Japanese authorities suggested that *if* there were such children, they numbered no more than 10,000. The lower the numbers cited, the less the shame for all concerned.

The American government considered the matter of mixed-blood children an issue under Japanese purview. It became an *American* problem only when soldiers wanted to take their wives and children home with them. Japanese authorities ignored the *ainokos* left behind. Most crept in the dust and slept in the shadows. One spoke of them in the hushed tones usually reserved for the condemned. If no one took care of them, neglect, starvation, and infanticide would.

I don't remember meeting any other families like ours—American soldiers with Japanese wives and their biracial children. Although meeting other families of our kind was beyond my experience, I was happy enough in the private warmth of our small family. My father's savings, combined with my mother's profiteering in the black market, made it possible for us to move to a home of our own in Tokyo. A garden harbored plants and flowers surrounded by pebbles that glowed. Inside, the new home was full of light, softened by rice-paper walls that glided open and shut. Father stayed with us more often and for longer periods. We slept on the floor next to each other, covered by bright comforters lined in silk. We'd slurp happily as we ate rice, miso, fish, and seaweed, our feet tucked underneath the *chabudai*.

My father was away as much as he was home. My mother told me that we were fortunate to see him as often as we did. After all, he was an American soldier and obligated to go where and when he was directed; otherwise, he'd be considered AWOL. Although my mother assured me that Father would never leave us behind, I resented that he couldn't stay as long as we pleased. The excuses annoyed me. I pretended that we'd be better off without him. I wouldn't have to listen to his tiresome reprimands about how I shouldn't interrupt when he or Mother was speaking.

When he was away, my mother intensified her trading activity. Cartons of cigarettes, soap, and sundries came and went through our back door. Some days, Mother's girlfriends visited us. I looked forward to their easy grace as they sipped tea, gossiped, and indulged me with their laughter as I showed off, rolling on the floor, contorting my face, and enjoying their attention.

As Mother told me he would, Father always returned. I felt generous enough to forgive him when he interrupted my conversations with Mother. I eagerly picked up the morsels of his language, one word at a time and one phrase at a time. Among the first American expressions I appropriated from my father was, "Pardon me, I lost my balance," which he invoked after he broke wind, followed by a chuckle. It inspired me to fart more frequently, just for the opportunity to gleefully apologize for losing my balance.

Mother seemed uninterested in pursuing the new language beyond what was necessary to communicate with Father. They understood each other through conversations that they constructed like jigsaw puzzles, one piece that fit here, another there, until it came together—or didn't. That's how it went for them. My father's language attracted and mystified me at the same time. For example, when we roughhoused in the yard, he'd pin me down, rub his unshaved cheek against my face, and demand, "Give up! Say uncle!"

"Uncle!" I'd squawk, repeating the word that, for some reason, meant surrender.

He told me he'd prefer that I call him Dad. "It's friendlier than 'Father,'" he explained.

I sat on his chest and put him in a headlock, like he had once shown me. "Yes, Dad," I said. "But for now, you must say uncle!"

I felt powerful, armed with American words, but when my father was absent, my power evaporated. When Dad returned to base, he'd tell me to behave and take care of business while he was gone. But in his absence one of our neighbors began to antagonize Mother and me. We were vulnerable. He knew about our weakness. Although my parents were married under Japanese law, their marriage wasn't recognized as official by the army. My father had already been demoted for *fraternizing* with a Japanese national.

If the wrinkled old coot saw us tending to our yard or approaching our house from a walk, he'd step up too close to my mother, lobbing questions like grenades. Where was my father stationed? When was he expected back? Did the American authorities know he was living with a Japanese woman? There was physical harm packed in the neighbor's sneer. He was committed to hurting us. We held our tongues and our breath and scurried into the house.

One day I was kicking a ball around our yard when the old snake shouted at me from his front door. He asked me where the smelly *gaijin*, the foreigner, was sleeping these days. He called me a little toad and asked me if I knew that the *gaijins* tried to kill all the true Japanese.

"Why is it that you, a *hafu*, are left to thrive? And of what family is your mother from? Perhaps she has no standing—just a *pan-pan girl.*"

Hideously, he laughed, bending over and holding his sides as if in pain. His pasty face grinned with malice. I wished that I could snap his head off, but all I did was stand there, afraid. When my mother overheard the taunting, she grabbed me and swept me back inside our house.

After Dad returned home, Mother told him about the disgusting troublemaker who threatened me and called her a woman who sells her body. Dad stormed to the neighbor's house and banged on the door. When the neighbor talked back, my father roared so loud that the rice-paper walls in our house hummed like bees, vibrating in the aftermath of his anger.

After that, if the neighbor should see me outside, he'd dart back into his house, a beetle scuttling from the light. It was as if the fear hopped off me and stuck itself on the neighbor, like a tick. It felt good to see it. I capitalized on the turn of events. I romped around his yard, shrieked and kicked pebbles toward his house. I celebrated my first revenge, such a dark and wonderful blessing!

I saw my father as a masterful giant, shoulders squared, chest expansive with promises, walking forward with long strides that left no doubt that he'd carry us to the United States of America, the land that he said teemed with cowboys, Indians, children, and dogs. He talked about General MacArthur, John Wayne, and Ted Williams, great men of America I hoped to meet. According to him, it wouldn't be long before we'd be trout fishing, playing baseball, and eating red meat in New Jersey. Though I lacked clear pictures of what these activities were, they sounded mysterious and wonderful. He said that America was the best country in the world, though it had its warts. It sounded like a fine place, except for the warts. I hoped that I'd find my own kind in the new world, where my face wasn't that of the enemy.

Mother tried to understand what Dad was saying about our plans to accompany him when he returned to America. Although their marriage had been officially sanctioned by the state department and the army, our passage to the U.S. remained uncertain. Each time we applied for passports and visas, the bureaucrats required more documents and authorizations. Mother asked him why. I watched his silhouette pace back and forth behind the walls that separated adjoining rooms. You could hear everything, except for the weakest whispers. In my twilight remembering, I hear his hybrid language of English and Japanese.

His commanding officer, a colonel, had wanted to *bust* him from sergeant to private for making a home with a Japanese woman. The colonel was *busting his chops*, he said. He was *playing games* with him. In the coming years, Dad would retell the story of that encounter:

"The little man took me into his office, *dressed me down, blew his stack*, and told me, 'You're becoming my number one headache. You go native on us, then you have a kid. Then you get married to a National. Now you want to bring the whole happy lot of you back home.' And then he pulled up another chair for a chaplain to have a chat with me—the last person I'd want advice from! The chaplain asked me, 'Don't you wonder how your parents are going to feel? Think of the shame you'd bring to your whole family. Maybe we should pray and reconsider.' It was all I could do to stop myself from punching that *holy roller* in the nose. I couldn't give a rat's ass what he had to say. That's when I walked out the door."

My father's shoulders sagged. "The bastards hold all the cards," he said.

I wondered who these *bastards* were and where they came from. These creatures sounded only part human, given their nature and the wicked things they wanted to do to my father—undress him, bust him, and blow up stacks, all the while playing games and holding all the cards, as if the torment they caused was wholesome fun. I began to wonder how these people could come from the America that Dad had praised so often.

Mother asked him if he would leave without us. She held her

breath for the answer.

"Yes, but just for now. We'll be together soon," he said.

She reminded him that her best friend was left behind by a GI who made similar promises.

"Never mind what that guy said or did." Dad poked a finger into his chest and said, "This guy will get his family home."

Chapter 5
SACHIKO FEELS TEARS BEFORE WRITING

In the spring, the army sent my father back to America without us. My mother managed the affairs of the household by herself. She continued to pray for help. She knelt before the same altar that she had brought from my grandfather's house. I wondered about our ancestors, those obscure presences who claimed to have such influence over our world. One day as she embroidered a lovely scene—a dragonfly hovering over a lily pad—I asked her what she said to her mother's ghost and the rest of our ancestors. She replied:

"What I say isn't so much in words. I remember my *okaasan* as she was, and I pray and stay silent. Sometimes I think I see a gate that opens to that other world, what I've told you is the Pure Land, and there she speaks to me."

"Where is the Pure Land?"

"It's found in many places. Some say their ancestors and *kami* reside in the mountains or the sky. Others say the sea. I think ours are in the Earth, in the deep magma."

"Under Mount Fuji?"

"Enough for now." My mother smiled, then finished stitching eyes for her dragonfly.

I didn't have confidence in those spirits, but I didn't argue. My faith was in my mother and the man who asked to be called Dad. Mother and I believed his promise that we would be together again. But my grandfather, always the doubter, felt otherwise. During a visit that would turn suddenly dark, my mother prepared tea, and knelt across from him.

He cradled his cup and said that the Americans were two-faced about what they did. Even if some soldiers thought they wanted to bring their Japanese wives and children to their homeland, they changed their minds once they went back. How could you blame them? Their people didn't want their sons bringing home children with mixed blood any more than our people wanted them here.

Imagine him trying to make sense to my mother.

"It doesn't make it right, but there it is," he said. "Sachiko, you should know that the Sergeant is well-meant but naive. He thinks these children are somehow exceptional, that they will get the best from their people and ours. These are grand ideas that seep out when you're drinking, but the next day you see it for what it is—just dreams. You will see, Sachiko."

"No, you will see!" Her voice erupted in the room, as if it belonged to someone else. Startled, my grandfather spilled tea on his shaking hands. Mother gasped, then dabbed his hands with a napkin. Never before had she spoken this way to him. She told my grandfather it was time for him to go. After he left, she collapsed in tears. I followed her into the next room. She stopped sobbing, just like that, making herself busy, taking inventory of her black-market goods, sorting through boxes of cigarettes, canned goods, sugar, and soap.

"When will we see him again?"

"Never mind," Mother would say, turning away. "There are other things to consider." She tells me not to worry, but as the passing months deepen the shadows on her face, I worry anyway. Waiting is torture.

Through a translator, Sachiko writes to convey her mounting concerns to Bill.

> *November 15, 1952*
>
> *My Dearest Bill,*
> *Very glad to receive your letter. Nothing happier than hearing you are fine. I recovered health, catching cold, and am in good spirits because I received the letter. The boy becomes clever recently and mimics my acts in a lovely way. His fourth birthday will soon be here. I hope you come back before the day. You used to write but recently I hear not a detail from you. I*

want to know more about you and to know what I was anxious about and asked you. I couldn't let every day go by merrily without you. Don't forget me and him and write a letter to me every day please, on your leisure.

I feel tears before writing when I take a pen, although I have many things to tell you. You know, I think, I used to be anxious about everything. I wish I would get out from this life and get in merry and hopeful life as fast as possible. Please come back earlier as possible. Take good care of your health. I will be waiting for the next letter from you. With a lot of love and kisses, far away from there.

Lonely, your Sachiko.

In the meantime, my father is stationed in Fort Bragg, North Carolina, close enough to his parents' home in New Jersey that he can hitchhike home over some weekends. My American grandparents write to a powerful man who is willing to help us. Senator Robert Hendrickson writes back, vowing, "I will do everything I can regarding the problem of the Sergeant in bringing his wife and child into the country." The senator's long reach into Occupation Japan persuades the state department to let us go. When it seems we will finally get our visas and passports, another obstacle intervenes. Mother tests positive for tuberculosis. Although her symptoms are mild, protocols require full recovery before we can leave.

Chapter 6
OF COWBOYS AND WHALES

Mother said we'd soon be on our way to America to reunite with Dad. She had repeated the same assurance for many months, which was on the boundaries of what I could remember. I thought of her promise the way a Japanese boy thinks about fairy tales—for example, "The Inch High Samurai." You wonder how a boy smaller than my pinky could become a samurai, but it happens. He grows and, in fact, marries a princess.

So, I wasn't completely surprised when, as impossible as it seemed, we finally boarded the ship for our two-week voyage from Yokohama to Seattle, where we would reunite with my father—just as Mother promised. That was in May 1953.

❦ ◆ ❦

Mother and I are on board the *General H.B. Freeman*, a military transport steaming across the Pacific Ocean from Yokohama to Seattle, where my father waits for us. The vessel commemorates a soldier whose service stretched from the Civil War to the Spanish American War. Except for his namesake vessel, General Freeman's legacy is otherwise unheralded, unlikely to be mentioned in American history classes or referenced in school commencement addresses. Despite its unglamorous bearing, I regard our ship as a wonder, a moving island resolutely steaming across the ocean. When Mother and I are not sitting in our room, we bask in the ocean air on the deck, or pick at American food in a mess hall with recently discharged soldiers and civilian administrators returning home. The Occupation of Japan is now officially over. Others on board are involved in the Korean War, now two months away from its bloody, stalemated end.

Mother and I speak only Japanese to each other. We rarely engage other passengers. My mother's poor English embarrasses her. I can speak it well enough to be understood, but I restrain myself. If

I speak for both of us, it diminishes her in the eyes of others. Our state is one of unease that sometimes swells into shame about who we are. I don't recall meeting any other Japanese on board, neither adults nor children.

Although meaningful conversations with other passengers are impossible, we exchange smiles and friendly greetings. But when my mother bids a passerby a simple "hello," she risks embarrassment, the word stumbling out of her as "herro." It might seem stilted to some, but she adopts "good day" and "good night" as her standard greetings because she can pronounce them flawlessly. For me, the new language isn't as formidable. Understanding it is a game, an aural jigsaw puzzle that requires trial and error. If I make a mistake, *I couldn't give a rat's-ass*. That's a phrase I heard my father use that mother told me not to repeat.

We see movies, old comedies and westerns that are repeated during our two-week voyage. One afternoon after lunch several ship stewards rearrange chairs in the mess hall, repurposing it as a screening room. My anticipation is almost too great to bear. Impatiently, I shift in my chair, asking Mother when the movie would start. She misunderstands and says it's a *cow boy* movie. She says cow boy slowly several times, testing its sound, then confesses she doesn't know what it means. We're about to see *Fort Apache*, arguably among the best of the classic westerns directed by John Ford. I do know something about cowboys—*and* about Indians. Dad told me about America, as much as he could in his fractured way. He'd try to speak Japanese but mangled the language so badly he'd revert to English. I absorbed some of his language and a basic understanding of America. According to Dad, we'd soon be playing baseball and watching movies in Technicolor in New Jersey. Whatever these activities are, you could count me in.

Fort Apache finally begins. It mesmerizes me to my very bones. I perch alert in my chair, pretending I am an Apache looking out for the cavalry. Horses gallop in mad waves back and forth, cavalry horns blare, guns blaze, Indians whoop out war cries, arrows slice through the air, men and beasts tumble to the desert floor, some rise again, lifted by sheer will. Although I don't fully grasp the dialogue, I admire the hero, Captain York, but I also root quietly for Cochise and his people.

In between battles, beautiful and sensible women ease the pain by making their men dance. There is music and stamping of feet. It lasts too long. I'm eager to get back to the desert where the stakes are life and death. Soon, the battles continue. My excitement is so intense I feel my bones will break through my skin and go rattling around the walls of the mess hall. Mother is restless, for different reasons. She's anxious about who we are, strangers groping their way to a strange land.

I see the movie several times during our voyage. I grasp more words, but not all. I understand that Captain York and Cochise, chief of the Apache, are heroes even though they are enemies. Both are fearless, but neither is bloodthirsty. They are two sides of the same coin. However, Colonel Owen, the smug commander, is bloodthirsty. I don't understand his oily speeches, but his gestures and tone tell me he wants to see men die, even if they are his own. I see he is insane. He doesn't give a rat's ass who dies. Though I lack command of the language, I *feel* all of this. I consider my father a man of honor like York and Cochise. He keeps his word. He said he'd send for us, and he did. Despite my penchant toward exaggeration and downright lies, I consider myself a likely hero, too.

Fort Apache is the first of a long wagon train of westerns that I'll see over the years to come that stretch from *Stagecoach, Shane, High Noon, The Searchers,* and *The Unforgiven,* all of which showed me that in America, justice and compassion are pursued by good people, but not necessarily always achieved.

My mother and I stand on the main deck, unconcerned about the world's troubles. We watch the waves capture flashes of sunlight that cast a halo around the horizon. My mother laughs, pushes her long black hair away from her eyes as the Pacific wind toys with us. Our coats billow like sails. When I look over the ship's deck railing, it seems a mile down into the water. The sky is cloudless and blue, though the ocean boils with white caps. I'm afraid, but at the same time emboldened by the power around me. The agitation of the sea and my inner excitement about what events lay ahead seem one and the same. I grip the deck's railing and wish for protection. My mother gently strokes the back of my head. "Look!" she yells, turning her palm up and sweeping her hand in an arc that presents the unified expanse of sea and horizon in front of us. "Whales make the waves in the ocean!"

Whether or not it is true is irrelevant. I accept it as part of my mother's world of the *kami*, the ancestor spirits who inform events that swirl into the future. She tilts my chin, so my face turns up to hers. The salt spray spumes to the heights of where we stand. Before pieces of the ocean land on your lips, you know it is delicious.

We are on our way to America. Below the waves, I sense that the great whales are thrusting the Pacific forward. They chaperone us to the land of cowboys and Indians and movies in Technicolor, just as Dad promised. There will be many movies to come. I *know* it and I *feel* it way down to my bones.

Chapter 7
AMERICA

May 1953

At first, I didn't recognize the man waiting for us at the end of our gangway. He was in civilian clothes and appeared bald. An imposter, I thought. After he scooped Mother and me into his arms and squeezed us, I remembered. He was my father, the hero-soldier who kept his promises. He wasn't bald, after all. It was his moustache that was missing. Little things can make a big difference. As we left that Seattle pier, I turned for my last look at the *General H.B. Freeman*, the military transport that brought us. I had regarded the ship with awe as it carried us across the giant blue swells of the Pacific. Now anchored and tethered to its berth, it looked rusty and dour, as if spent from its labors ushering thousands of soldiers to and from distant bloody wars. My family was an incidental consequence of the war. But for the war, I would not be.

We flew on a small military plane from Seattle to New Jersey, making unscheduled stops because of storms. Our plane leapfrogged across the continent. Rain, lightning, thunder, and wind threatened to swat us to the ground. I considered it fun until the first chorus of fear rippled through the cabin, passengers gasping and yelping. Mother gripped her armrest and Dad said something about *Christ's sake*. I took my parents' cues about how scared I should be. Mother placed her warm palm over my eyes and told me not to worry and go to sleep. With her, I could sleep anywhere and soundly. I woke up as our plane wobbled to an airport in the Midwest. We spent the night in a hangar with the crew and other passengers—soldiers, sailors, and civilians connected with the services. When I put my coat on the floor to go to sleep, Mother insisted that I sit on a bench like everyone else. I slept on and off, sprawled partially on her lap and the bench, the night howling and banging on the roof.

The next morning, we returned to the sky, which was a rowdy shade of blue, as if celebrating itself for chasing away the storm. We flew to New Jersey, landing at Newark Airport. It was good to walk on Earth again, though it seemed a different planet.

The journey had glittered with first-ever experiences for me—the ship across the Pacific, the plane across the continent, and now, riding in an automobile that catapulted us to my grandparents' home. I sat between my parents, clutched Mother's arm as Dad navigated our way through a maze of highways that teemed with traffic of all sorts—sedans, station wagons, trucks, and buses. They were nothing like the rickety vehicles that I saw nosing their way cautiously on the unreliable roads of postwar Yokohama.

> *Feel the spring air rush through the wide-open windows. Look at my father grip the steering wheel. I consider him masterful, navigating over tall bridges and elevated highways that pitch upward toward the sky, then plunge us to the industry below. Dark rivers twist among factories that blow brown clouds from their smokestacks. I watch skyscrapers coalesce before me—monuments built for giants. Dad said it was New York City, where my grandfather worked. I assumed he held a position of great importance. The dusty landscape of Yokohama, its people and their taunts, blinked across my mind. It seemed long ago. As we drove onward, traffic began to ebb, roads narrowed, and wave after wave of hills, woods, and meadows rolled toward us.*

I wondered about the children and dogs I'd meet. The car ride stretched out like a good dream. We were together again. Hope and mystery surged inside me—what ordinary people like us considered adventure. You never knew for sure what would happen next. I fell asleep on my mother's shoulder. It was the simplest and happiest moment of my life.

When I woke up, we were in Millington, New Jersey. As my father turned into my grandparents' driveway of grass and dirt, an old dog yapped at us until Dad rolled down his window and scolded him.

"Prince, quiet down, boy! It's just me."

Once we were out of the car, Prince sniffed my feet, then ambled away, peeing every few steps, pooped, and then collapsed under a crab-apple tree to sleep. When Dad first told me about Prince, I had fantasized about a dog that would romp at my side as we hunted wild animals or protected our land from evil men. But Prince's scraggly fur, cloudy eyes, and lethargy repulsed me. As he lay under a tree occasionally snapping at flies, I saw a huge black cat skulk by. His name was Sam, my father said. As I approached the cat, he arched his back and hissed at me. I ran back to my parents—if these animals didn't want a new friend, I didn't want them either.

The screen door of what Dad called a farmhouse swung open, and my father's mother greeted us. She was a short old lady with silver hair and gray-green eyes. She limped a little, but before I knew it, she had swooped down and was all over me. She smelled very good—what I'd later recognize as the smell of lilacs, sweet, but with the lightest bite. That aroma drifted into my nose and etched itself there, forever. Clusters of purple and white lilac blossoms swayed outside and posed in vases around the house. The old lady clasped my face in her palms, looked down at me and made sure her eyes looked straight into mine. Then she said:

"You'll call me Grandma, OK?"

I shrugged. My father spoke for me and said that, of course, I'd call her Grandma.

My mother started to bow to greet my father's parents, but before she could complete it, the old lady took her hand and shook it. The tall old man who was my grandfather ran his big paw back and forth on my head. I didn't mind. He puffed on a cigarette, and then he, too, shook my mother's hand. "How'd you do?" he said. My mother, puzzled, looked to Dad for guidance.

"Bill, why don't you take Sachiko and Billy upstairs and get settled." Grandma said. As we turned, she asked, "Oh, have I pronounced 'Sach-i-ko' correctly?" My mother looked at Dad, unsure.

"Close enough," he said.

"Yes, good," Mother said.

When I asked Mother if I could play outside, she said fine. Prince dozed fitfully in the shade, occasionally snapping at insects that buzzed around his hindquarters. I wandered into the backyard and found Sam toying with a little brown creature. He clutched it in his mouth, then released it, only to bat it around and then again put the bite on it. I pitied the tiny mole and plucked it from Sam. It groped blindly on my open palm, but instead of cuddling there, it bit me on a finger. Though it didn't draw blood, I dropped the ingrate by Sam's eager forepaws. I had a fleeting pang of guilt, but I had no tolerance for its betrayal.

My parents were still unpacking when I came back. Dad said:

"Our new beginning."

Mother nodded and smiled. I snooped around the room, inspecting American things. When Dad went to the car again to get more luggage, Mother spoke in Japanese.

"Nothing seems ordinary right now," she said, "But we'll get accustomed."

I wondered if that was possible, but I kept my wondering to myself. Our first night, rather than sleeping side-by-side next to them on the tatami, I slept in a different room. Mother helped me get into my bed, which was high above the floor. After she left, the room changed. Moonlight cast asymmetric shadows across the walls. Breezes annoyed tree branches that rattled against the house. I saw swaying figures hide inside of shadows, then reemerge like ghosts. I tucked my head deep under the bed covers. I wondered if the shadows were the ghosts of those who once lived in the house, picturing them as versions of my grandparents—but far more decrepit and dangerous. Just in thinking about it, I feared I had summoned them to get me.

By the end of our first week, I told Grandma in my version of English that I was afraid of *ghostas*. She said that there were no such things as *ghostas* but smiled when I said it. She said that the house made noises because it was old—so old that George Washington may have slept here. Whoever he was, he was long dead. I suspected he still wandered around the house, bumping into doorways, drifting restlessly from one room to another. I wanted Grandma to know about my ancestors' spirit world called *the Pure Land* but refrained from bringing it up. Mother hadn't unpacked her *butsudan* or prayed to the *kami* since we arrived. She told me we should be as American as possible. It would be rude to act like we were still in Japan.

As if to confirm our conversion as Americans, my mother would adopt Sarah as her first name. Looking back, I don't think it was her idea.

❧ ◆ ☙

Much in this new land seemed larger than necessary, and strange.

> *Look at the couches, floating like boats in the cavern called the "living room." Are the other rooms for the dead? Instead of chopsticks, we eat with utensils better suited for garden work—heavy pitchforks and swords! Look at these people enter the home, in full stride, with their shoes on!*

I shared my concern with Mother. We spoke freely in Japanese when we were alone but used it sparingly when we were with the rest of the family. It would be disrespectful otherwise.

"Yes, they clomp through the house in their big shoes like horses," she whispered. "But it is the custom here, so we will keep our complaints to ourselves."

I felt relieved that she shared my dismay. I could trust her as a confidante. She ran her hand along the sill of the bedroom window, looked at her fingertips, and shivered. I wondered if it was dust that provoked the shiver or something else. Perhaps she missed Japan. I did not. Yokohama had been unkind, even cruel to us. When my parents strolled in our neighborhood, the sight of my mother's delicate hand clutched in the gorilla palm of the American soldier had provoked insults. My face stirred suspicion and disgust because it was neither Japanese nor American.

Despite adversity, I believed good fortune would come to us. Children are born with a reservoir of optimism, like the albumen in an egg that nourishes the forming life inside. In our case, there was other cause for optimism. A family that had sustained itself in the ruins of a failed empire could surely succeed here—in the new land on the greenest side of Earth.

Chapter 8
LANGUAGE MAKES US

During our first spring and summer with my grandparents in Millington, my voice found words and arranged them in the American way, all by itself. But my mother and I still spoke to each other in Japanese. I was amenable to speak Japanese at home, but when we went to the market or walked in town, I'd choose to speak only English, as if to spite our old language. Because Dad addressed his mother as "Mom," I thought it was a good and American thing for me to do the same with my mother. The first time I called her "Mom," she flinched as if stung. Still, I wanted her to keep up with me and embrace the new ways and words.

She struggled with English, making conversations awkward with the rest of the family. I was eager to help her with pronunciation but did it in a haughty way, prideful of my growing command of the language. One night at dinner, Grandpa talked about a rabbit that we saw invading his vegetable garden. He and I had tossed stones at it, chasing it from the rows of greens that were just coming up. I mimicked gunshot noises, pretending to shoot the interloper as it scampered away. Grandpa said that one rabbit could eat a row of lettuce in no time.

"Lobbit very hungry then," my mother replied. It was still difficult for her to distinguish *l*'s and *r*'s.

"Not *lobbit!* Say *rabbit*," I said, pointing to my mouth for emphasis each time I repeated the word. *Rrrabbit. Rrrabbit. Rrrabbit.*

"That's enough, Billy. Don't be a show-off," my father scolded.

"What is show-off?" I asked.

"To be smart in a stupid way."

"Then should I be stupid in a smart way?"

"Enough! You just don't know when to stop, do you?"

"Yes, I do," I said. "Very much." The last word was important to me.

Whispering in Japanese, Mom told me to listen to Dad and

be quiet. I sulked, and turned my attention to the food, cautiously regarding my plate, as if what was on it might leap out at me.

"This is a casserole with lamb and mashed potatoes," said Grandma. "It won't bite."

I was unconvinced. When I pushed the weird brown mass around my plate, my mother told me not to be fussy. I longed for fish and rice.

"Don't play with your food!" Dad said.

"Please pass the shepherd's pie," said Grandpa.

Whoever the shepherd was, I didn't want anything to do with him, or his pie.

"Well, I'm glad someone's enjoying the house cuisine," Grandma said, passing the casserole dish.

Though the new food took some getting used to, there were American customs I considered to be highly civilized. For example, Grandpa gave me 15 cents a week for my *allowance*. But there was a catch. Grandma told me that, in turn, I should do *chores*, which I found shocking, since up to this point, I was never expected to work. My first assignment was to set each place for dinner, not just once but, as I understood it, *forever*.

I told her in a fevered jumble of words and gestures that I wanted to quit. She asked me why, and I explained to her that Dad gave me 25 cents every week for doing nothing and when Grandpa gave me 15 cents, he said nothing about *chores*. Summing things up, I said:

"Work is large. Money too small."

You would have thought I was making a joke, the way she laughed. She composed herself, smiled, and said:

"Set the table anyway."

I did the job with my face pinched in pain and my shoulders slumped, the postures of forced labor. Eventually, I was proud of my work, inspecting the glasses, plates, and shiny silverware I had set in place, and pleased with myself for all the money I had amassed from my toil. My grandmother was my first supervisor and would continue to be for domestic assignments to come. Beyond introducing me to the American work ethic, she was my key to unlocking the mysteries of English, as well as introducing me to a variety of French and Spanish terms that she considered useful, like *Bon Appetit, Hasta la Vista, Merci,* and *Gracias.* Unlike most women of her time, she had gone to college and studied the world, though she had never traveled farther than a day's train ride from home.

As days rolled forward, I'd sink my hands in the pockets of my shorts and let my fingers loll in the fortune of loose change I had hoarded. I planned to unleash every coin when Grandma took Mom and me to shop in Bernardsville, which, compared to Millington, was a teeming city where ladies strolled in pairs on the sidewalks with the children in tow or pushed baby carriages, chattering as they window-shopped. I wandered ahead of my limping Grandma and Mom, who lagged behind.

> *Look at my grandmother and mother, how they walk with too much space and too much silence between them. It is a beautiful day, and they are not smiling.*

I suffered as we browsed in what I regarded as a wasteland of clothing and shoe shops, but I perked up for what would usually be the last call of our venture—the five-and-dime store, which offered a sprawling cornucopia of toys—the proof that my new homeland was a civilization that was superior to the old one. I never saw such a place in Japan. I swooped down to the basement level, where a treasure trove of toys beckoned me. Bins overflowed with products that had no purpose but play—water pistols, rubber knives, rabbits' feet of every color, yo-yos, all kinds of balls (including ones attached to paddles), jacks, pirates' swords, play money, cards like "Old Maid," tiny cars, trucks, ships, and airplanes. There were also more serious goods but in miniature, such as pen knives, compasses, binoculars, telescopes, and magic tricks. I bought an arsenal of toy guns, a green penknife to protect myself from thieves, a yellow compass to help me find my way, and four blue rabbits' feet to bring me luck from the north, south, east, and west.

We lived on a country road where houses were far apart. Compared to Yokohama, the arrangement seemed a form of isolation. But kids appeared from nowhere, as if tugged toward one other by the gravitational force of common childhood. One day, in a meadow between our house and the next, I slashed tall milkweeds with a stick, sending one imaginary foe after another collapsing to the ground. That's where I met Eddie, at the edge of the woods where raspberry bushes grew.

He stood between his two little sisters, holding hands with both. They had been watching me. I stopped and considered them. They all had blue eyes, light brown hair, and the same bowl haircuts—bangs snipped across their foreheads that were the approximate width of a pocket comb. The boy let go of his sisters, bent down and picked up a stick. He walked over to me and tapped my stick, which I held idly at my side. I tapped his stick back, then he tapped mine a little harder, and so forth, until the July afternoon swept us up in an endless reprise of dueling and dying. When we broke from our sword fight, Eddie asked me if I knew Judo. I said I didn't know him.

"It's not a *him*!" he said. "It's a kind of fighting." He showed me how to do it, moving so fast he appeared to fling multiple arms and legs around him. I showed him that I could do that, too. His sisters were a good audience, sitting in the wild wheatgrass while they watched us, eating wild red raspberries, one at a time.

Eddie and his sisters lived with their mother; I never saw the father and he wasn't mentioned. Their house was just a short walk away. Some windowpanes had wood slats instead of glass in them, and there were bald spots on the roof where shingles had blown off. Language posed no problems for Eddie and me, or with his two sisters. We were about action, not talk. We shot each other with pretend guns, played hide-and-seek, tag, or chased coppery-coated chickens that pecked freely about their yard. One afternoon, Eddie's mother announced that they'd have chicken for dinner that night. We followed her as she walked to a tree in the backyard, her arm clamped around the biggest bird.

> *Watch her bind its feet to a thin piece of rope and tie the other end to a branch, hoisting the chicken so it hangs upside-down. Consider how deftly she takes a carving knife from her apron, slices its head off, then backs away, to avoid the spurting blood. Though unable to squawk, the headless chicken makes a furious racket, beating its wings against the air and itself, flying in wild arcs under the branch to which it is still tethered.*

We recoiled from the bird and its awful blood circle until it was finally limp and dead. The rope was as taut and straight as a plumb line from the branch overhead to the chicken dangling below. Eddie's mother clutched the knife in one hand and wiped her forehead with the back of the other and told us she hadn't expected this ruckus. She said that she usually cut off the head, then let the chicken run until it dropped, which was a *God-awful* thing to watch. When she lifted her apron to wipe some specks of blood from our faces, she sighed, "I thought doing it this way would be kinder than wringing its neck." This was the first and last time I'd see the end of something that was a pet one moment and dinner the next. I saw suffering at both ends of that knife.

Quickly and mysteriously, Eddie and his family had moved by summer's end. Grandpa said that they did it to beat the landlord. I didn't believe a word of it. They wouldn't beat anyone.

My new life in America puzzled me, but like my mother promised, eventually we'd get accustomed. I'd begin the day running out of the house, recklessly bullying an old screen door wide open and letting it go, stuttering shut behind me. I'd launch myself into the lush summer of flowers and berries, a sea of jewels. I'd carry a rabbit's foot for luck, a cap gun for protection, and my yellow compass so I couldn't get lost. I could choose a direction, run with my eyes closed until I ran out of breath, and pretend to be fearless. When it was time to go back home, I was the Lone Ranger, galloping home to my new family.

Dad worked at a golf course during the day, tending to the grounds, which turned the back of his neck and his arms bright red. He worked evenings as the *maître d'* at the Old Mill Inn, a restaurant in Bernardsville. Mom stayed at home and tried to help Grandma with household chores. She told Dad that Grandma didn't want her help, which made her feel useless. On nice days, she sat in a lawn chair in the backyard, where she wrote letters to Japan, and in the evening, she embroidered her latest scene—fallen leaves around a weeping willow. Mom asked me something in Japanese. I asked her to repeat what she said in English, because her language was drifting away from me. She asked me if I was *hoppy*. I said yes, then asked her if she was happy, too, but she didn't answer. Mother looked past me, then turned her attention back to her stitching.

Sometimes Grandma took me with her to pick up Grandpa at the train station. We'd wait for the Erie - Lackawanna train from New York City to come clanking and squealing toward the station. My grandfather would step out of one of the chocolate-brown cars with a newspaper coiled under his arm and slide next to my grandmother in the Buick and give her a peck on the cheek. When we returned home, I'd take the *World Telegram* into the living room, splay it on the rug and look at the funny pages, all those cartoons of people and animals with clouds full of words over their heads that showed what they were saying and thinking. Though I couldn't read the words, I liked to imagine what was on the cartoon characters' minds. It was good practice for reading what was on the minds of real people, like my family.

Chapter 9
NORTHBOUND AND BACK

We drove to New Hampshire where my father would study chemistry at the state university, and I would begin kindergarten. We made the long trip in an old Cadillac, belching clouds of smoke as it labored to climb the steep hills of New England. Dad called the car a mixed blessing because it gobbled gas and oil. It was a gift from my grandmother's sister, Aunt Jean. I remember her as a stern old lady who I thought tolerated Mother and me but had no special feeling for us. I was wary of her.

Dad would get something called the GI Bill, which Mom assumed meant more money, perhaps even abundance. But our new circumstances disappointed her. We lived in a monotonous settlement of two-story beige buildings, army barracks converted to apartments for veterans and their families. My father went to classes during the day and worked nights in the shipyards of Portsmouth. Although he complained that the work was hard, the pay was too good to pass up. This was not the life my mother expected. I didn't know what to expect, which was okay with me.

Dad and I had our own interests in the outside world, but my mother stayed alone at home. The only outsider who came into our home was the Ice Man, who carried a block of ice pinched between a huge pair of tongs as he trudged up our apartment stairs. Everyday life was tedious at home, but elsewhere there was enough monkey business to keep my life interesting.

It seemed a lifetime ago that neighborhood bullies had chased me in the ragged alleys of Yokohama. They had called me an ainoko—a half-breed, a mongrel boy. But now, barely a year later and 8,000 miles away in New Hampshire, a new color of kids disapproved of me.

Pale, wide-eyed boys with crewcuts heckled me on the school playground because I was half-something else. Once again, I wore the face of the enemy. I ran away from them, weaving around seesaws, swings, and swarms of other children who were jumping rope, hanging upside-down on the monkey bars, and playing tag. But the boys caught up with me, pulling the corners of their eyes so they were barely slits. They blocked my way, and chanted ching-chong-ching. I would've liked to have smashed their bright faces in, even though none laid a hand on me. I claimed that my father was a sergeant in the U.S. Army; that he was a war hero, and that I was 100 percent American. I felt righteous, in that at least one of my claims was true. They snorted with disbelief, so I warned them that I knew judo, those acrobatic maneuvers that my friend Eddie had taught me. Furiously, I chopped the air like my hands were meat cleavers, kicked like a wild horse, and spun like a windmill.

"Run or die!" I yelled.

Instead of running away they started laughing, which was fine with me. I was ready to join them, but they walked away, arms on each other's shoulders, chattering and having a swell time. I coveted what they had, ached to be among them. They had each other to hold on to. I held on to grudges. The trio of bullies were the exception, not the rule. A few other kids were kind of snooty, but most treated me the same as they did others. The exceptions are what stick out in your memory.

Out of breath in those 20 minutes of each school morning that was called recess, I stood alone—but just for a moment—then dived into the currents of children that twisted this way and that, like river rapids. As I skimmed my way among the other kids, my face was regarded as no different from the others, all of us set free, screeching, and wild. This was America, and for now, it was perfect.

Occasional reprises of playground taunts would percolate as part of my growing up—dealing with boys and later on, full-grown men who twanged nonsensical oriental jibber-jabber. Sometimes, their antics provoked a scuffle, which usually exposed my judo chop as more artifice than chop.

Although we rarely socialized with other families, I remember visiting a friend Dad made, who, like him, was a veteran studying at the university and also like him, a family man. A pretty blond lady greeted us at the door with a baby in her arms, ushered us in, then excused herself to put her child to bed. After the usual introductions, handshakes, and howdies, Dad and his big-bellied friend sat down, smoked, drank beer from a glass, and talked about the army and college. Mom and I sat across from them and drank ginger ale. The blond lady returned and said that the boys should quit smoking because cigarettes can kill you, then lit one for herself anyway, the three of them laughing.

She pulled Mom out of her chair and said she wanted to show her the *five-cent tour* of her home. I tagged along as she showed my mother around the rooms, pointing to special objects—a vase here, a music box there, with a ballerina spinning on top of it, and photos of relatives splashed on the walls—such as Aunt Roberta (*dead now, poor thing*) or Uncle Joe (*what a card!*). Mom gave me a nudge when I got fidgety and told me in Japanese to be polite. She could see that the boring things were important to our hostess and her husband. She was chirpy, her blue eyes widening when she emphasized something, laughing in short bursts, and taking another sip of beer from her glass before she started talking about a special rug, of all things! Mom squeezed my hand extra hard to remind me to be polite through the tour that seemed to last forever. My mother nodded and smiled, and said, "Yes, nice," and "Oh, lovely," pretending that she understood more than she did.

When the baby cried from another room, our hostess left the kitchen to take care of it, and returned to cooking, managing everything with apparent ease. After dinner, we sat down in the living room to watch television. Our hostess, turning knobs on the device, announced, "We're going to watch *Disneyland*! We watched short vignettes about Mickey Mouse, a friendly rodent in short pants, and Donald Duck, a white bird with a bad temper who wore a sailor's cap, and an excerpt about Sleeping Beauty, a princess with an entourage of odd little men who sang while they worked in a coal mine. What spectacles went on in that little box! It was like going to the movies in your own house. This was an unexpected treat, since we didn't have a TV—just the radio in the kitchen where I'd listen to Gene Autrey and "The Long Ranger." I was envious of that family and all the good stuff they had. I sulked when we had to leave. Through most of our visit, my mother was quiet, withdrawn. I wondered if she was shy, or if she was "being difficult," as Dad said, when we got home.

Although we didn't have a TV, we went to the movies, which showed people with lives more interesting and desirable than our own. A movie based on real life, *The Bob Mathias Story*, made me hunger for possibilities of *what could be*. It was about a once-sickly American teenager who became an Olympic champion. I wished that I, another puny weakling, might grow up to be like him. I asked my father if I might be a great athlete. He told me probably not, because *I didn't have the dexterity or focus*.

Regardless, I wasn't about to give up. I made a silent vow to become like Bobby. I practiced long-jumping over brooks, heaved rocks to hone my shotput skills, used a broomstick to pole-vault, ran as hard and far as I could, imagining thousands of people cheering me on. I imagined breaking every record there was to break. With the passing of that one afternoon of intense training, I got bored, and quit preparing for the Olympics.

Occasionally, Mom went with us to the movies. The three of us saw *Seven Brides for Seven Brothers*. The movie posters said it was a western, which was an out-and-out lie. It was punishment watching it. Every time I suffered through a song or a dance and it finally ended, another one started. The only good thing about it was that we did something together besides bickering or fighting. I think Mom enjoyed it, the three of us munching popcorn through a fake cowboy movie with no real cowboys.

Target Earth was more up my alley, where a mystery army of robots from Venus attacked an American city that was now almost deserted. Mom didn't come with Dad and me because it looked like a war story, even if it was science fiction and hard to believe. For example, the heads of the robots looked like TV sets plopped on their shoulders. Still, I chose to believe the story. They spurted out cheesy death rays that disintegrated their human targets. Only a few survivors had escaped being disintegrated, but they had more than aliens to worry about. The humans began blaming each other and fighting among themselves because of the fix they were in. In the end, the scientists figured out that piercing sounds would paralyze the robots. Soldiers saved the day by driving around in jeeps with sirens on full blast. Regardless of its cheap special effects, the movie still made me wonder.

I asked Dad, "What if the Venusians really attacked us?"

He waved his hand dismissively and said, "First of all, no intelligent life could survive there. They say the atmosphere on Venus is like a radioactive steam bath. If there's something to worry about, it's the Russians. Just itching to blow us all to *kingdom come* with their newly tested H-bombs."

I could still depend on westerns, like *Shane*, to bring common sense and justice to the big screen. Nobody killed bad guys better than Shane—a reluctant-gunslinger-turned-farmer—and nobody deserved to be shot dead more than Wilson, an evil gunslinger. At the end, a boy named Joey saw Shane shoot Wilson. Like Joey, I wished that my father was more like the masterful Shane. Just thinking it, I felt like a traitor.

The snow arrived in early October and stayed through March.

My mother did housework, wrote letters, and finished a new embroidery, a black bird perched on a fence. I wondered if it was bad luck. I asked her why the crow. She said it was from real life, next to a New Hampshire field. Our days were spattered with trouble, whether it was Dad complaining about Mom's cooking or Mom complaining that Dad was away too much or that there was not enough money. She accused him of seeing other women. He asked her to consider when it might happen. *Between classes? Or before or after he worked all night and came home at four in the morning, coated with muck from working on the docks in Portsmouth?* It was a war. *No fighting,* I wanted to say. When we went to the store, Mom said people made fun of us. If she heard people laughing in a passing car, she said that they were laughing because our eyes and skin were not like theirs. I wasn't certain if what she said was so, but I hated them anyway, yet wanted them to like us.

Winter reluctantly turned into spring. I'd escape outside and play. When I played with kids outside of school, we were of one kind, unhindered by the yoke of the classroom. We rounded ourselves up in the neighborhood and played cowboys and Indians by the pine forest that went on for as far as you could see. We reenacted battle scenes from westerns, and whooped, ran, killed, died, got up, and did it all over again — a taste of immortality. No cowboys or Indians died for good until it was time to go home for supper.

When warm weather arrived to stay, I began to see gelatinous continents of black dots, floating in the shallows of a pond. They were frogs' eggs.

> *Look at how they become something else after they hatch. Watch those black dots become tadpoles and wiggle away, swollen little sacks with lips and eyes on one end and long tails on the other. Notice how they lose their tails and grow legs, then turn into the frogs that sun themselves at the pond's edge, eyes half-closed, until you lunge for them. Listen to them chirp before they disappear underwater, leaving behind a widening ring on the surface. How beautiful and strange the same creature becomes a completely different creature. In America, miracles happened. I wondered, what might I become?*

I sat with Mom and Dad at a kitchen table so small that our

plates almost touched. Even so, we were slipping away, silent rings in a pond moving ever apart. After Dad's classes ended, we left New Hampshire. We took a long and cold highway back home to Grandma and Grandpa's.

◈

A dry and joyless summer revealed nothing bright about our future. The plan was to return to the university in September. For the time being, my father returned to his old jobs at the golf course and at the restaurant. But when the leaves turned, we stayed in New Jersey. Dad decided not to go back to the University of New Hampshire—it was just the way it was. Until he got on his feet, we'd stay with Grandma and Grandpa, and I would go to first grade at Millington School, not far from the train station.

I heard them talking by the garden, Grandpa taking down the pole beans, and Grandma collecting an end-of-season bouquet of zinnias and cosmos. When Grandma asked, "*For pity's sake*, why can't Bill just finish college and get his degree?"

Grandpa said that finishing a thing was not Dad's *strong suit*. What was *pity's sake*? And what did a *strong suit* have to do with it? Sometimes I thought they talked in a secret language, although I understood the gist of it, at least in a refracted way. I wanted to chime in and say that maybe Dad didn't have the *dexterity and focus* to finish college.

Mom spoke little when we were all together, stayed in her room or sat outside, wrote letters to Japan, and embroidered—the latest scene, a peony, beyond its bloom, its scarlet petals tumbling softly below—pretty in a sad way. Our family's response to her sullenness, as with other matters of feeling, was to leave her alone until it went away. In her case, it turned out to be as dangerous as ignoring frayed wiring. I couldn't explain what was happening to me or my parents.

Though the new language poured itself into me, there were no words I heard that were powerful enough to bring us together. Tension coursed through each day; a steady electric hum interrupted by jolts of suspicion that something terrible was approaching. It was coming faster and growing larger than my family could bear. I waited for the thing to happen, the thing for which I had no words.

Chapter 10
FUGITIVES AND PUNISHMENT

Soon after I began the first grade in Millington, the familiar sound of *ching-chong* and its variants pealed like bells on the playground. As had become my custom, I assumed my menacing poses and told my new tormentors I'd kill them. But instead of settling it with me and having some fun, they reported me to the teacher. I was still figuring things out in my new country.

Miss Carter called me to her desk and told me to face the class. I stood there as she turned to the class and said that she expected everyone to play nice and to work hard and to learn not only about reading and numbers, but also, and maybe most important, to treat each other with kindness. Some kids were nodding their heads in agreement, and it sounded fine to me, too. Miss Carter looked at me and said, "But sometimes we misbehave and do or say things we shouldn't. Does anyone in class know what we do after we've done something mean?"

Several hands fluttered in the air and Miss Carter pointed to Merle, a red-haired girl with thick glasses, who replied, "*We* say we're sorry." So pleased with herself, I thought. Merle and her best friend, Linda of the Dutch-boy haircut and polka-dot dresses, double-teamed against me, sticking out their tongues when Miss Carter wasn't looking. At least they noticed me. Maybe it was the start of something good. I was an optimist.

"That's right, Merle," said Miss Carter, rising behind her desk, and giving me a bifocal stare over her glasses and addressing me firmly, her thin lips tightening. "So, Billy, after you apologize to the class for the poor deportment today, you can take your seat."

I didn't understand what she was getting at, other than that I should return to my seat. I stood in front of her, dumbly waiting for Earth to turn in another direction. I fiddled in my pockets with my rabbit's foot and compass. I wondered why she didn't like me. I told myself I didn't care. The kids shifted in their seats, getting worked up from the tension. They looked like they were all set to pee in their pants. When the mumbling and tittering got feverish, Miss Carter slapped her desk and barked, "Quiet!" then turned back to me and said, "Well? Say something!"

"So long," I said at last. It was a friendly, cowboy way of saying good-bye. I returned slowly and deliberately to my seat like we were supposed to, as in *Walk! Don't run!*

That made her even madder. "Sashaying like you're in charge," she said, "This just takes the cake!" Why she would accuse me of taking the cake, who could say? I slunk in my chair as Miss Carter squinted at me, so angry she seemed to be trembling. She called me *mister* and said that I wasn't going anywhere except to the principal, if I kept it up.

That was how I launched my school career as a recidivist troublemaker. I annoyed and enraged teachers and administrators, whether doing something or doing nothing. Despite my best efforts to make friends, my classmates treated me like a disease. When I began to chat with these little girls, they shrank from me. "Yuck, he has cooties," they'd say. Most of the boys just avoided me. Still, I was undeterred, and thirsty for conversation.

"Get back in your seat and stop talking out of turn!" Miss Carter demanded. I knew what she meant and tried to behave. Regardless, I'd be swept away by impulses that compelled me to get out of my chair and see what was happening outside a classroom window, or roam through an aisle to spark a conversation with another kid. These disturbances provoked Miss Carter to strap me into a chair with masking tape and put a strip over my mouth. I could have forgiven her for taping me to the chair, but I hated her for taking away my voice.

After school, she handed me an envelope and told me to give it to my parents. My family discussed it at dinner that night. I told them my version of what happened.

"For pity's sake, the idea of tying a child to a chair is beyond the pale. You should speak to the principal," Grandma told Dad.

"But what's this about you threatening the boys?" Dad asked, ignoring what Grandma said.

"They called me names. Like *Jap!*"

"You need be good," Mom sighed.

"Listen, mister, you're in enough trouble, with this business of judo and getting in and out of your seat," Dad said. "Stop acting like a nut. Things would be a lot easier if you'd just do what the teacher says."

"I didn't do anything bad."

"You told these kids you'd kill them."

"But I didn't kill them, did I?"

"You just don't know when to stop!"

"You watch. I can stop!"

"Always you with the last word!"

"Listen to me stop—just like this," I said, folding my arms.

"Next time," said Grandpa, "just belt the kid who's teasing you and leave it at that."

My father said he'd call the school office the next day and straighten things out. I doubted that he would. For my part, he told me to apologize to Miss Carter and *to mean* it.

"Maybe—maybe not," I said.

Dad sent me to my room, which I didn't mind. It was simply furnished with a dresser, a small table, a chair, and a bed covered with an old-timey quilt. A large dartboard hung on my closet door, depicting the sun and the nine planets of our solar system. Instead of steel points, the darts had suction cups that stuck to the board. The board gave me a sense of where I was, here on Earth, spinning around the sun. There were bigger things to consider than getting into trouble at school.

Except for occasional reprimands, I avoided serious trouble at school. At home, I caught wisps of conversations about my mother going back to Japan, words that settled in uneasy silence. When Mom was upstairs, I heard my grandparents and Dad whispering in the kitchen. When I walked in, they stopped talking. Another time, I eavesdropped on Mom and Grandpa. Because he worked in New York City, Mom asked him to find out how much one-way tickets cost for a ship to Japan. Dad brushed past me from behind and told her, "Can't you ease up on this thing just for one *God-blessed* moment?"

I went outside and played by myself, pretending to shoot bad guys in between trees. It was New Jersey, but it was my American Wild West. I stood in Grandpa's vegetable garden remembering how, just a year before, he had helped me unearth *real* Indian arrowheads. It was a different world then.

For a long time, I could feel *it* loping toward us. Maybe it was just a nightmare. During a sticky August night when everyone else was sleeping, Mom shook me awake. Urgently, she whispered that we were going back to Yokohama. As she helped me get dressed, she asked me if I'd go back with her, and I nodded yes. What else could I have said? I asked her if we should tell them that we were going. She knew who I meant, but told me, "Never mind."

The night began to spill, a toppled bottle of a terrible dreams. I grabbed a rabbit's foot and my compass but couldn't find my penknife. We snuck out my bedroom window to avoid opening the creaky front door and began a long, silent walk into the night, her heels clicking on the road. Pulling me along, Mom finally stopped opposite the parking lot of a tavern, where we began hitchhiking.

A car left the parking lot and swerved to our side of the road. The driver seemed happy to see us. After choppy back-and-forth talk, he finally understood that my mother wanted to get to the airport. He said it was her lucky night or something like that and told her to put her suitcase in the back seat, so we could sit up front. He talked incessantly, but after what seemed like hours, he finally shut up. Rather than paying attention to the road, he kept stealing looks at my mother. When he slid a hand toward her lap, she slapped it, shrieked at him, and said something about the police.

Mom scrunched away from him, leaning into me as far as she

could. When he tried to touch her again, I began yelling too, told him he was bad, threw my rabbit's foot at his head, which bounced right back into my hands—*so lucky*! He cursed and swerved to the highway's narrow shoulder, barely giving us enough room from a guardrail to get ourselves and the bags out of the car. My mother yelled at him in Japanese, if only to drown out his torrent of curses. He slammed the door behind us and sped away.

We stood on the edge of a miserable world. I heard the faint drones of airplanes far above, while tattered billboards rattled in the wind. In the marshland beyond the guardrail, tall reeds whipped themselves into a frenzy. Neon lights from a gas station, a diner, and a motel across the highway beckoned us. A concrete barrier divided the double lanes. Doppler waves of roaring motors, spinning tires, and honking horns terrorized us. Headlights from both directions skipped over my mother's face. Debris skittered on the highway's shoulder. Pieces of newspaper and empty cigarette packs sputtered briefly aloft with each passing car. Sensing a break in traffic, Mom grabbed my trembling hand and our bags. We lunged into the highway, scrambling over the divider, ran across the road, then stepped over the guardrail. Finally, we reached the other side, panting and exhausted. Mom looked back across the highway that we had crossed and smiled, as if admiring her work.

The clerk in the motel office looked unnerved when we came in. Perhaps he had seen us make our crazy run across the highway. This Oriental woman and her kid weren't like his usual wayfarers. If we provoked suspicion, you couldn't blame him. Asia had swelled with fanatics in Japan, Red China, and North Korea. If he had seen us plunging across the highway, maybe it looked like we were on a suicide mission. Regardless, he was patient and courteous. My mother seemed unruffled by the night's events, capably registering us and paying for the room. Briefly, I regarded her with pride. She had engineered our escape from the criminal in the car and then navigated our run across the road without us getting killed.

But all of it was a nightmare of her making. I distrusted her judgment and I ached with the shame of wanting to be away from her. As she unpacked, she spoke Japanese to reassure me and, maybe as well, *to convince herself* that everything would be all right.

She took familiar objects from her overnight bag and arranged them on a bureau. I watched her from my bed as she lit incense and bowed before the Buddha. After praying, she told me we wouldn't make it all the way to Yokohama on this trip. Next time, she would plan better. When the time came, would I again go with her? When I said yes, my own voice sounded as if it belonged to someone else.

"Always my *Akachan*," Mom said. It had been a long time since she called me that, a term of affection appropriate for infants and toddlers, not ones like me, old enough to be goaded by their mothers to run across a highway in the bitter dark. I sank into the strange bed but couldn't sleep. This night had a life of its own, spreading in ways beyond our knowing.

"Are you asleep, *Akachan*?"

I kept my eyes closed and didn't answer. I didn't want to talk to her. I lay in bed wondering about Dad, Grandma, and Grandpa, and worrying about whether they'd take us back. I thought about our wild ride and was afraid of what I would see in my dreams.

When Mom woke me up in the morning, it felt like I had never fallen asleep. She called Dad. I wished they would make up. Instead, when he picked us up, they barely said a word to each other. The momentum of dreadful things rolled silently forward and faster.

> *Look at my father clenching the Buick's steering wheel, as if he was choking it. See my mother staring through the windshield and making her eyes dead.*

I was afraid of their ferocious silence and stopped looking at either of them. I rubbed the lens of my cheap yellow compass, its needle frozen in place, just like us.

When we arrived home after that night, Grandma said that she was glad we were still in one piece. That was that. No one said anything about what happened. It reminded me of having my mouth taped shut. For days, the quiet inside our house throbbed silently like a fever that wouldn't break. I was afraid it would last forever, but kinder events distracted us and sparked optimistic chatter—the lush red of Grandpa's tomatoes, the growing chorus of Grandma's colorful snapdragons, Dad's job interviews, and updates on apartment-hunting forays that he and Mom took. Through the rest of the summer, I played outside whenever and for as long I could, trying to forget a night that for the rest of my family, seemed never to have happened.

Chapter 11
ARSON, MARTIANS, AND BANKERS

In the summer of 1956, we moved from Millington to a house in Summit, a short drive from my grandparents. As we prepared to leave my grandparents' home, there had been half-hearted chatter again about fresh starts. We would move to a new town. Dad would start a new job. I would start second grade at a new school.

But while our circumstances had changed, we had not. Rather than hope for a new beginning, we faced the dread of repetition.

❧ ◆ ☙

Our new home was an apartment on the top floor of an unremarkable three-story house, similar to others in the neighborhood that were converted to multifamily dwellings. Dad was hired as a lab technician at Celanese, a plastics company. The job sounded personally promising for me. I imagined him bringing armloads of plastic toys home, a greedy fantasy that never materialized. My parents argued about what they could afford. They economized by buying furniture in thrift shops. Mom suspected that salesclerks and customers were gossiping about her. Conversations she overheard were slights about her and me.

"They make fun," she told Dad.

"It's all in your head," he said, but she wasn't convinced.

We bought one luxury item, a second-hand television. While possessions accumulated, the promise of the future continued to diminish. The conversations between Mom and Dad, as meager as they were, often turned bad. One evening, Dad's attitude about Mom's cooking didn't need translation. He pushed his dinner plate away. Mom said that if we had more money, we'd eat better food. Dad said that he ate better meals in the army and dumped his plate into the kitchen sink.

"*Shinjimae!* Drop dead!" Mom jumped from her chair, grabbed a knife from the kitchen counter and lunged at my father. Dad backed away as she flailed the air around him. She shrieked, "Nothing is good!"

Dad grabbed Mom's wrist and called out to her, as if she was far away. "Sachiko!" and tried to calm her down. I ran frantically around the table and groped for calming words in Japanese, which I could not find. Dad grabbed Mom's wrist until she dropped the knife. The fighting ended as suddenly as it began. We stood in the kitchen, breathless and beyond weeping. There wasn't a scratch on any of us, yet we were a family bleeding to death.

I sat in the dormer attic of our apartment, used for storage and as a makeshift playroom for me. It was cheerless and windowless, one ceiling bulb casting light into the room. The room was my sanctuary from the troubles that simmered and boiled between my mother and father. I sat by my toy box and played with matches there. It became a habit. I'd light a match, hold it, watch the flame creep toward my fingertip, and blow it out. The box was crammed with old favorites, now lame and used up: a one-eyed stuffed rabbit I had coddled to death; a robot with no legs; my once-treasured "Fanner 50" cowboy cap gun, its trigger frozen; and Fort Apache, a plastic rendering of a miniature western outpost populated by cavalrymen on the inside, and marauding Indians on the outside. There were losers in the box, too—broken crayons, and dried-up paint boxes—all that should have been thrown in the trash. I leafed through a Japanese comic book about mice that lived in castles on the clouds. At one time I understood the story, but now the Japanese form of character-writing, *kanji*, was unfathomable to me. I got bored taking inventory of my toy box and went back to playing with matches.

The ritual of fire fascinated me. The scratch of the match head across the striker. The hiss of ignition. The burst and blossom of flame. The acrid smell of sulfur. Wisps of smoke trailed behind as I tossed spent matches into my toy box. I snapped out of my reverie when Mom called me to set the table. By the time I got to the kitchen, she sniffed the air and asked me if I smelled smoke. I lied and told her I didn't. When the smell became intense, she screamed, "Fire!" but froze in the kitchen.

I saw Dad bolt from the living room and followed him into the dormer where smoke was gathering. He pulled a ragged army blanket from a pile and used it to smother the nascent flames in my toy box. Sweating and panting, he looked at me, trying to figure me out. He didn't yell, and asked me in a regular voice, because he really wanted to know.

"What's the matter with you? Don't you know you could've burned the house down?"

"I didn't mean to. It was an accident. It just happened. I don't know what made me do it."

"Stay here and help me clean up this mess," he said.

I promised that I'd never do it again, sounding so earnest that both Dad and I believed it.

Movies distracted me from the storms at home. I never knew when Mom might throw a lightning bolt of worry my way. I didn't help matters. I stole money from Dad to finance my Saturday matinees in downtown Summit. I can't recall consciously scheming to steal from him. The opportunity materialized when he began driving a taxi on weekends. I'd filch money from a coin dispenser he used to make change for fares. He kept it by the daybed in the living room, where he slept. The circumstances of where we slept had changed. I slept in the same room as Mom, in a twin bed across from her.

Because my parents were absorbed in their own separate worlds, I shaped one of my own making, invisible to them. To support my movie-going habit, I needed 25 cents for admission to Saturday matinees—which included the feature and usually a half-hour of cartoons before the feature. Occasionally, there'd be special *live entertainment*—a magician, jugglers, a clown! I also needed 30 cents for round-trip bus fare to downtown Summit. Along with my weekly allowance from Dad, which was still a quarter, I'd treat myself to a soda and a comic book after the movie. I hated myself for stealing from him, but it was a numb hate, the kind that makes no difference.

A movie that impressed me most was *Invaders from Mars*. Repulsive creatures from the Red Planet landed their flying saucer in the desert and burrowed it underground. The Martians kidnapped upstanding citizens and plunged huge needles into the back of their necks. Now mindless slaves, the victims returned to their homes, with telltale scars on the back of their necks. The hero was a boy about my age. He convinced everyone, including army generals, that there were people under the Martians' sway who were not who they seemed. The boy stopped the Martians from taking over Earth. *The End.* Or was it? You just didn't know for sure. Regardless, going to the movie was a relief from the problems at home. The theater was packed with kids gasping and yelling as the Martians took one victim after another. It would have been more fun if I had seen the movie with friends. The boy in *Invasion from Mars* didn't have friends either.

When the show was over, I walked outside, shading my eyes from the afternoon glare. I listened to older kids laughing and jostling each other, just to show they weren't scared. Others were more concerned. I heard them say things like, "It gives you something to think about, doesn't it?" and "Do you believe in people from outer space?" I had different questions. I wondered about my parents. Who could trust anybody? Who could trust me?

Mom prayed in front of the *butsudan* arranged on her bedroom dresser. If our ancestors and spirits existed, I thought they had lost interest. The dainty teacup, scattered incense ashes, and little Buddha reminded me of my grandfather in Japan. I had almost forgotten him, the old man who scoffed at my mother's rituals. He had it right—the ancestors just made things worse. During this time, I came straight home after school, concerned in a general way about my friendless mother.

Though she prayed and embroidered, what she did most was watch TV. *Queen for a Day* was among her favorite afternoon shows, where tired ladies told sad stories of illness and loss that befell their families. The contestant who told the saddest story won furniture or appliances as the grand prize. They would usually cry as they told their stories of woe, then shrieked with joy when the host of the show told them that they had won. When he presented the winner with a washing machine or dining room set, they'd collapse again with happy tears. I thought I'd keep crying, too, if I won a lousy prize like that. On the other hand, Mom could have used a washing machine, rather than having to scrub laundry with a washboard in the sink.

I looked over her shoulder when she told me she had finished a new embroidery scene. She had stitched white thread on the blank field of white linen. I asked her what it was supposed to be, and she laughed, told me that it might be the inside of a cloud, or it could be nothing. She laughed in a way that made me shiver.

She had started a feud with our downstairs neighbor by clomping her heel on the floor when she watched TV, just to annoy him. I told her to stop it, because I expected he would get mad. She did it anyway and when the man came upstairs and knocked on our door, she didn't answer it, but just snickered. Mom started banging her heel on the floor again as soon as he left. I squatted behind a chair on the other side of the room and begged her to stop and when she didn't, I took off a shoe and threatened to throw it at her. Mom eventually tired of harassing the neighbor but began to tease me in mean ways. If I bumped my head, tripped, or did something clumsy, instead of sympathizing, she'd bark, "God punishes you!" and laugh. When I called my father *Dad*, she'd chortle and say, "You call him 'Dead,' hah!" I asked Mom to cook a Japanese dish that she used to make, and she told me she didn't know what I was talking about. I tried to describe it to her. The best I could do was say it was like an eggplant, but you squeezed it like fruit, and it was delicious with rice. That struck her as hilarious, and she told me to go into the kitchen and make it myself. I searched in the refrigerator and the cupboards for ingredients that might refresh my memory, but it was no use. Good meals and the sweet of the past were gone, replaced by the mean and the bitter. The sting of her words lasted long after she uttered them. I resented her and felt guilty because I probably deserved it.

I knew it was far-fetched to believe that Martians had stolen our minds, but still, I'd try to check the back of my mother's neck for evidence of puncture wounds. I rubbed the back of my own neck, feeling for those Martian scars.

One Saturday morning, I stood by our living room windows and looked out into the street. Mom was still in bed around eleven, which was not unusual. She often stayed in bed until after I went to school. Dad was already out. I checked in on her and saw she was sleeping soundly. I took a box of matches from her dresser and went back to the living room. I pushed the white curtains to the side, looked at the impressed figures of flowers and leaves, and felt the fabric's texture between my fingers. I wondered if the material would catch fire. If it did, how fast would it burn? It was an interesting question that provoked research. In this way, I considered myself a scientist, embarking on an experiment. I expected that the flame would crawl up the fabric. When I touched a lit match to the bottom of a curtain, it didn't burn, so much as it exploded, then flamed out of existence. I ran to the kitchen to fetch a glass of water to extinguish the fire. Mom saw me scurrying past the bedroom.

"Something is happening?"

"Nothing," I told her.

I held the glass of water in my hopeless hand, standing in the living room where two panels of the white lace curtains were transformed into a hanging veil of spidery, smoky black strings. The window trims and sills smoldered and pulsated with the boils and blisters of super-heated paint. My mother stood behind me, shaking. Her face was ashen. Fire, once hurled at her from the sky in Yokohama, had found her again, this time on the other side of the world. For the second time, I had invited fire inside our home. She fled back to her bed, sobbing. I promised to fix what I had done and ran out the door.

Yelling at myself for being so stupid, I careened down the stairs out to the street. So much was going wrong, who could keep track? I was a troublemaker in school. A thief and firebug at home. A liar everywhere I went. I needed to get to the bank and get enough money for paint, so I could repair the mess. When I got to the street, a taxi pulled alongside. It was Dad. He said he was between fares. Like the day, his disposition was sunny, and he seemed cheered by seeing me, which made me feel even more ashamed of what I had done. When he asked me what I was up to, I said I was meeting friends. He told me to have fun and that he'd see me before supper.

"And keep yourself out of trouble," he said, smiling as he drove away.

I wished myself dead and waited for him to get out of sight so I could catch a bus. I had conjured a plan with three steps that seemed reasonable: first get money at the bank; then buy paint, a brush, and whatever else I needed; then paint the woodwork around the windows to make our living room look like new.

But the bank people stood between me and my money. When I presented my bankbook to the teller, she pushed it back to me and told me I'd need my father with me to make the withdrawal.

"But it's *my* money!" I said, pointing to the seventeen dollars inscribed in my bankbook. "My money! I just want *some* of it, just five dollars."

The teller was unmoved and repeated that the rules are the rules. My father needs to be there because it is a custodial account.

I stooped to begging and bargaining. "Please lady, I need that money to fix something! *For real!* How about three dollars?" But there was no convincing her. When I walked away from the teller's window, a man stood up behind his desk to let me know he was important. His suit jacket was unbuttoned so his big gut could have some breathing room. I took a step in his direction, but he waved me away.

"Don't bother coming over here, boy. I heard the whole thing. Rules are rules."

Rules! I stared hard at him, wishing I could answer him by sinking my fist into his soft belly, then make off with a bag of money the bank owed me. Instead, I stalked out of the bank, angry at the rule makers and at myself because I didn't know what to do. Although I could have bought paint if I had gotten the money, I still wouldn't know how to paint or fix anything.

I wanted to believe that something magical might happen. *I'd get home, and Mom would've fixed the room back to what it was before; or, this was just a bad dream, and all I had to do was wake up.*

But when I got back home, ashen detritus hung in weepy strands from the curtain rods— just as I had left it.

When Dad came home and saw the mess, he tried to yell at me, but got so worked up that he lost his voice for a moment. He told me in a croaky sputter that he might give me a spanking, or worse. But hitting me wasn't in his nature. Later that day he sentenced me to write 500 times, "I will not play with matches," and told me I couldn't go out for two weeks, and no allowance, maybe forever.

The punishment was harder than I expected. Gripping pencils until I squeezed them down to the nub, my fingers kept cramping up as I wrote 500 lines of "I will not play with matches," smudging soft lead on page after page of cheap paper. Isolated among those lines, I sprinkled in my own vows:

> *I will not play with matches. I will not play with matches. We will not be crazy. I will not play with matches. No more fighting. I will not play with matches. No more fighting.*

I buried my runic messages in those monotonous fields of boxy, sloppy print. I wondered if Dad saw any of them when he checked the pages of my punishment. He never said anything.

In the years to come I'll carry the burden of the remorseful arsonist, afraid that I will unwittingly burn down whatever I leave behind. Ritual inspections are required. It isn't enough for me to confirm that I've turned off the toaster, stove, and other appliances. Other sources of possible pyrotechnic disaster haunt me. Static on the radio, a warm switch plate, the erratic hum of a refrigerator, or the tiny white dot that lingers in the center of a television after turning it off. Everything is a candidate for spontaneous combustion. Just as a pianist collects music in his fingers, I hold flames in mine. My judgment can't be trusted. I force myself to leave and shut the door behind me, then test the knob to make sure it's locked. I jiggle it to the left, then to the right, and back to the left again, just to be sure. Always three times. When I conduct the final checks for burning embers in the toaster, in the oven, it's always three times. One of the reasons I quit smoking was that it took half an hour to leave my home, inspecting every ashtray for evidence of the slightest heat. Why three times? After my mother left, I intuited that the ritual of 3X had powers strong enough to bring our family—the trinity of father, mother, and son—back together. Although I stopped believing that long ago, it's a legacy habit.

Still, sometimes all the checking is not enough. Driving to work I wonder if I left the stove or the toaster on. The idea glows like an ember until it ignites a vision of flame and rubble that panics me back home. Do I expect to see the living-room curtains on fire? Am I a fool, or is it a faulty attempt at restoration, these returns to the scene of the crime? Regardless, this is how it is for the arsonist who set the fire that chased his mother back to Yokohama, her city made of kindling.

Chapter 12
THE GOODNESS OF MRS. THURLUR

When I began second grade in Summit, Dad gave me a pep talk at the kitchen table, telling me that going to a new school offered a fresh start so I should do what the teacher said. "It's not that hard," he said, poking a finger on the kitchen tabletop for emphasis. "You're old enough to have more self-control. Don't let yourself *go to pieces*." Despite making a sea of trouble at home, I had, so far, avoided serious problems at school.

Mom washed the dishes at the sink, turned to me and spoke Japanese, which was fading for me, but I got the gist of it: *don't make trouble*. Later, I vowed to Mom and Dad separately—because they weren't speaking to each other, that I'd behave. Truly, I wanted to be good, to fit in.

My new school made it easier. I sat near Fred and Sally. They and my second-grade teacher were engines of happiness. In class, Mrs. Thurlur glided from aisle to aisle in no hurry. Tall and willowy, she stooped over each child's shoulder to check their work, answer questions, and encourage the frustrated. When she smiled at others, then turned to me, her face didn't change. I dared to think her smile grew wider. She taught us to read, improved our penmanship, built confidence, and helped us enjoy the world.

Even her writing on the blackboard was soothing; her chalk never squealed or screeched. If Mrs. Thurlur wasn't bliss, she was its first cousin. Yet with all her goodness, my impulses continued to uncoil. During her brief absences, I'd make fart sounds or sit idly in my seat and hang pencils from my nose. I appropriated techniques from TV shows like *Abbott and Costello* and from old movies that featured Laurel and Hardy. I did it all to entertain Sally, the blond German girl who sat across the aisle from me. What I liked most about her was how easy it was to get her to laugh. I imagined us inside a special cloud, at the exclusion of everyone else.

"Billy, stop! You'll get me in trouble!" She muffled her laughter by pasting both of her palms over her mouth. As innocent as my intentions were, I sensed that caution was needed. A vague and sinister power tugged at me. Glimpses of the panties of freewheeling girls who swung heedlessly on the playground monkey bars bewitched me. Sometimes I'd keep looking. Other times I'd run away as fast as I could, as if to save myself. It was dubious comfort to know that some other boys were as depraved as I was, hypnotized by girls' underwear. Sometimes we'd stand together in pairs or threes, just staring.

Meanwhile, the grown-up world bumped into us, intruding on our play and daydreams. I saw sadness and danger in other homes, even in those that seemed perfect. Take Fred, for instance. We were classmates and friends until his mother ruined things. He lived in a grand house with a slate roof in one of the best neighborhoods in Summit, not a third-floor apartment like I did. Fred had magnificent toys I coveted, yet I wouldn't have traded places with him for anything.

His basement was dedicated to a Lionel train layout, a paradise of miniature tunnels, bridges, villages, and tiny people that became animated as soon as we flicked the overhead lamps on. We'd watch the locomotive pluming white smoke from its stack, whistling and pulling its freight cars around a bend, and then disappearing under a green mountain. If we got bored, we'd place cars, trees, farm animals, and even people on the tracks. We'd shout with demonic glee, "Here it comes!" as the train careened toward railroad crossings, promising wonderful carnage and mayhem. In our world, disasters were decoupled from tragedy.

The only real disaster in the house was Fred's mom. Sometimes she'd drift downstairs, a ghost determined to haunt our happy, imaginary world. With the hint of a smile, she'd whisper awful things to Fred, just loud enough for me to hear. "Your father wants to destroy me, if the cancer doesn't kill me first." She might stand next to me, ask me how I was, and turn to Fred and say, as if pondering an interesting idea, "Freddie, you *do* know I'm the *good and kind* parent and that *your* father only thinks of *himself*." Then she'd turn back up the stairs, muttering about the husband who had left her months before.

Fred would try to suck it up, but he'd soon be overwhelmed by sobs. That's when I'd say good-bye and see myself up the stairs and out the door. The last thing he needed was for me to hang around and watch him cry. I wouldn't do that to him. No, not in a million years. He was as close to a best friend as I had. He was a good guy, for real. Even though both of our mothers were not right, there wasn't anything I could do for him or anything he could do for me. Once outside, I kept the smell of smoke in my head, smoke that puffed out from the toy trains. The smoke reminded me of my mother's incense, the perfume of ghosts.

One day during recess, Fred and I watched the girls on the playground.

"Hey, Billy, look at me!" said Sally, up-side down, her knees draped over the monkey bars. "The world's topsy-turvy!"

"Hold on tight!" I yelled, as I forced myself to turn away from teddy bears that danced upside-down on Sally's underwear. Fred kept looking. "It's not polite to stare," I said, yanking him away with me. "Anyway, I want to show you something." I handed an incense stick to Fred.

"What is it?"

"It's magic. From Japan. Light it with a match and blow the flame out. You make a wish while it's smoking."

He told me that he wasn't allowed to light matches, and I thought it was just as well.

Back in class, Mrs. Thurlur stood over my shoulder, watching me practice printing on ruled paper. She told me to take my time, not press so hard. She said I didn't have to make it perfect. When Mrs. Thurlur talked to me, she'd often begin or end a sentence by addressing me by name. It helped me remember I was somebody worthy.

"Take your time. What you put on paper tells other people not only who you are, but also *what kind of person you are, Billy.*"

But when she said that to me, my pencil jolted out of my hand onto the floor. I didn't want her to know what kind of person I was—a showoff, a peeper, a lost cause. She bent down to get the pencil for me, her hand brushing against mine as she reviewed my printing and said that it showed I was a thoughtful and funny boy. I felt like a million dollars when she said that, but I couldn't say anything or even look at her. I held my breath until she turned to help another kid. Anything to keep myself from going to pieces.

Chapter 13
A BOY CHOOSES

Mom's dark moods would smolder, then either break into a rage or evaporate. I couldn't tell which direction these moods would take. She spoke more often about returning to Japan. Bad signs fluttered everywhere. I saw my principal open his umbrella inside the school before he walked out on a sunny day. Dark birds congregated on a gnarly tree across the street. I stumbled over a gaping crack on the sidewalk curb and fell. After Mom prayed before the Buddha, I thought I saw him smirk. I saw blood in the toilet one morning after Mom neglected to flush it. A terrible sign. I told Dad I was scared she might be bleeding to death. He said that it was something that happened to women.

More troubles. Grandma invited us for dinner to celebrate Mom's birthday with cake and candle blowing for good wishes. When Grandma presented Mom with a festively wrapped box, Mom wouldn't open it.

"Go ahead and unwrap it, Sarah. I think you'll like it," she said.

"Not now. Maybe later," my mother said.

"Very well, then, later."

When we returned to our apartment, Mom lifted a dress out of the gift box. It looked pretty to me. Mom glared at it for what seemed a long time, then began ripping it apart, shrieking in Japanese.

Dad tried to calm her down and kept saying "Now, now, now," but she wouldn't stop. I ran from the room, covering my ears. Everything was tearing apart, inside and out.

Sometimes Mom would disappear when Dad and I went out on an errand. When we returned, she'd be gone. Her disappearances swelled inside me, distorting how long she was missing. I fretted through what seemed like a long ordeal. After she came home, Dad would ask her where she went. She'd say it was none of his business. Although I became good at not crying, it didn't ease the peculiar new hurt that crawled inside me. I had been afraid for her, but now

I began to be afraid *of* her.

She badgered Dad until he finally agreed to arrange her return to Yokohama. How that information was first conveyed to me I don't remember. It was a matter of fact that I absorbed. She seemed calmer after her decision to leave was settled. The absence of constant chaos seemed a good thing.

While we watched TV one afternoon, Mom asked me again if I would go back to Japan with her, because it would be *soon*. I told her yes, but I didn't know for sure if I was saying yes truly or just saying yes because it was easy. It felt worse than saying a bald-faced lie.

My mother and I bused into town to shop for clothes. The bus ride was familiar, the route I took to go to the Summit movie theater. When we were done shopping, she decided I needed a haircut. She took me to a barbershop that was empty except for a hefty guy who sat smoking a cigar and reading a newspaper. He snuffed out the cigar, then grunted himself up, overcoming his body as if lifting dead weight. He ushered me into a chair and draped a barber's cloth on me, panting from the effort. I faced a large mirror and saw Mom's reflection behind us. She leafed through the pages of *Life*, a magazine that boasted it brought you the world in pictures. Since she barely read English, it was easy for her to thumb through. The barber asked what kind of haircut I wanted, then reconsidered, and said to Mom in a fake-friendly way:

"Maybe I should ask the pretty lady who brought you."

She glanced up but didn't say anything. I thought the barber mumbled something about her being stuck-up. He asked:

"What'll it be?"

I said I wanted a crew cut like the other boys, but not too short. He asked me what country we were from, and I told him. As he sheared my hair with electric clippers, he kept sneaking glances at Mom. She sat, one leg crossed over the other, and continued to flip pages. I tried to stab him with my eyes to let him know that I didn't like the way he was looking at her.

"Aren't you the tough guy," he said, buzzing away, then looked back into the mirror and said, as if talking to himself, "She's a nice-looking woman—tall for a Japanese girl."

Though it sounded like a compliment, there was more to it than that, and it gave me a bad feeling. There was nothing I could do. If we were in the Old West, I'd draw my gun, like *Shane*, and blow his head off—then, as he fell backward into the barbershop mirror, I'd shoot him in the gut a few times. Instead, I sat in the chair as he plowed through my hair, cutting it so short that when he finished, I looked like a lightbulb with slanted eyes. My mother was upset, and her hands were shaking when she paid the barber. She grabbed my hand and swept us both out the door. Alert and wide-eyed, we quick-walked to the bus stop, like frightened prey.

One day in March, my father spoke to me in the way grown men talked to each other. I was proud that we talked in serious, low voices. It meant I was becoming a man.

"You know Mom wants to go back to Japan, right?" he said. "She's been at me for a long time, and I don't see any other way but to give in. The big question ….do you want to go back to Japan or stay home with me? You don't have to answer now; I want you to think it through, then …."

"Stay with you," I blurted, even though I had already told Mom I'd go with her. All I wanted was for things to be all right.

"OK," he said, "then that's that."

How could it be that that was that, when it was all wrong? All I wanted was that we could stay together. I knew that we could not fix my broken mother. I also feared that after misery broke her in half, it would in turn break me and Dad. When I was angry at her, I'd silently wish that she'd go away forever, and after that anger dissolved, guilt swam inside me. What kind of boy would wish his mother to disappear?

Now the day of her leaving was here. It was a week or two after

Easter, a complicated religious holiday that I understood in part. I eagerly accepted the chocolate rabbits, marshmallow chicks, and jellybeans that were somehow connected to Jesus dying and coming back to life.

On that last day with her, my family planned things we had never done before. We'd drive into New York City, have an expensive dinner *and* dessert, marvel at the synchronized high kicks of the Rockettes, and watch the feature at Radio City Music Hall. For the grand finale, we'd bring Mom to the ship that would take her back to Yokohama. The day would be a shipwreck, masquerading as a *bon voyage* party.

Chapter 14
SAYONARA

April 1956

The preparations for my mother's departure had begun that morning. Mom helped me get dressed, straightened my suit jacket and fixed my bowtie. Dad told us to hurry up because Grandma and Grandpa were already here. I looked from our living-room window down to the street and saw Grandpa standing beside his car, smoking. While Mom fussed with her hair, Dad and I lurched her swollen suitcases downstairs from the third floor. Though my mother wasn't due to board her ship until evening, we had a full agenda.

We rarely dined out, no less at a restaurant in New York City. Dad worked two jobs and still had no extra money. My grandparents' habits teetered between thrifty and frugal. Still, there we were, in a restaurant with a name that was hard to pronounce. Dad joked that it was a *rule of thumb* that if you couldn't pronounce the name of a restaurant, you probably couldn't afford to eat there. Mom and I didn't get it. How thumbs made the rules, we had no idea. We sat at a table with shining silver, glittering glasses, and white napkins folded into the figure of birds. My mother held my arty napkin, appraising it. She whispered to me in her fractured English that it looked like origami made by monkey hands. She unfurled the napkin with a flourishing snap, then put it on my lap. The table conversation was thin, about how good the food was and how wicked the weather was. We spoke more to the waiter than to each other.

Afterward we went to see *The Teahouse of the August Moon* at Radio City Music Hall. I was excited about seeing a movie and a live show, which Grandma had told me would feature the Rockettes. I inferred that missiles and fireworks were in the offing. But instead of being awed by indoor pyrotechnics, I sat grimly through a series of dance numbers by almost naked women who kicked their legs impossibly high and smiled impossibly wide. Embarrassed for all concerned, I buried myself in a box of Raisinets and finished them before the movie began.

The movie was about American soldiers helping Japanese villagers solve their problems after the war. The hapless villagers had many problems. As my grandmother liked to say, *it's just one thing after another*. The Americans were silly, but the Japanese men were stupid, shuffled about, and hardly mattered. People around us giggled and laughed. Although it was the first movie I saw with Orientals in it, the main Japanese character was played by an American.

Grandma nudged me and said, "That's Marlon Brando, *very famous*."

Mom leaned to me from my other side and said, "Marlon the Brando, very famous, not Japanese. He look like a ghosta!"

I agreed that he did look like a ghosta, with his pasty face and his squid-like eyes. I felt nauseated. The candy I had gobbled began to gurgle and stomp in my stomach. Marlon the Brando, *very famous*, played the part of Sakani, who said clever things that made the audience laugh. I thought he was a jerk. The men who were actually Japanese were small and wretched morons compared with the tall and handsome American soldiers. A beautiful Japanese girl seemed to be in love with an American officer who was, of course, very handsome.

The movie ended when Sakani, played by Marlon the Brando, very famous, turned to the audience and made a long, boring speech about the moon and sleep, and finally said, "*Sayonara.*" The audience burst with applause, but Mom and I didn't clap. I was relieved it was over.

Grandma rose slowly out of her seat and asked me, "Well, what did you think of that?"

I couldn't answer her. I had squirmed in my seat through the story. I wanted to say that I felt like I was one of *them*, not one of *us*. As we filed out, I wondered if others thought I looked like Marlon the Brando, the way he was in his ugly Japanese makeup. I hung my coat over my head to be invisible until Dad told me, "Put your coat on the right way and stop acting like a nut."

When we drove to the pier, it was twilight. Once on board, my father rebuked me again about my posture. "Stand up straight. You look like you've got the weight of the world on your shoulders." Yes, I felt the weight of something pressing down on me. Didn't he feel it, too? After I glared up at him, I slipped away to the other side of the so-called stateroom. I was still small enough so that I could weave my way around my parents and grandparents. If they wanted to change position in the cramped cabin, they had to sidle past each other.

I watched my mother from across the room but avoided looking directly at her. I could not bear it if our eyes met. She had her hair up and wore the blue suit and white silk blouse that she saved for special occasions. Instead of being happy and proud about how beautiful she looked, what leaked into my mind was the fat barber who Mom had taken me to earlier that week. He had talked to her in a nasty, hungry way. I hated him for making that sly remark about my mother being tall for a Japanese girl. What he meant was something ugly, covered in gift wrapping. If only I had had a tomahawk to sink into his fat head. I wanted to kill him, *for real*.

Across from me in the cabin, Dad and Mom stood silently next to each other like strangers at a bus stop. Dad looked older than he had that morning. He fidgeted with his hair, which was blown around by the wind when we came on board. When Dad saw me watching him, he turned away. He took Mom's elbow and ushered her to a corner where he whispered to her and handed her a large roll of money.

Standing by the room's only porthole, Grandpa puffed on a cigarette and gazed at the choppy waves on the Hudson River. When he exhaled, the smoke hung around him in layers. He looked like a well-dressed tough guy. I liked that. He mumbled something about April, the cigarette bobbing between his lips. No one else paid attention, and it didn't make any sense to me anyway.

Grandma had her back to him and hobbled a couple of short steps toward me, listing as she moved. Polio had damaged her left leg when she was a girl. Her other leg was fine. Once, I had asked her about her bad leg and all she said about it was, "I managed. Others had it much worse." She told me it wasn't polite to ask, then pinched my cheek for emphasis. That was as close as she would ever come to talking about it. She was in charge of our family's unspoken rule to keep our feelings to ourselves.

Without anyone telling me so, I came to understand that feelings, once let loose, would become beasts, turn on us, then devour us. Look at my mother—she was what happens once you lost control.

Grandma rummaged through her purse, said "Presto!" and presented me with a small chocolate egg, left over from Easter.

When I turned my palm up for it, Mom tapped my shoulder from behind and told me, "Always say 'thank you,' *Akachan*." She gave me a soft push back to Grandma, who dropped the candy into my hand. I unwrapped the foil and popped the chocolate into my mouth.

"Thank you," I said, and opened my mouth wide to show off the gooey brown mess inside.

"That's enough of that," Grandma said, giving me a fake slap on the behind. I was bored and asked if I could walk around outside on the deck. She replied, "In this weather? Don't be silly. *Just hold your horses* and be patient."

Mom and Dad continued to stand in their corner and Grandma whispered something to Grandpa, all of us waiting for who-knows-what. I felt trapped in that smoky room, feelings buzzing around me that I couldn't swat away. I saw a red button on the wall by the cabin door. I pressed it hard for a long time, but nothing happened. A few minutes later, a steward came into the room and asked us if we needed help. Everyone was confused. He explained that someone in the cabin had paged the stewards by pressing the red button.

"That one," he said, pointing to it. Raising an eyebrow toward me, he wondered out loud, "Maybe someone leaned on it by accident."

After they figured out that I had pushed the button, they all laughed. Hesitantly, I joined in and laughed weakly. I was just glad that I didn't get scolded. They kept laughing too hard and too long. I knew it wasn't *that* funny. They finally stopped when the steward gave us a wave, turned, and left the room. It was time for us to leave, too. When I said *sayonara* to Mom, she told me in Japanese that I had it wrong. I barely had enough of the old language to understand what she was saying. "No, *Akachan*," she said. "Sayonara means 'it has to be this way'—that this is all there is for you and me. Better you just say good-bye or farewell in the American way."

I thought she might tell everyone right then and there that I had promised to go back with her. But she didn't, and I said good-bye to her without looking into her eyes. I turned from her and wished that the wind would sweep us all away. We could have a *fresh start*. I begged silently, asked God and the *kami* to give us another chance, but I knew it wouldn't happen, not in a million years.

Our parting came and went, as if a random wind had blown us into the cramped cabin of the ship bound for Yokohama, then tossed us back outside when it was time to go. One moment I was standing next to my mother, the next I was outside holding on to the cold railing of the steep gangway. We scurried down to the dock, as if to break the gravitational pull of what we left behind—my mother. We were rid of her. We had lost her.

Walking back to the car, I stayed a step or two behind Dad and copied him, shoved my hands into my pants pockets and hunched my shoulders into the cruel wind. Grandma and Grandpa followed well behind us. Hudson River gusts whipped my face, a good excuse for the tears that seeped out. I didn't want to be exposed as a crybaby. Dad and I slowed down, then stopped, waiting for Grandma and Grandpa to catch up.

That is one big boat, Grandpa said, looking back over his shoulder at the behemoth that had swallowed up my mother.

It is, indeed, Grandma said. *It is indeed.*

I sat in the back seat with Dad as Grandpa drove through the Holland Tunnel to New Jersey. Dad's head was tilted back, his eyes squeezed shut. I sat the same way on the other side of the seat. I rubbed my hand over the bristles on my head which reminded me again about the barber who butchered my head and made eyes at Mom. I thought about how great it would be if Dad and I got together and beat the crap out of him. I knew that wouldn't happen, not in a million years. All I could do in the meantime was keep track of my grudges and, someday, get even.

Dad reached across to rub my stubbly head the way I had just done, and he said, "You really got your ears lowered." I nodded, and he curled back into the far side of the seat. After he fell asleep, I slipped my hand into his coat pocket, where there was some loose change, an almost-empty pack of Lucky Strikes, and a book of matches. I tucked the matches, a cigarette, and a few coins into my pants pocket.

It was warm in the car, and I felt sleepy in that good way when you can't remember anything you were worried about. I was drowsy and, at one point, I thought I called out, "Mom!" I startled myself, but no one seemed to have heard me. When would I see her again? Other than Grandma clearing her throat, no one said anything, so I guessed that I said it just to myself. I got drowsy again but stirred when Dad and Grandpa argued about which was the fastest way to get to my grandparents' house from the Holland Tunnel. The plan was to stay with them for a couple of nights. Grandma interrupted their bickering by saying, "It's been a time today, hasn't it?" No one answered one way or the other.

The day had been something, all right. I worried about my mother sleeping alone in that stuffy cabin and pictured her opening the porthole to expel the smoke and admit fresh air and I thought all of us should be punished for ruining what we were. But just in the thinking of it, I knew I was making things worse. No one told me she might be gone forever—but it could be so, like when someone dies.

The orbits of this new world and my old world intersected

so often, I didn't know whether to appeal to God, Jesus, or my ancestors. the *kami*, for help. The only thing I knew for sure was that I had broken my promise to go back to Japan with Mom and that whatever choices I made would rest on the back of this terrible thing. My choices were doomed to be the wrong ones, the kind that would leech on me day after day. My mother's absence seemed ambiguous and temporary at first, but as the days and years passed, her desertion became fixed, like an ancient creature trapped forever in amber. I wondered what would become of me.

⋄ ♦ ⋄

That night, I slept in my old bedroom at my grandparent's house. I buried my face in my pillow and for a while, allowed myself the guilty comfort of knowing I wouldn't have to worry about Mom making trouble for us tomorrow or the day after that. She wouldn't pick a fight with a neighbor, or try to stab Dad with a knife, or make fun of me when I stumbled on a step or bumped my head, then snidely tell me that, "God punishes you."

It was hard to fall asleep thinking about the lies you told, the money you stole, the fires you set, and worse—all those times when your mother asked, you'd look right into her eyes and promise you'd go back to Japan with her. But you knew all the time that you wouldn't go back to where the people hated you. No, not in a million years.

> *In the long shadow of her leaving, I'd mourn her in my own way. When awake, I took it like a man and didn't complain. When asleep, I cried out not in Japanese or English, but in a child's language of nightmares, where darkness worked its way from the ceiling and settled in your insides. I feared my father and grandparents would turn against me. I wanted to be tough like The Ringo Kid, not a cry baby. My worries ricocheted across the room during the first night that*

Mom and I were ever apart. Desperately, I wanted to remember her and the three of us together. In between the creases of my tossing and turning, the idea that we might forget each other taunted me. I promised myself to stay awake until she returned but sank into an ocean of sleep.

Part Two
A Tepid Harmony

In the long run, nothing is more unbearable than a tepid harmony in personal relations brought about by withholding emotion.

— *C. G. Jung*

Chapter 15
BACHELOR LIFE

This fresh start was different. Now it was just the two of us in our Summit apartment. Dad said he was glad that I chose to stay with him, to the degree you could be glad in this *situation*. By situation he meant the one in which our family had exploded to bits. He didn't say that, but that's how it seemed. I wasn't so troubled in the mornings. Launching myself from the apartment, I felt I could shed the disaster behind me. I went at a pace of my own choosing. I'd run, walk, or even walk backward if I wanted. Sometimes I'd slow down at street crossings until the traffic signal changed to yellow, then as the light switched to red, I'd race through the intersection, dodging cars like I was a matador. After school, I walked home slowly and reluctantly. Entering the empty apartment made me want to turn around and go home, although of course, I was already there. The only sounds were my own—the rustling of my jacket when I took it off, my footsteps, the squeak of cabinet doors as I opened them to get bread, peanut butter, and jelly. From the street below, I'd hear cars driving by and the faint sounds of people coming and going in our neighborhood. By evening, I'd listen for Dad coming up the stairs.

"What's for dinner?" I'd say, as soon as he came in.

"*Pasta e fagioli!*" he'd reply, regardless of what he had bought at the market. I had no idea what *Pasta e fagioli* meant, but I knew he said it to make me laugh, so I did, every time.

It was okay the first few nights we were alone, pretending we were celebrating. He'd whistle as he made a cheese omelet, showing off by flipping it in the air. "How about that—just like the pros!"

"Like in fancy restaurants!"

"I think we'll do just fine—just the two of us bachelors and a fresh start. Don't you?"

"Better than fine. And the eggs are good, too."

The first week or so when we were on our own, I didn't mind pretending it was good. Dad outlined Plan A for me. He'd continue to work at Celanese, and I'd finish the second grade in Summit. Our routines were intact. My school was just a short walk away. If we needed help, Grandma and Grandpa were just a half hour away in Millington. That was as detailed as Plan A got. I wondered aloud about Plan B, and Dad said that we should keep it simple. We'd cross that bridge when we came to it.

One afternoon the sound of kids drew me to a huge clapboard building that squatted at the town's edge. Train tracks and a few shacks were next to it, some that belonged to the railroad, others to families who lived in them. Dad had said the neighborhood was poor and told me to stay away. Laundry hung outside on the porches that wrapped around the perimeter of each of its four floors. Black and brown boys and girls ran up and down the outdoor stairs to return to their apartments or to go out to play hopscotch and jump rope in the dusty, unpaved parking lot below. They started in with the *ching-chong* routines, but quickly got it out of their systems. I posed my judo moves for them, and they howled. Once that ritual was behind us, we played tag and hide-and-seek until dusk. I was glad to find new friends. I showed up more often to play, until one day a couple of older kids said I had to go home. Their mothers said I looked like trouble, and that I should stick to my own neighborhood. I wanted to tell those mothers that I was just like their kids, so leave us alone and let us have fun.

Despite Mrs. Thurlur's general kindness, I couldn't sit still, and kept checking the clock, like I had somewhere important to go. Outside, all was lush and sleepy. Summer vacation was two weeks away. One morning, after Dad left for work, I decided to stay home. I got bored watching TV, so I went fishing for bluegills in a local pond. A few classmates saw me and asked me why I hadn't been in school. I told them it was my birthday—I could do whatever I wanted. The next day, I stayed home again. Before I decided what to do or where to go, there was a knock on our door.

It was my school's truant officer. Immense in his uniform, he filled the doorway with blue. He poked his head inside, looking right and left, his jaw jutting out as if he wanted to ram something with it. He asked:

"Are you William?"

I hesitated, and I said, "No, I'm Billy."

"Are your parents here?"

"Not really."

"Don't be a wise guy. In or not?"

For me, the answer was more complicated. Dad was out, but still here. My mother was out, but out forever. The truant officer bellied past me through the doorway. He told me to stay put. I told him it was *my* house, but before I could say more, he tramped through the apartment, nosing around, like he owned the place. His blue uniform glinted chrome, like fishing lures. The morning light bounced off his badge and small chains that looped from his belt. He wasn't a real policeman because he didn't have a gun. Still, this new level of big trouble seemed to erupt from nowhere. He told me that he'd have to drive me to school because I couldn't be left *unsupervised*.

"It's the law," he said.

I was disappointed when we drove to school in an ordinary sedan rather than a police car with sirens and flashing lights. When we arrived, he told the principal that I was a *piece of work*. The principal scowled. He told me to sit in one of the two chairs that faced his desk.

It was to be an interrogation.

"Why didn't you come to school yesterday or this morning?"

"I'm very sick. Can I go to the bathroom?"

"Go ahead. And you mean, *may* I go, not *can* I," he said, pointing to his personal lavatory in his office.

When I was in the bathroom, I shook my fist at the mirror, imagining the principal's big, important face. I would've liked to ask him, "*May* I punch you in the nose?" But I thought of a way out. I made loud gagging sounds like I was throwing up and flushed the toilet several times. When I returned, he was still unconvinced I was sick. He told me the truant officer said I was home alone. He asked me how long this had been going on. I said that Dad took care of me and that he was at work now and that I was sick yesterday and today.

"You couldn't have been too sick. I hear you went fishing yesterday."

"No, I didn't. I was home sick. *For real.*"

"That isn't what your classmates told your teacher."

This is how it is, I thought. *Your friends turn on you, like the communists.* I told him that I was sick in the morning, and after I felt better, I went out fishing. Then after I fished, I got sick again. As I polished my lie, I began losing my breath, panting, and it was *for real*. The principal snorted. He said that I was excused for now and he'd send for me later. He turned to his secretary and told her to bring me to my class.

Then I heard him say, "When you get back, get his grandmother on the phone for me."

No! I thought, horrified that the principal was dragging Grandma into this mess. Things were now officially out of control. I needed another fresh start. As the secretary escorted me through the halls, I closed my eyes and prayed, *Please God, let this be a bad dream.* When Mrs. Thurlur opened the classroom door, my classmates turned their eyes on me, sizing me up. Lots of murmuring. I considered myself a figure of some importance. I took my time, and casually slid into my seat. I glanced at Sally and Fred to receive a warm look or smile, but neither looked me in the eye. Just like the saying goes, they deserted me *like rats jumping off a sinking ship.*

"Children, quiet please! Let's get back to our lesson." Mrs. Thurlur went to the blackboard, jotting something that I couldn't read. She could just as well have been writing in a foreign language. I turned around in my seat and scowled at the boys, the good-looking class favorites who I figured had snitched on me. I prayed. *Please God, help me get even.* Time passed. I couldn't pay attention to what Mrs. Thurlur said until she said that I had to go with Miss so-and-so, the secretary, back to the principal's office. I got out of my seat, looked straight ahead and floated out the door, which elicited more murmuring and another scolding to the class from Mrs. Thurlur.

Returning to the principal's office, I saw Grandma seated in front of the principal's desk. "Suppose you tell your grandmother what you did," he said, gesturing for me to take the seat next to Grandma.

"I'm very sick. My stomach hurts, so I stayed home." I winced and held my belly. By this time, my stomach was genuinely hurting.

"The boy is lying," said the principal.

"Are you really sick, Billy?" Grandma asked. I was too far gone for the truth.

"I have a bad headache, too, for real," I said, rubbing the sides of my head. "It feels like there's thumping inside my head. I think I'm going to throw up." Then I asked, "*May* I use the bathroom?"

"Go ahead, if you must," the principal said, waving me away like I was a bug.

Inside the bathroom, I wretched and coughed, as if my guts were turning inside-out. I flushed the toilet repeatedly, until the principal knocked on the door and said, "That's enough nonsense for today. Knock it off right now and come on out, Billy!" he scolded. "The boy is quite the actor, a show-off," he told my grandmother, agitating himself back into his seat. He told me to wait by the secretary's desk. While she typed, I heard the principal and Grandma making noises that told me they were agreeing on something.

Driving away from school, Grandma said that I was making an unpleasant situation even worse. She told me that I had caused quite a *stir* and that I needed to get a *hold of myself*. "Actions have consequences," she said.

I started to get a better idea of who I was, and it wasn't good. We drove beyond Summit toward Millington. A thunderstorm rammed the afternoon into the dark. Grandma said something about boarding schools for me if I didn't behave better. I stopped listening to the details, which were drowned out by sounds of windshield wipers churning in the rain, tires sloshing through puddles.

Chapter 16
SPECKS OF DUST

Like Grandma said, there were consequences. When school ended, I was back in Millington, where my life as an American began. But this wasn't a triumphant return. It was a forced retreat of my own making. I was ashamed for bringing me and my own problems into my grandparents' house. But it was summer, and I looked forward to what I considered the best of the seasons—at least until Grandma enrolled me in Shiloh Bible Camp, a bare-bones day camp.

There were two cabins, one for Bible lessons, the other for arts and crafts. A few outbuildings were scattered in the woods and clearing by a sad pond, more of a big mud puddle. Except for me, the dozen or so campers were schoolboys who attended a church in Basking Ridge. I'd run around briefly in the heat with a few other kids, then rest, swat away the bugs and then attend a Bible lesson that was taught by the minister's assistant, a student from a nearby seminary.

I learned about the American God and his son, Jesus, who died, came back to life, and, to this day, still walks among us. I was open to these ideas, having watched my mother speak with the spirits who occupied the Pure Land, which I supposed, was like heaven. After the lessons, we'd eat our lunches at picnic tables on the patio between the two cabins; then we'd run around for a while and try to skip rocks across the murky pond. For the daily grand finale, I'd sit on a stone wall with other kids, each of us waiting for our rides home by mid-afternoon.

No one else in my family went to church, except Grandpa, who attended occasionally. Grandma wasn't a church goer, but she thought it was a good idea for me to have some *grounding* in religion. According to my father there was no God, no heaven or hell. One night at dinner I mentioned a few Bible stories from day camp. Dad added his two cents to the conversation.

"There's no life after death. No God in the sky who's looking out for us. We're just specks, specks of dust in the universe. Just nothing." Then, as if for emphasis, he stabbed the last two slices of Grandma's delicious meat loaf and shook them on his plate. I caught Grandpa's eye as we cast resentful glances at Dad, the quick-draw meat-loaf rustler who took all the leftovers.

Over the years, I'd listen to my father give different versions of those sentiments, trying to render them with a fatherly authority that I, like all sons, eventually came to doubt. As for me, I liked the Bible stories and how matter of fact it was for Jesus, God's son, to walk on water, make the blind see, and bring the dead back to life. With all those powers, it must have been great to be God's son, except of course, getting crucified.

I considered ways of bargaining with the American God and with the Japanese spirits of the other world that my mother had prayed to. Even if I could have articulated my worries, who else could I ask for help? My father had his own troubles to nurse. As for my grandparents, they were like camels of a special sort, beasts of burden who could plod over long expanses of troubles with barely a sip of talk.

We had no heart-to-heart chats, like they had on *Father Knows Best*, a TV show about the Andersons, a family that solved its tiny problems in a sparkly way. In my family, we didn't dwell on problems. When I went to bed, I said goodnight and shook hands with Grandma and Grandpa. It wasn't cuddly, but the good thing was that every morning, I knew I'd find them in the same steady mood as the night before. They wouldn't drag me out of bed in the middle of the night, like Mom did, to hitchhike back to Japan.

My mother's desertion, as an event, was swift, like a quick beheading. Once she decided, she got on the ship and she was gone, and that was supposed to be that. By comparison, my father slowly cut himself out of the picture with a dull blade, without conviction. He still worked at Celanese, but now had his own place in Newark. The tacit agreement was that he would stay with us on weekends, but he came up with new excuses for making his stays shorter and less frequent.

He'd make excuses like, "I better get going. Got to get an early start at the lab tomorrow. See you next weekend." With that, he'd push himself away from the dinner table on Sunday nights and be off. Agitated, Grandma would shift in her chair next to me. Dad's alibis irritated her, too. But we didn't complain about Dad, at least not out loud.

"Well, so we'll see you next week," she'd say.

I'd follow Dad out to his car, we'd shake hands good-bye, and, as often as not, we'd part after his tiresome observations about my poor posture, then he'd step into his banana-colored Studebaker convertible and drive off into the night.

I heard my grandparents talking as I walked back into the house. "I'm just *fit to be tied*," said Grandma. "Every week he leaves earlier and earlier. Did you talk to him?"

"Not yet," Grandpa said, which meant he wasn't going to pursue the matter.

I pretended I hadn't heard them. Though my father disappointed me, I knew I'd still wait anxiously for him like Prince, the old dog now dead, used to do. Though I didn't think Dad's absences were fair, I buttoned my lip.

I had trouble sleeping. I'd walk quietly through the house. Sometimes, when the weather was nice, I'd wander in the yard and garden. When I was too tired to host the opaque thoughts that had kept me awake, I'd return to my bedroom and try to sleep.

One night I was jolted awake by a thunderstorm. The old house conspired against me as I walked with no purpose in mind. The stairs and floorboards shifted and creaked with each footstep, but not loud enough to wake my grandparents. When I returned to my room, I pulled my mother's travel bag from my closet, the same one she used when we tried to run away to Japan. Grandma had put it in my closet, along with a kimono, sandals, and other Japanese things that Mom left behind. I opened the bag and removed the Buddha and an incense stick and arranged them on my chest of drawers, then prayed to the American God and the three Jesuses—the baby Jesus, the grown-up, and the ghost. I told them I was sorry for my sins and that I would never sin again if they brought her back. *Amen*. Though I had no matches, I smelled the wisps of burning incense. Folding my hands together, I reached out to the *kami* not with words, but with silent intent as I remembered my mother doing. If I had conviction, my appeals would penetrate the deep magma where, perhaps on the other side, she directed *her* prayers. I tried hard to imagine that world where I could find the gate, unlatch it, let it swing open, and there, on the other side, I'd see Mom, rising from *her* prayer to greet me, her arms wide open to receive me.

I fell in a hollow half-sleep. An image coalesced before me that shoved me into wakefulness. What poked into my mind was Sakani, also known as Marlon the Brando, very famous. How I hated that faker! The more I told myself not to think of him, the worse it got. I put everything back into my mother's bag, then tucked it in the closet. No spirits or ancestors were going to guide me to a magical path.

Trying to figure things out in my head was like eavesdropping on muffled voices from the other side of a thick wall. I strained to hear answers about why my mother left and where she was. But there was no one on the other side of that wall, just me on this side, mumbling nonsense inside the echo chamber of my head.

Chapter 17
OF FISH AND FISHERMEN

During the remainder of that first summer without her, Dad took me on fishing and camping trips, which paroled me from my echo chamber. I watched him build a boat from a do-it-yourself kit in my grandparents' yard. He often lost interest in things before they were done, but this time, he eventually finished his project, putting the finishing touches on an odd-looking boat, which was called a pram. It was a couple of feet longer than he was tall, just big enough for the two of us. He said it would be great for lake fishing.

He swabbed the hull with green paint, his favorite color, and mine too. Unlike boats I had seen, this one's bow was squared-off, instead of v-shaped. I wondered how it could cut through the water. But Dad was proud of his work, and I felt good for the both of us.

"How long does it take to dry?" I pressed my hand onto the hull to test it and left my handprint there.

"For crying out loud! If you had half a brain, you'd be dangerous!" He took a turpentine-soaked rag, cleaned the green paint off my hand and took a brush to the smudges. "If you can't do something useful, stay out of my hair until I finish this, OK?"

I went out back to the vegetable garden, where Grandpa stooped over a row of green beans, tossing the pickings into a paper bag. "How about giving me a hand, Willie?" he said. "I can use the company."

"Sure," I said. We picked together for a few minutes, but I got bored and tried to sidle away without him noticing.

"Hey, is that all? You need to develop more staying power," Grandpa laughed. "I guess the apple doesn't fall far from the tree, does it?"

It was a joke that I figured out, but I was in no mood for it. Rabbits loitered nearby in the meadow. I tossed stones at them, missing by a mile, and muttered, "Stupid boat."

The next Sunday, we woke up early for our maiden voyage. Dad slid the boat into the back of his new used car, a Plymouth station wagon. Triumphantly, he honked the horn as we pulled out of our driveway and onto the open road to Lake Hopatcong. The July sky was cloudless, bright blue and promising.

When we arrived at the lake, I was nervous because I began thinking about a model jet that Dad had built a few months earlier, a disaster that crashed and burned—created by the same two hands as this boat. Then, there was the time that he couldn't properly assemble my bicycle. His biggest failure was that he couldn't fix my mother. But each time I doubted him, guilt banged in my chest.

We waded down the public launch, and Dad wrestled the boat into the water. It settled in quietly until I hopped on board, which rocked the pram so hard that it almost tipped over, but just for a moment. Dad glowered at me, told me to sit down on the seat at the bow, and cautioned me to keep still. He tinkered with the settings on the outboard motor, and after pulling the cord a few times, the motor sputtered, then roared to life. The boat moved slowly at first, then sliced through the water, its bow rising into the air as if we were going a hundred miles an hour.

"Look at us!" I leaned over the bow, the square nose of the boat thump-thump-thumping over every little wave. When sleek speedboats zipped past us, it seemed like we were dead in the water. But I didn't care. I looked back over my shoulder and saw my father smiling, captain of our so-called pram, as we cruised across the huge lake.

We spent the day out on the water catching sunfish and perch, which we tossed back. The day was hot, but in that good way—when the breeze dries the sweat off you, before it beads up on your forehead, or above your lips. Dad and I didn't have much to say, except to guess that the few hard hits we missed may have been trout or bass. My butt was sore from sitting on the hard seat all day, and I was getting tired. I was glad when Dad finally said, "Time to call it a day," and we headed home. We stopped at a roadside stand on Route 46 and ate chili dogs and drank chocolate milkshakes—a perfect meal for a perfect day.

In August, we drove to Maine to go camping and fish for pike and lake trout. The trip seemed to take forever. Whenever I told Dad I had to take a leak or asked him how far we were from Maine, he'd get annoyed. "You just asked me that five minutes ago!" he'd complain, and I'd stare out the window, until I guessed that enough time had passed to ask again without getting yelled at.

One mile was the same as the next. Pine trees flanked us on both sides of the highway and hid everything beyond them. Along the way, a series of signs that advertised men's shaving cream broke the monotony. For example—*The Monkey Took/ One Look at Jim/ And Threw the Peanuts/ Back at Him/ He Needed/* BURMA SHAVE! We got a kick out of taking turns reading those signs out loud.

After driving all day, we reached our campground. Our site was beside a lake so wide you could barely see the other side. We (mostly Dad) unloaded our gear and set up the tent. I told him I could build a fire, get it ready to cook dinner. He didn't think it was a good idea, considering my history with matches. I didn't need to be reminded that I set our home on fire, twice.

"Instead, why not walk down to the lake and see what's what," Dad said.

I stood at the water's edge and watched boats on the far side, trolling slowly back and forth. They weren't catching anything. The wind picked up and the water was choppy. A few yards offshore, a snapping turtle cruised in front of me, its beaked head and neck thrusting forward, the rest of it cloaked in a shell propelled by its paddle-like legs below the waterline. I looked around for other people, hoping to see or hear some other kids. Only a few campsites had tents pitched on them.

When Dad yelled, "Come and get it," I ran back to our campsite. The fire was going good. He lopped canned meat ravioli and corn on our aluminum plates, next to slices of Wonder Bread. We sat on stumps by the fire pit and got ready to dig in, cowboy-style. "At long last," Dad said, "And bless you, *Chef Boyardee.*" He lifted his fork and smiled with well-deserved anticipation. Suddenly, a gust of Maine wind raced over the lake and through our campsite, flipping his aluminum plate, tossing ravioli across his shirt and on his lap. The wind stopped as suddenly as it began. I laughed hysterically, but he didn't think it was funny. "You might not be laughing so hard if it happened to you," he said. That made me laugh even more.

After we ate, Dad said it looked like it might rain, so he chopped wood for what seemed a week's worth of fires. It seemed like a good idea. I liked it when he planned ahead. We stacked up wood and put a tarp over it. We crept into our sleeping bags with that good feeling when you're too tired to worry about anything.

On our first day on the lake, we caught the same small fry that we had caught at Lake Hopatcong, only more of them. It started raining that afternoon. We didn't see the sun for the rest of our vacation in Maine. We sat in our tent looking out at the lake through light rain, hard rain, downpours, and all kinds of rain in between. We swatted mosquitoes and scratched the blisters on our ankles from poison ivy. There were nights I rubbed my itchy feet together so hard that they seemed about to burst into flames.

When the rain relaxed, I'd get out of my sleeping bag, sit outside the tent, and gaze into the silent, dark world of trees. I'd doze off until startled by the sudden cracking of tree limbs, the thud of a rain-sodden branch falling on the loamy forest floor. A figure moved among the pines, a shadow within a shadow, the memory that Dad and I shoved deep inside, a topic not to be discussed. The more I pretended to forget, the more her absence dragged me down.

When the rain let up, Dad showed me how to build a fire by stacking the wood teepee-style. We kept feeding the fire until it was a bonfire, its orange reflection ablaze across the lake. It started drizzling again, which turned into another monsoon. We were tent-bound through the next day. We played card games like War and Canasta, and he taught me new games like Rummy and Poker. We used M&Ms as poker chips. He read *Field & Stream* and *True, the*

Magazine for Men, and I read *Superman* and *Little Archie* comics. We farted and apologized for losing our balance.

We tried our best, but the soggy weather took the fun out of camping. Rain thwarted our cook fires, dampened the linings of our sleeping bags. Running in the pouring rain and dark to the campground latrine just to take a nighttime crap was the last straw. We abandoned camp the next morning, cutting our vacation in half. It felt good to be on the road home.

Dad said, "Well, the weather could have been better, but it was fun, don't you think?"

"It was," I said, thinking that things could always be worse.

We passed more of those shaving cream road signs on the way home. *Hardly a driver/ is now alive/ who passed/ on hills/ at 75/* BURMA SHAVE! We both laughed, and I liked how it felt, two men scoffing at the grim message. Even if we're just specks in the universe, I'd take it.

During the rest of that summer at home, I often fished alone in the Passaic River. I'd strap my rod, creel, and other gear onto my rickety bike, and hide it in the woods by one of my favorite spots. Wading in my shorts and sneakers, I'd take my time casting from bank to bank, meandering with the river through the woods and meadows by Millington and Long Hill. I always stayed far upstream from the train station because there was a Johns Manville plant nearby. Everyone knew to stay away from the plant that manufactured asbestos and sent debris slobbering into the Passaic.

Having the river to myself, I felt free and successful, even though I rarely caught anything except eels and suckers. I'd see a red hawk soaring overhead, screeching and casting its fleeting shadow below on skunk cabbage, ferns, and the river. I'd hear muskrats plopping into still pools and watch their slick underwater glides to their dens. I'd watch black water snakes silently and quickly weaving their way on the river's skin. All these creatures were on the move. They were either looking for someone to eat or scurrying away from someone that wanted to eat them.

When Dad fished in streams, he used a fly rod. He prided himself on tying his own dry flies, delicate imitations of insects with names like *woolly bugger*, *hare's ear*, and *blue-winged olive*. I fished artlessly, with a spinning rod. One afternoon I fished a familiar stretch where quick-flowing riffles settled quietly into a deep, cold pool. I had tied a silver spinner to my line and, for good measure, knitted a couple of worms on the spinner's hooks. Lazily, I reeled my line in, unprepared for a hard strike that jangled the rod out of my hands. I flailed into the shallow water on all fours like a crab and lunged for the rod, as desperate as the creature at the other end of my line. I jerked the fish in and dragged it to the riverbank. It was a brown trout, as long as my forearm, the biggest fish I ever caught. I almost cried I was so happy. My catch was too big to pack in my creel, so I used fishing line to tether the trout to the handlebars of my bike. I took the longest way home, so the folks in passing cars might admire my trophy.

I stopped at the sweet shop by the Millington train station, where I usually bought my comic books. After gulping down a Coke, I hung around the comic-book rack and leafed through *Forbidden Worlds* and *Strange Tales*, until the shop owner told me not to touch any more comics because I smelled like fish. I told him about the big brown and asked him if he wanted to see it. He wasn't interested and told me to go home and clean up. Insulted, I slammed the door on my way out. But he had a point. The smell of dead fish was imprinted on me. Even as I coasted briskly downhill, my trophy fish attracted flies. The trout, suspended between the handlebars, was stiffening quickly, rigor mortis setting in. When I got home, I untied the trout and carried it to the kitchen counter for Grandma to admire. The thin leader line had cut into my trophy catch, forming hash marks all over its hefty body. Its mouth was open, and its once bright, dark eyes had turned milky. Grandma was husking corn for dinner, and I waited impatiently for her to get a good look.

"Isn't it the biggest trout you've ever seen?"

"It's big all right, but it's gone bad," she said, pressing the back of her hand to her mouth.

A few minutes later, I was digging a hole in the garden. Grandma told me to dig deep enough so animals wouldn't get at it. She said it wasn't all a waste—the Indians buried fish for fertilizer. It was great for making vegetables grow.

Chapter 18
A STONE PORCH IN AN OLD HOUSE

It was sheathed in tired white clapboard and chipped blue trim. Like my grandparents, the house was worn but not worn out, despite the usual indignities that come with age. The front door was off plumb and required two hands, and sometimes a shoulder, before it cooperated. It was more efficient and pleasant to come and go through the door of the stone porch, the original footprint of this house, built when one room and a fireplace was enough to make a home.

※ ◆ ※

During the dog days of summer, you peel off your shoes and socks and pad barefoot on the porch floor, its blue stone slabs a cool celebration on your feet. You sit Indian style in front of the idle stone fireplace and remember when you could stand up inside it. From the stone porch, you enter the kitchen, which was just big enough to accommodate a tin country sink, a short counter, an icebox, and a puny white gas range that, along with your grandmother, are the kitchen's chief laborers. The kitchen abuts a small pantry, where crooked stairs lead up to two bedrooms separated by the upstairs bathroom.

You remember that in Japan, you squatted over an oval hole in the floor where you dropped your turds and squirted pee. You remember "honey buckets," the ironic euphemism for pails filled with human waste. Lowly workmen called night-soil collectors recovered the excrement from a holding tank under the house and carted it away to fertilize rice paddies— far enough away that you stopped gagging from the smell. You still gag reflexively when you smell shit that belongs to someone or something else, including dogs.

But here in America, you can sit on a toilet like a king on a throne while leafing through a comic book. Then when done with your business, you tug a handle, and it disappears! Now you take such things for granted. The bathroom is a huge chamber, sparsely furnished with a claw-foot tub, a pedestal sink, a small mirror, and the toilet. When you sit there, you study the floor, which is covered by a huge map of the United States—a single sheet of linoleum that spans the length of the bathroom. All the 48 contiguous states are imprinted on it. Red stars mark the state capitals. This is how you get a head start on American geography.

When a teacher asks the class, "What's the capital of Wyoming?" your hand shoots up like a missile and you proudly shout, "Cheyenne!" You impress no one. On the contrary, you feel humiliated, exposed again as a loudmouthed show-off.

Several times each day you pass by a peculiar half-door, shut tight, off the upstairs hallway. About four feet off the floor, it accesses the attic. A decorative bowl full of wax fruit is arranged on a side table, placed against the wall, right below the door. It looks like an offering to whatever is inside the attic. Although your grandmother insists there's nothing of interest in there, secrets and dark matters beckon you from behind the door. How long can you resist the attic of no interest?

The dining room, living room, and two more bedrooms are downstairs. In the summer, a blade of grass or a sprig of wildflower might sprout up through the plank-board floor of the dining room, where crickets and an occasional praying mantis might visit. During windy winter nights, puffs of snow collect in those same cracks. You watch your grandfather angle down the narrow steps to the cellar, where he shovels coal into the furnace until it rattles to life. Squatting at the top of the cellar steps, you watch sparks dance in the open furnace door. Feeble warmth clangs in the water pipes, making its way toward the iron radiators upstairs. The glowing furnace reminds you of when your grandfather complained that your father had no *fire in the belly.*

Sometimes this house is a glass barely half full. You cannot pour your mother into it, because she has left for good, neither can you pour your father into it, because he prefers to be elsewhere than here with you. But this house is never a glass that is empty—you and your grandparents find each other every morning, although sometimes, when you encounter each other, it seems a minor surprise.

In the world outside, you love America fiercely. There are so many colors to see, accents to hear, flavors to taste, and textures to touch, all of which fill you with longing for your kind. Who they were and where to find them was another matter. You wish you could fall asleep like you used to, when it was the easiest thing.

Chapter 19
MY CROOKED PATH

I heard two words that were new to me: *incorrigible* and *miscreant*. This was during the first week of third grade at Liberty Corner Elementary. When I asked Grandma what they meant, she asked me why I wanted to know, grimacing as she waited for the answer. It was kind of a long story and one I knew she wouldn't like. Although it was my new school, the circumstances were familiar. I watched the minute hand of the classroom clock reluctantly jerk forward one eternity at a time. While I fidgeted and doodled, Mrs. Jamison, hefty and pale, droned on. I went to the pencil sharpener often, just to break the monotony, and made a big deal of grinding a pencil down to its nub.

"No sooner do you arrive at our school than you begin showing off like a clown who owns the place. Who do you think you are?" she said. As she clenched her teeth, I thought about horses.

But back to the question at hand, *who did I think I was?* That was a perplexing question I had heard before. It was more of an accusation than a question. *Who did I think I was?* I wanted to know, too. I thought about the idea for a few beats as I stood by the pencil sharpener, and held my chin in a pondering pose, to show I took the question seriously. This incensed Mrs. Jamison. She huffed that it was the last straw, ordered the class to stay put, and told me to follow her. She walked apace down the hall, her horsey shoes clacking on the shiny linoleum floor. I broke into a semi-trot just to keep up, her bottom swaying back and forth in front of me. Without bothering to knock on the office door, she swooped by the secretary and told her never mind, then before you knew it, we stood in front of the principal's desk. She placed me by her side, so that we both faced him. He looked at us as if we had just sprouted from the floor. His bald pate glowed bright pink. She told him what I did and called him by his first name, as if he were just a kid himself.

"So, Charles, this thing is your problem, not mine. He's

incorrigible!" She pivoted and snorted out of the office. It took a long moment for the principal to pull himself together. Then he began interrogating me.

"What possessed you to behave like that?"

"Nothing," I said, staring at the floor.

"You think you're a comedian? You think you're funny?"

"No."

"If you don't change your ways, you're well on your way to becoming a first-rate *miscreant!*"

Furiously, he scribbled on a notepad. I could tell when he ended a sentence. That's when he stabbed a period on the pad—like he wanted to kill it. After he finished, he slipped the note into a folder. He told me to sit outside his office and think about what I had done. After the principal figured I had been thinking long enough, he had his secretary bring me to my classroom.

In a day or two, I was in trouble again. Instead of listening to whatever Mrs. Jamison was talking about, I drew pictures of airplanes in a dogfight high in the sky, while ships fired at them from the sea below. Bombs and gunfire rained over the sea. I didn't notice her hovering over me. She scowled and shook her head. She examined my drawing, took the paper, and crumpled it in her fist. She asked me if war was all I had on my mind. She tossed the wad in a waste basket.

"That'll be enough of that," she said, "Enough of your wicked ways. You're just … I don't know what."

Before long, everyone knew I was a troublemaker. During one recess, the class do-gooder scampered toward me, then stopped just short of my face and yipped, "No wonder she hates you. Japs killed her son!" and stomped off, back to his snickering friends.

I was stuck between the urge to apologize for something and another urge to pick a fight. That's how it was when you wore the face of the enemy.

That day when Mrs. Jamison had asked me, "Who do you think you are?" the answer was on the tip of my tongue. It stopped there, when she took me to the principal—just before I could say *nobody*.

Because I had a bad reputation, I couldn't be choosy about who I played with. I made friends with the lowest-hanging fruit—the damaged, bruised, and undesirable—Billy Haddon and Eddie Graham. They were rotten kids like me. Grandma told me to stay away from the Haddons' house, but I went anyway. Billy lived with his mother and his crazy grandfather up the road. He was a year older than me. When we played, we might be having fun, and it would suddenly turn bad. Billy might look at me, his dark brown eyes widening, like a great idea came to him. For instance, when we were playing a game of catch, he lunged several steps closer, then threw the baseball as hard as he could.

"What's the matter, can't you catch?" he'd say, as I ducked to avoid the missile.

Or, riding bikes and coasting downhill, he swerved into me just for the heck of it. To avoid him, I had to tumble into the weeds and brambles off the road.

"Why'd you shove me off the road?" I asked, and he denied it.

"I didn't touch you, you sissy! Don't blame me just because you can't ride."

The inside of Billy's house was dim and swollen with stale air. The windows were always closed. His mother sat in their murky living room, smoking and watching TV. I was afraid of his grandfather, who sometimes charged the door, shrieking nonsense when I knocked. I'd run away, but would come back another day, so desperate was I for friendship. Sometimes the old man would misbehave so much that he'd have to be put away for a while at the veterans' hospital, which was conveniently close by. For these reasons, I felt sorry for Billy, but it was hard to sympathize with a guy who tried to knock your head off with a baseball or wanted to run you off the road. Eventually, I'd stop going over there.

I was supposed to make friends with Eddie Graham. Both Grandma and Mrs. Graham arranged for us to get together. When I biked to the Graham's house, I had to navigate my way around their pet, a huge white goose that patrolled their yard. As soon as I got off my bike, the bird—which seemed larger than most dogs—would swoop toward me, his powerful but flightless wings thumping on his flanks, his pumpkin-colored beak nipping at my legs and hands.

The only good thing about Eddie was his mother. When I went over to their house to play on a rainy day, the three of us watched a puppet show. The show was for babies. I hated it. But Mrs. Graham just loved Lamb Chop, the star puppet. "Isn't that Lamb Chop a darling!" Afterward, she'd make us a snack, then Eddie and I would go outside.

One afternoon we picked up small branches to play swords. We dueled, clacking our sticks, thrusting at each other but without serious contact, until Eddie gave me several stinging whacks on my arms and back. I gave him a couple of good ones in return. Instantly, he started whining. "Oww! You hurt me!" he whined, rubbing his forearm, like it was gushing blood. It looked okay to me. He got sulky and said he was going inside for some water. I was beating the crap out of a tree trunk when Mrs. Graham came out of the house and looked at me grimly.

"I am *so* disappointed in you, Billy. It's obvious you don't know how to play nice. I put some ice on the welts you gave Eddie. You might be glad to know the swelling's going down."

Her eyes welled up with tears, and her lips were twitching, and her face was red. She took a deep breath and said, "Please leave. *Now.*"

Biking home, I had to ask myself, how the heck did I get into these messes? I was glad that I wouldn't have to play with Eddie again or deal with that violent goose, but sad that Mrs. Graham thought I was a criminal. I worried that she would call my grandmother, telling her a story that wasn't true. When I got home, Mrs. Graham had already called. I told Grandma my side of story and stuck pretty much to the truth.

She asked me, "Billy, can't you just stop making things so complicated?"

It seemed to me that it was just as much other people who made things complicated. But I kept the thought to myself.

For a while, I was on a good path. When school ended, I was very busy selling boxes of YMCA cookies door-to-door so I could go to sleepaway camp for two weeks. I rode my bike around Millington until there were no more doors to knock on, all in the service of going to Camp Washington, set in the bucolic hills of western New Jersey. The deal was that Grandma would match whatever money I made. I made so much that it astonished her. Dad drove me to the camp and dropped me off. I looked forward to what I expected to be the adventures of a lifetime, including horseback riding, the dream of any cowboy.

I had my sleeping bag, fishing gear, and an old-time suitcase that Grandma had used when she was a college girl. When I got into the cabin with the other nine-year-olds, one of them made a remark about the suitcase. One thing led to another, and I was in a shoving match with another camper. I cut my arm from bumping into an exposed screw that stuck out from a bunk frame. There was enough blood for my cabin counselor to send me to the infirmary. The camp nurse dressed the cut and sent me back to my group. Back in the cabin, I said "shit" out loud, just for the shock value of it, and the counselor told me to wash my mouth out with soap and watched while I did it. That was all on day one.

Things calmed down after that. I enjoyed boating and swimming in Lake Nichecronk. I passed all the swimming tests to become a Flying Fish. I came close to becoming a Shark, but I failed the test from the high dive. Once I got up to the diving board, it looked like the water was 100 feet down. I'd be crazy to dive from there. I chickened out. The boys in line behind me had to back down on the ladder to make room for me. They made clucking noises as I clambered down.

Besides activities on the waterfront, my favorites were archery and arts and crafts, not because I was especially good at either. In both cases, I liked the way your eyes took everything in and then you depended on your hands to make what you imagined actually happen. Though I had looked forward to horseback riding, I was disappointed. Rather than galloping wildly across the meadows and thrashing through the forest on horseback, younger boys like me were restricted to a corral, riding tired old nags in slow circles, their heads bobbing monotonously, the noose of supervision wringing every ounce of adventure from horseback riding.

On a clear July afternoon that was just too perfect to waste on the day's schedule, I took off after lunch. I began fishing in a brook that ran into the lake and followed it upstream on Schooley's Mountain. The brook meandered between rocks on each side and, as I went farther, pools formed where small fish milled about, feasting on the insects that skimmed the water. The fish were too little for catching. I left my rod and tackle box there because I needed to climb on all fours to go over or around the boulders and follow the brook. I'd rest and turn around to look down at the camp, the big lodge at one end of the lake, the roofs of the dozen or so cabins nestled below, the kids and counselors on the dock of the waterfront. I lost track of time, but I didn't care. This was not an ordinary path, but one that I was blazing, the most beautiful path I had ever been on. When dusk started to settle in the woods, I turned back down the mountain. I got back after dinner was over and the mess hall was closed. My counselor scolded me because he said they sent out a search party for me. He told me that I had upset a lot of people, including him. He told me that the only person I thought about was myself. He let that sink in and wouldn't you know it, he asked me, "Who do you think you are?"

"What about dinner?" I asked, "I'm starving!"

"You missed a great dinner–spaghetti and meatballs," he said, disgusted with me.

Just my luck. Spaghetti and meatballs were my favorite dish. To boot, the counselor confined me to the cabin, which meant I would miss the camp's big bonfire that everyone had been talking about for days.

All the campers were obliged to write to their parents. I wrote to Dad and told him I was having fun, staying out of trouble, and I asked him to visit on parents' day the following week. Other campers in my cabin heard from home and, along with the letters, received cookies and candy. The only thing I had asked Dad to do was to send my toothbrush, which I had forgotten. He didn't show up or write back. When he picked me up at the end of the two weeks, I'd be among the last campers waiting for their ride. Just time enough to do something bad before I went home. While waiting by the parking lot, I saw two magnificent lanyards hanging out of an untended backpack that belonged to one of the junior counselors. Furtively, I looked around to make sure no one could see me, then stuffed the lanyards into my suitcase. Once we got home, I told my father that I had made them.

"Look, Dad! These turned out great and this one's for you," I chirped, and handed him the fanciest and most beautiful of the two.

"Hmm," he murmured, "Did you make these all on your own?" He inspected the lanyard, then narrowed his eyes at me.

"I had a little help."

"I thought so. For the time being, just hold on to it for me."

He was barely impressed. Dad's approval was as slippery as an eel, regardless of whether my points of pride were true or not.

The horsing around, the swearing, the hike by myself up the mountain were things I could live with. Stealing something a guy made with his own hands was behavior that Grandma would say was *beyond the pale*. Soon after summer ended, I lost track of the lanyards and couldn't remember where I had put them. I had robbed that counselor of the beautiful things that he first imagined in his mind's eye, then twisted and wove with his fingers. When I pulled the lanyards from his backpack, I knew that what I had stolen from the boy was more than just things. In the aftermath of my theft, I understood, however obscurely, that I may have robbed him of the trust he took for granted in day-to-day life. What if my thievery changed everything in his life for the worse? I didn't want to think about it. If I kept my theft a secret, no one would ever know who I really was.

Back home on one of Dad's weekend visits, I overheard him and Grandma talking about sending me away to a boarding school, which they said might be the best thing all around. But then they talked about how expensive it would be. For now, I guessed they were stuck with me.

In the meantime, my family was concerned about developments in the news that were far more important than the problems I created. Those Russians were at it again. While waiting for Grandpa's train at Millington station, Grandma and I sat in the Buick, staring through the windshield up into the night sky to spot a blinking light that might be Sputnik, the satellite that the Soviet Union had launched into outer space. It was orbiting Earth, cruising high above us.

As far as we knew, we were no longer as safe as we thought. Experts talked to each other on news programs and wondered how the Russians had reached outer space before we did. It was more than an embarrassment. Some experts said the problem was that American schools failed us.

"They say our children don't do as well in math and science as the Russian children," Grandma said, straining to glimpse the nasty little satellite.

The autumn night was clear, and the sky pulsed with so many stars it was impossible to differentiate Sputnik. Regardless, we suspected it was up there watching us—like God, but in a bad way.

Chapter 20
FOREIGNER GO HOME

Summer vacation slumped into fourth grade, and I was anxious about going to a new school, Cedar Hill Elementary, which had just opened in Basking Ridge. "If you get off on the right foot, you can make things easy for yourself," Grandma told me. "A good attitude can make all the difference." I didn't reply but figured that at least, I could pretend to have a good attitude.

Although its facilities were sparkling and new, I sensed the familiar vibrations that pushed me to the edges of social life at school. I was part of the cohort populated by the outsiders and undesirables. You know when you are one. After being picked on or ignored by those with pedigrees in popularity, misfits like me might turn on one other to keep from sliding to the very bottom of the bottom. I could be as cruel as the next little bottom-feeder, so long as they were easy prey. The cafeteria, playground, and classrooms may have looked benign from the outside, but from the inside I recognized school as a jungle. Still, I tried to keep Grandma's advice in mind.

Crossing her arms, I knew Miss Crowell was serious. On the first day of school, she told us, "I'm going to expect the very best from all of you, and you can expect the best from me." She was stocky and had copper-colored hair. I liked her very much. If I didn't give her cause to get cross at me, I thought she'd treat me fine.

The first several weeks went well, despite a couple of dustups, which didn't draw any teacher's attention. At recess, a twerp gave me the slant-eyes routine. I shoved him as payback. Another time, a sixth grader who stood behind me in the cafeteria line told me to forget lunch because they were all out of rice. A buddy of his slapped him on the back and snorted, "You should be on TV!" His face was like a large dish with its eyes, nose, and mouth huddled in the middle. As I brought my lunch tray to the return stack, I gave Dish Face my *I-dare-you* sneer, but he stared right back at me, like he'd wring my skinny neck. Intimidated, I walked briskly toward my table, breaking into a jog until the teacher on lunch duty barked, "Walk, don't run!" Fortunately, the kid peeled off in another direction.

My attitude was pretty good until John the Brit got on my nerves, not for anything he did but because he was so popular. Everyone slobbered over John because he came from "abroad." He and his family had moved from London. His father was a big shot whose company had transferred him to New York City. John, with his curly brown hair, easy grin, and quaint accent had it all going for him. When teachers chitchatted on the playground or in the cafeteria, I overheard them talking about the many charms of the new boy from England. "He has such a gentlemanly demeanor." "He's so mature for his age." "I wish I had *him* in my class."

"*So mature,*" I muttered to myself. You would have thought that he was Baby Jesus or something, if there could be a mature Baby Jesus.

The three teachers who taught fourth grade anointed John as the star in a joint class play that was tailor-made for him, a story that portrayed the trials and tribulations of an English schoolboy who, having moved to America with his family, had to cope with severe cultural challenges—for example, differing accents and national holidays. My class got to attend some rehearsals. The plot was about a plucky British boy who endured the hardships of being in a new country. How could the poor lad survive, having to cope with the American accents and all? He would not only survive; he'd clear up the big mysteries of life for us. For example, we learned that "fortnight" in England meant two weeks. That the music for "My Country 'Tis of Thee" was lifted note-for-note from the "God Save the Queen," the British national anthem. That he had to cross the "pond" to get here. Well, *righto* and *blimey!* What about the "pond" I had to cross? In fact, the pond I had to cross, the Pacific, made his pond, the Atlantic, look like a pee hole in the snow. What about the wildly different language I had to learn? My ardent wish was that John the Brit pack his bags and return to his pale, upper-crusty homeland and do it sooner than later. I watched John sitting at his desk across the aisle from me, always busy and intent. Occasionally, he'd look up and catch me glowering at him, silently wishing a school bus would run over him. He'd give me that British trademark grin of a mouthful of crooked teeth and say something like, "Is everything okay with you, mate?" For all the bad looks I tossed his way, he never spoke a cross word to me. I'd go back to minding my own business, while grinding my teeth on a pencil. If only the charming foreigner would go back home where he belonged, maybe I could be one of Miss Crowell's favorites.

One October morning before class started, I told Miss Crowell that I spoke Japanese and said a few phrases I could remember like, *arigato gozaimasu* for thank you, and *ohayō gozaimasu* for good morning. She was so impressed that I told her I also knew how to write in Japanese. She said it would be marvelous if I'd write something on the blackboard. Although I was illiterate when it came to Japanese, I told her I was happy to do it. I scratched out a vertical series of crazy hash marks as reasonable facsimiles of Japanese characters.

"This means 'In 1492 Columbus sailed the ocean blue,'" I said.

"Oh really?" she said.

The air leaked out of me, and I had to confess, "No, it's not for real."

"I gathered that. Maybe you can learn it someday."

I tried other tactics to curry her favor, like becoming a teacher's snitch. Bunny, the girl who sat in front of me, made a habit of picking her nose and pasting it under her seat or eating it. This was the truth and, I thought, useful information for the good of the order. Rhetorically, I asked Miss Crowell, "Isn't that disgusting?"

"Well, just don't look," she advised.

When I told her that John the Brit was cheating on quizzes by stealing glances at my answers, she said, "Then he'd be making a big mistake, wouldn't he?"

One morning I was drawn to a cluster of kids who were chattering around another kid outside the school doors, a second grader who was crying because someone had thrown a horse chestnut that struck him on the back of his neck. The other boys sidled away and melted into the building as the assistant principal, drawn by the commotion, asked the kid what had happened.

"They threw this at me," he said, holding out the evidence in his palm.

I thought it was good entertainment to start the day, and I snickered. The assistant principal snarled, "You think this is funny, Fellenberg?"

"No," I lied.

He turned back to the boy. "Who threw the chestnut? Was it Fellenberg?"

The boy shook his head no. I walked behind them as the assistant principal put a friendly arm around the kid's shoulder and guided him inside. When any grown-up called me by my last name, it gave me the willies. That's how guards addressed the convicts in old-time prison movies. I shuffled down the hall toward my classroom, wanting to shout out, "I'm innocent!"

◈ ◆ ◈

It's May, and the school auditorium is packed with teachers, staff, and kids for the much-anticipated fourth-grade show. I'm surprised, even pleasantly so, because watching the play has been fun, mainly because John the Brit's so engaging. He draws in his breath as the school band starts the music that segues into the star's big closing number. Meanwhile, Dish Face, the big sixth-grader, sits behind me and pokes me in the back with a pencil. I twitch in my seat to avoid the jabs. I glance behind and see the assistant principal sweep past Dish Face's row and head toward me. He gestures for me to leave my seat, grabs my elbow and ushers me out to the hall.

He says, "All that fidgeting in your seat. Why do you have to be the center of attention?"

I press my back against the wall to avoid getting the full blast of his sour breath. "Fellenberg, what's to be done with you? You're an insult to your race."

There he goes calling me *Fellenberg* again.

Not to be a smart aleck, rather because his question puzzles me, I ask, "Which one?" I mean, one side or the other of my heritage seemed to rankle certain people. His face reddens, tenses up like the skin of a balloon just before it pops. Instead, he takes a deep breath and exhales a cloud of bad air that wafts like an evil spirit around me and tells me wait in the hall for the rest of the show. "Join your class when it's over," he says.

> *The assistant principal had it on good authority that my kind was a bad idea. "Anyone who has traveled in the Far East knows that the mingling of Asiatic blood with European and American blood produces, in nine cases out of ten, the most unfortunate results." That was Franklin D. Roosevelt's opinion. Under his watch as a war President, he imprisoned 120,000 people because they had Japanese blood, and in the process, took their homes, livelihoods, and dignity. FDR was long dead, but his views still resonated. To some, I posed a risk.*

Though the doors are closed, I hear John the Brit warble his country's national anthem which ends with, *Happy and glorious, long to reign over us, God save the Queen!* That's the part where we Americans sing, *Land of the pilgrims' pride, from every mountainside, let freedom ring!*

I have to admit to myself that he's a pretty good singer. If I was the crying kind, I could've shed a tear. From the hallway, I hear applause swelling inside the auditorium as the show ends. I clap, too. John's the kind of guy you'd like to have for a friend.

The author's paternal grandparents

Chapter 21
ADVENTURES WITH THE ANCIENT ONES

Grandma was my best friend, even though I wasn't consciously aware that she was. But, I never would have admitted it. I mean, it's embarrassing for a ten-year old boy to have an old lady as a pal. Regardless, I enjoyed our small adventures together. When she asked if I wanted to celebrate my tenth birthday by seeing a movie, I jumped on it.

"Yes, I want to see *Dracula!*"

"I don't know. It's horror, you know. Could give you nightmares."

"It would be good to see something… *different*," I said. What I meant was that it'd be a welcome departure from other Wednesday matinees we saw together, like *Auntie Mame* and *Around the World in 80 Days*. She thought they were grand. When she asked if I liked them, I told her they were okay. But now she had dangled an opportunity to choose my birthday movie and was about to renege. Before I got mad, I'd reason with her. I reminded her that I saw *Godzilla* on TV and it didn't scare me. If a radioactive dinosaur didn't faze me, a creep with fangs in a silly cape wasn't going to give me nightmares.

"Well, he's a vampire, a bit more than a creep."

"Look, I even felt sorry for Godzilla. The A-bomb made him a killer. In the end, the Japanese army killed him, and everything returned to normal."

"None of that sounds very normal."

"What I mean is, I knew it was just a movie, not real. No nightmares."

Finally, Grandma relented, and we went to a double feature in Morristown, *The Horror of Dracula* and *The Thing That Wouldn't Die*. Grandma paused under the theater's marquee, reading the posters displayed outside.

"Look at that blood dripping from the vampire's teeth. And listen to this, '*Those who come to end his realm of terror stay to become* his victims.' Or this, 'The line between vampire and human is a fragile one.'" Grandma shivered and said, "I still have my doubts. We could go to Schrafft's for a cup of cocoa and slice of cake instead."

"The posters exaggerate. The shows are never as scary as you want them to be," I said.

"All right, then, but you can't say I didn't warn you."

Well, Grandma did warn me, and I was soon convinced that there was just a thin line between vampire and human. Dracula sucked the life out of beautiful girls while their feckless family and boyfriends stood around and did nothing. His victims became vampires. Garlic, crosses, and holy water made him hiss, but he kept coming back for more. Though Grandma had bought me Raisinets, I had barely eaten any, and the box was damp from my sweaty hands. I was terrified.

"Are you okay?" Grandma asked.

"Of course." I bared my teeth at her to show her how unfazed I was. In the spirit of my horsing around, she curled her upper lip, flashed her gleaming incisors at me. I thought I'd pee in my pants right there in my seat. I choked out a weak laugh.

"Well, I'm glad you're enjoying it," Grandma said.

My blood drained to the carpeted floor. This movie said it all. Things are not what they seem! Despite their magnificent house with all their fancy stuff, cozy setup, and upper-crusty English accents, these sorry dopes didn't know the difference between a fiend and a friend. Worst of all, the beautiful Lucy became a vampire. I persevered to the torturous end, where Dracula met his doom, staked through the heart and set on fire by sunlight. Still, I wasn't convinced he wouldn't come back. We stayed for the opening scenes of the second feature, *The Thing That Wouldn't Die*, but left early. It was a story about teenagers on a beach who find a partially buried chest and instead of treasure inside, they find a pirate's head that does a lot of talking. Grandma saw me yawning and asked me if I wanted to leave.

"It's a pretty cheesy movie. I'm ready to go." After seeing Dracula, this show was about as scary as Howdy Doody.

Walking out past the lobby, I read a poster that cautioned, *"Beware the bedeviled master of all that is evil!"* Who could say that he was dead for good? Who could say that he wouldn't come back to turn people into blood-sucking ghouls? On the ride home, I had a horrible feeling about where the leering vampire was heading.

That night, I saw Dracula climb out of the half door of our attic. He swooped past my doorway, his cape rustling. The tricky ghoul skulked outside my bedroom and then disappeared. To repel him, I arranged pencils in my room and improvised crosses, laying short ones perpendicular across longer ones. I crossed myself, then drew crosses in the air above my bed and by the doorway to infuse the atmosphere with goodness and begged God to keep me safe from Dracula. For good measure, I reached out to the ancestor spirits of the Pure Land and asked them to protect me from the Bedeviled Master.

Though I survived that night, I bolstered my defenses for the next. I took the antique cross that lay on my grandmother's dresser. It was a likely vampire repellent, and a fancy one at that, framed by silver filigree that was inlaid with rose-colored glass. Jesus would work his magic through the cross and send Dracula cowering back into the shadows. I planned to press the holy jewel on his chalky forehead or cheek, sizzling his skin just like it did in the movie. The night came and went without incident. When I came home from school, Grandma asked me if I had taken the silver cross off her bureau. I told her that I just needed to borrow it for a while.

"Why on earth would you need to do that?"

I confessed that I was scared and wanted the cross to ward off Dracula.

"Of course, you know vampires don't exist, right?" Grandma said.

"Maybe not," I said, "but I saw what I saw."

"I should never have taken you to see that miserable show. I could just kick myself!"

After several more nights blighted by vampires, Grandma moved me from the upstairs bedroom to the spare room downstairs. It was a relief to have more distance from the undead. I worried less about Dracula and rarely saw him.

I thought about my mother and how she had changed into a person I did not know. Something not of this world, like a vampire, might have taken hold of her. It made sense in a crazy way.

Grandpa took me with him to the bank where he worked in New York City. I was astonished from the moment we went inside the subway and boarded the train that swayed and screeched, like a carnival ride. Lights inside sputtered off and on like flashbulbs. Sometimes the train jerked to a stop for no reason. Annoyed and sweaty, passengers pressed against each other and muttered things like, "Now what?" or slapped a newspaper against their legs. Others just bowed their heads with their eyes closed, hanging on to the hand straps overhead. The car was crowded with hot, weary, angry people—and they were just starting the day!

"Willy, give me your hand," said Grandpa as we got off the train. I resisted holding his hand at first—it wasn't like I was a little kid. I soon changed my mind, as we got jostled and pushed by the stampede of people that rumbled all around us. The underground air smelled alternately like wet socks, ashtrays, bad cheese, and, less frequently, nice perfume. I gripped his big paw and held on tight in his wake, the two of us in tandem swept along in a tidal wave of people that gushed through subway turnstiles and spouted up two long flights of stairs.

On the street corner, taxis, trucks, and buses honked, fumed, loomed, and lurched past stone-faced men in suits and women in fancy dresses, all dodging through and past the roiling tramp of people to the safety of the other side of the street. After reaching safety there, we had to repeat the same madness at the next crossing. Waiting for the light to change, my grandfather paused to light a cigarette and exhaled a big puff of smoke. I could use one of those, I thought. It looked very relaxing.

Grandpa worked at the Federation Bank and Trust, which was in a huge building called the Coliseum, on Columbus Circle, just off Central Park. He was the head teller, something I figured was like the president of the bank. He introduced me to the men and ladies he worked with. I walked into gleaming vaults where they kept the money. One of the bank ladies showed me $1,000 and $5,000 bills.

When lunchtime came, Grandpa took me to a restaurant called the Automat. I saw the future! Walls of chrome compartments with glass doors presented plates of meat and mashed potatoes, sandwiches of all kinds, slices of pie or cake, scoops of potato salad and coleslaw, all at your fingertips... and untouched by human hands! I imagined that robots worked relentlessly behind the chrome and glass, preparing thousands of dishes with conveyer-belt precision.

After lunch, Grandpa took me to see a movie in Times Square called *Run Silent, Run Deep*, which was about a submarine in World War II. I was glad it was about us, the Americans, against the Nazis– the Germans– and not the Japanese. I didn't want to be nervous about someone looking at me like I was the enemy, although no one ever figured me as part German and shouted at me, like, "Hey, you lousy Kraut boy!"

Our last stop was to visit my great uncle Ed. I hadn't met him before, but Grandpa told me about him as we took an elevator to the 50th-something floor. Uncle Ed's office was in a skyscraper that was so tall that when I looked out the window, I couldn't see the street below us. Cautiously, I backed away from the precipice, afraid I might fall away into oblivion. Meanwhile, Grandpa and Uncle Ed smoked and sort of yakked it up, but only a few words at a time and spaced apart. Uncle Ed owned ships that worked in the New York harbor. He was rich. When we left and shook hands, he put a five-dollar bill in my palm, clasped it shut, and winked at me. Loved that old man! Then we were on our way home, struggling with the crowds the same way we did on the way in. Only now, everyone was hotter and angrier.

When Grandma picked us up at the Millington station, I told her about the day we had, about the vault in the bank, the Automat, the five bucks Uncle Ed gave me, the noise and the city crowds.

"Did you thank Grandpa?" she asked.

"Of course."

"Did you learn anything?"

"Yes. I'd like to have a job like Grandpa's. Go to the bank, talk to his ladies, count money, go to lunch and the movies, stop and say hello to Uncle Ed, then come back home."

"What's that about 'his' ladies?" Grandma asked.

Grandpa was approaching retirement and, together with Grandma, they had a vision, a plan to move farther south in New Jersey and start their own antique shop. For now, Grandma and Grandpa scoured public auctions from one weekend to the next in the outback of New Jersey, in places called Ringoes, Belvedere, and Beemerville. The drive seemed interminable as we traveled west on Route 46 to the boondocks of New Jersey at 35 miles an hour. My grandfather considered it reckless to drive any faster. As we inched toward an antique auction that my grandparents had doped out as particularly promising, I'd see familiar billboards alongside the highway that barked, "Just 10 more miles to Wild West City!" or "Just two miles to Space Farms!"

"Can't we stop there, maybe on the way back?" I'd beg for consideration to visit those places. Who would not want to experience the inspired theater of stagecoach robberies, battles between cowboys and Indians, gunfights, and other tests of human values and manly determination? Who would not want to see native lizards of Sussex County or cuddle with a real llama in a petting zoo?

"We're not going to waste our time at either of those seedy roadside attractions. They look hideous," Grandma said.

"But cowboys!" I whined. Wild West City looked like the town in *Stagecoach*, where the Ringo Kid gives the murderous Plummer boys their just desserts. I saw the movie many times on *Million Dollar Movie* or *The Early Show*, but the story got to me every time. My throat would close up and my eyes would tear up when Ringo says, "Well, there are some things a man just can't run away from," and rides out of town with Dallas, the saloon girl. I wished I'd end up with a girl like her.

A side trip to Wild West City was never in the cards for me. Invariably, our weekend destinations wound up at auctions where old fossils smoked cigarettes, milled around and inspected furniture, china, ceramics, farm implements, paintings, maps, quilts, cribs, and, worst of all, old dolls, little ogres with cracked skin and bug eyes.

"Oh, aren't they sweet?" Grandma might say, lifting one of the doll's palsied arms. "A very nice Victorian piece," she'd say, fluffing up the doll's matted hair, nodding approval to Grandpa.

I sneezed under canvas tents or in mildewed barns that were stacked full of detritus from dead centuries. Always, these auction venues were out in the middle of nowhere, often next to a deserted diner or gas station, or at a crossroad that was hopeless to a boy who daydreamed about a gunfight or, at least, looking at a giant tortoise eye-to-eye. Instead, I was stranded in an alternate universe of dusty obsolescence—a postapocalyptic world of old folks and old stuff.

Before the auction started, they sniffed and poked around items that would be brought to bid. They muttered approvals, scoffed casual disgust, hemmed and hawed over various lots of items. This is what my grandparents did for fun.

This ritual pre-inspection was a warm-up to what would be the main event, when the auctioneer's assistant stood in front of the auction table and told everyone to take their seats and announce, "If you haven't already, you've got to register at the table to get your paddle. No paddle, no bid."

Then the auctioneer, Colonel So-and-So, would step up to the auction block and enthusiastically describe an old curiosity, a steamer trunk that two sturdy minions held aloft over their heads. That first item would start a constant parade of sleep-inducing inventory: dark, morose furniture with ornate carving, dainty porcelain and ceramics, silverware, pewter, jewelry, and tools from homes and farms of long ago.

When it came to raising their hands to buy and hoard old things that they wanted, these collectors scorned those who bid against them. They shifted in their seats, lifted their wrinkled hands and paddles in a variety of personal styles, sometimes with a twitch, a nod, or a frown, as they responded to the rhythmic urging of the Colonel, whose cadence became increasingly agitated, until the final bidder prevailed and he'd stop breathlessly and announce, "Going once, going twice, gone!" Then, with a resolute flourish, he'd slam down his mallet and shout, "Sold!"

On the way home from auctions, Grandma and Grandpa would whisper conspiratorially about what they had bought, as if they had executed some grand heist, getting away with what they considered fine examples of antique majolica, cranberry glass, cut glass, Frederick Remington, and Currier & Ives prints—to me, just boxes of junk taking up more of my precious space in the back seat.

Wild West City or Space Farms were so close, but ever so far. I stared out the car window, sulked over the opportunities forgone, and resented my grandparents for their stodginess, stinginess, and for just being so old. And yet, I understood I hadn't had it this good in a long time.

Chapter 22
WHAT I TOOK FOR GRANTED

After dinner we'd watch TV for a while, shows like *Lassie* and *Jack Benny*. Grandma would say it was time for me to get ready for bed. After I changed into my pajamas, I'd return to the living room, I'd shake Grandpa's hand goodnight, then go to my room. A few minutes later I'd hear Grandma approach, rising from her couch in the living room and making her way to me, her form slightly swaying as she compensated for her bad leg. As she smoothed my covers, she would say silly things like, "Sleep tight, don't let the bedbugs bite."

Lying in my bed, I'd watch her walk away, serenely managing her hobble, then listen as she returned to the living room toward the faint sounds of the opening theme song of *The Perry Mason Show*. As it was most nights, I was restless and kept flipping my pillow to its cool side. In between awake and asleep, I saw my mother with a bamboo embroidery hoop in her lap, quietly stitching an image. I couldn't discern what it was. I stopped looking, afraid she'd turn her head and start cawing at me.

Perhaps my need for Dad to love me back was pushing him further away. He didn't desert me so much as he sidled away into the tall jungle grass. His increasing absences left me and my grandparents to bridge the chasm that separated us.

The half-century difference in age between my grandparents and me seemed as wide as a geologic epoch. The distance between our origins, might as well have been from here to Saturn. Then there were the challenges posed by our disparate cultures and language. As I searched for my place, my kind, and myself during those early years, the Ancient Ones were steadfast and trustworthy. I knew that they would not flee into the night or spin into a rage, like my mother. They would never drop out of sight for weeks at a time without a word, like my father. They saved me. Who were they?

Ida Kipp was born in Mechanicville, New York, in 1898. William

Fellenberg was born in Hell's Kitchen, New York City, in 1900. Each of my paternal grandparents survived the childhood deaths of brothers and sisters, the Great Depression, and two world wars.

◈ ◆ ◈

Grandpa's father was German, his mother a French Huguenot. He told me her last name was Germond, as if verifying his lineage. He quit school in the eighth grade and took care of his kid sister, Emily. When he was a young man, Grandpa headed west, working as a lineman in Oregon and California. He returned to New York, where he met Ida, a social worker assigned to the settlement house where he roomed. They married, and for more than 40 years, he commuted from New Jersey to the Coliseum Building on Columbus Circle working at the same bank, eventually as the head teller. He was chatty with customers and neighbors, but not a big talker with his family. He enjoyed raising his chickens and gave them names, treating them like pets. They followed him as he turned shovels full of earth and worms in his vegetable garden. Dad would tell me that Grandpa assigned him the job of killing and dressing the chickens. Dad asked him why neither of his brothers, Donald or Richard, had to share these grim duties.

"You're the oldest, that's why," Grandpa told him. During the Depression, Grandpa sold those chickens to customers or colleagues at the bank. To his colleagues and customers in the city, he called the home in Millington his "farm," exaggerating the circumstances of renting an old house with a garden out in the fields of New Jersey.

He smoked all of his life. I watched his loyalties shift from Camels, Chesterfields, Old Golds, and then to Pall Malls—all unfiltered brands that caused tobacco shreds to stick to his lips and tongue. By the time I was twelve, I'd filch cigarettes from his packs as he dozed off on the couch. When he was well into retirement and had emphysema, he developed a casual concern about his health and switched to 100-millimeter filtered cigarettes, Virginia Slims and Mores. He never drove faster than 45 miles per hour and that was for a minor emergency, like the time he had almost forgotten that it was Election Day, and the polls were about to close.

Whenever he was relaxing on his couch, he'd read a book while listening to Wagner on the hi-fi. He'd always have a cigarette lit in the ashtray on the end table. He'd sometimes neglect them, his smoldering cigarettes toppling out of the ashtray and scarring the hardwood floor with forms and shapes that could have inspired an abstract expressionist. Of course, the habit crazed my grandmother.

Listen to my grandparents arguing.

"Honestly, Bill, you could end up burning down our house and everything in it, including the antique shop. If you're feeling drowsy, put your cigarette out first."

Rhetorically, Grandma said, "That's not too much to ask, is it?" She'd repeat the same complaint for emphasis.

> *Listen to my grandfather groan, and mutter sotto voce, "On and on and on. It just goes on and on and on." Watch the old man fire up another Virginia Slim. This is as close as they get to rage.*

Grandpa rarely swore. When most agitated, he might blurt "For the Christ's sake!" which represented his most extreme oath. I never heard him raise his voice to Grandma, or to me, for that matter. I never saw him lose his temper. According to my father, that wasn't the case when he was growing up. Dad would tell me that Grandpa occasionally beat the hell out of him. "Grandma would tell him about something I did or said that was out of line, then when he came home from work, he'd charge into my room and start throwing windmill punches at me—not casual punches, but hard, sustained body blows. I swear, I thought he wanted to kill me."

"What did you do that made him so mad?" I had asked.

"I don't remember," he said, "Anyway, the last beating he gave me I was about 16. I told him if he ever hit me again, I'd hit him back. That was the end of it."

My grandmother was the middle of the three daughters of Myron and Elizabeth Kipp. The girls were named Jean, Ida, and Helen. They were of Dutch and Scottish descent. Myron worked part-time as a train conductor but was primarily a carpenter. When I first arrived from Japan, I became the incidental beneficiary of a menagerie of wooden animals, among the few extant artifacts of Myron's hardscrabble career. All of the creatures were painted in three colors—black and red details on a background of white. Though he had been stingy with the colors, red spots and black stripes were enough to transform the animals from wood to flesh, springing them to life and adventure. I played with those giraffes, zebras, and tigers relentlessly, until they collapsed or splintered, reduced again to pieces of wood. My favorite was a rocking horse large enough that I could straddle. I brought that poor beast outside on the lawn, rocking it brutishly across our backyard, although it wasn't built to withstand such punishment. It eventually collapsed from exhaustion.

My great-grandfather's work showed a thoughtful eye and accomplished hand, but pictures of him, the unsmiling carpenter, suggest why my grandmother said little about him. Her mother's name was Elizabeth, and when Grandma invoked her memory, there was a patina of mourning in it. In the only photograph I remember of my great-grandmother, she is standing in front of a flower garden in a soft, evanescent light, as if poised to disappear. When Grandma spoke of her, it was with commiseration. I inferred that her mother deserved a kinder husband than the miserly carpenter.

Grandma had a brother, born first, who died when he was still a boy. Stoically, my grandmother recalled her brother and his untimely death. I was myself a boy when she told me about him. She had told me his name, which I have long forgotten. Although my grandmother did not drop a tear, I absorbed a wordless understanding that her brother lived just long enough to be ardently loved, dying at the age when a father and mother began to imagine the man that their boy might become. Perhaps that's what caused the old man to turn inward and hard, and why his wife seemed to surrender herself to the garden in the background.

The three daughters graduated from Wells College, a rich girls' college in upstate New York. The girls' education was made possible by the generosity of the eldest sister's in-laws. Jean had married well. The college experience freed the girls from the narrow destiny of Mechanicville and, most important, from the fixed scowl of their father. Grandma worked as a teacher and social worker, and then married the big German. They held on tight to each dollar and to each emotion, as if letting go of either might plummet them into poverty or emotional collapse. They raised a family of three sons, the first of whom, my father, William Kipp, was born in 1928.

Even in their wildest dreams, Grandma and Grandpa couldn't have imagined the circumstances that would call on them to raise a grandson who was born a world away. No, not in a million years.

Chapter 23
CONGA

You look for connections wherever you go. Funerals, christenings, and weddings are supposed to affirm family ties. That's the idea, anyway. I was excited about going to the wedding of my Uncle Don and his bride-to-be, Audrey. It was the first wedding I went to, and before the day was over, I had about as much excitement as I could handle. I don't remember anything about a church or the ceremony. The reception is what I remember. Hope and misery pulled me in opposite directions all in one day. I met a girl who called herself George and spent the better part of the reception with her, which seemed the most exhilarating two hours of my life. Also, I had a beer and danced, both for the first time. Dad got drunk, fought with Richard, his youngest brother, and passed out next to me on the long ride home.

I was standing by the bar, sipping a ginger ale through a swizzle stick. My father began to sound sloppy as he argued with Uncle Richard.

Dad said, "Let's go outside and settle it."

Richard said, "Don't be ridiculous, you're drunk." When he glanced down and saw me watching all this, he told Dad, "And stop making a fool of yourself in front of your son."

I could tell he was saying it because he wanted me to think he was on my side or something. If Dad had hit his brother's smirky face right then and there, I wouldn't have blamed him. I still rooted for Dad, whether he was right or wrong. All the same, I didn't know what started it and I didn't want to be near either of them. I thought they might mix it up right then and there, but Richard turned around and walked away, laughing and shaking his head as Dad's face got redder and redder.

Except for us, everyone's attention was on the wedding party's table. Dad and Richard were supposed to be there, too, because they were the groom's ushers. My Uncle Don and Audrey were at the table with the bridesmaids and best man. When people clinked their glasses, which seemed to happen every other minute, Uncle Don had to lean over and kiss Audrey. Our small family was outnumbered by the bride's side, and I thought that it was just as well. Her family and friends seemed to know how to have fun, especially compared to mine. When the bride's family wasn't on the dance floor, they were talking up a storm at their tables. My family sat and watched Dad and Uncle Richard stalking back to the wedding party's table.

I took a detour before returning to the table where Grandma and Grandpa were, so I could be by myself for a while. There were no other kids that I knew and the only so-called cousins I saw were old like my father and his brothers. *Some party* is what I muttered to myself. I hung around where the band played, watching a few couples dance. Soon, the ballroom throbbed with music and people dancing.

I saw a tall glass half-full of beer on a tray, took a couple of sips, then gulped down the rest before anyone saw me. Just like the cowboys in the movies, I swiped the back of my wrist across my mouth. It tasted lousy, but it felt good after it passed my mouth and swirled down to my stomach. I burped, then noticed the little kid looking up at me and giving me the once-over. He had a crew cut and blond hair so light that for a second, I thought he was bald. He fidgeted with his dumb-looking plaid bowtie and pointed to the empty glass that I had put back on the tray.

"Was that good?" the kid asked me.

"None of your beeswax."

"What's your name? I'm Jack."

"Billy," I said, turning my back to him.

"How old are you?"

"None of your beeswax."

"I'm five, and I know how old you are."

"Yeah, sure. How old am I?"

"You're not old enough to drink beer! And I'm telling!"

"Wait a sec!" I held on to the little wise guy's arm to keep him from scampering away and tattling on me.

"So how old are you?" he asked again. I figured I'd be better off telling him.

"I'm ten, okay? Going on eleven." I turned my attention to the dance floor, the band playing faster, and everybody dancing. Everything was loud. You had to yell to make yourself heard. The swirling of dresses, the sashaying back and forth, and the laughing was like school recess for grown-ups, as if they just got permission to be noisy and wild.

The kid tugged my sleeve, asking me, "And what's with the eyes?"
"What?"
"Are you squinting or what?"
"It's because I'm part Japanese."
"That's nice," said Jack. "But what's with the eyes?"

He just didn't get it. But it was kind of a relief that he didn't make Chinaman eyes at me or say something stupid. I was about to explain it to him when a girl, at least a head taller than me, approached us, tossing her long brown hair behind her so that it hung midway down her back. She sipped a Pepsi, straight from the bottle.

"Is Francis bothering you?" she asked.

"Francis? He told me his name was Jack."

Francis shrugged his narrow shoulders, his open palms out, like he had been caught red-handed for something. He said:

"I like being called Jack better," he said.

"That's my brother for you," the girl said. "Is he being a pest?"

"Sort of," I said. Then the poor little twerp bent his head, ruefully staring at the floor. I knew that feeling. "But he's not bothering me. He's okay."

The girl said her name was Georgette and it was the -ette part that she *just couldn't stand*, so she told me to call her just George, for now.

"Okay, Just George," I said, trying to be clever.

"Both Francis and I think our parents were drunk when they named us," she said, tousling the top of Jack-Francis's hair.

"So, I heard you tell Francis you were half Japanese. That's cool. Your mother's side?"

"How did you know?"

"Just guessing. Where is she?" Just George scanned the room for someone that looked like my mother.

"She's not here. She went back to Japan."

"For good?"

"Nobody knows for sure," I said.

"How come?" asked Jack-Francis.

"Never mind, Francis." Just George gently muzzled him with her palm.

"It's just a question!" Jack-Francis said, squirming away from his sister.

George wore a lavender dress, which made her bright brown eyes even more painfully beautiful. I could barely look at her. But she talked a blue streak, too, which made things easier. Just George was twelve, went to an all-girls' school somewhere I never heard of, and she *just loved* a bunch of things—ballet lessons, tennis, reading, and R and B music (whatever that was), and today she was stuck looking after her kid brother while her parents had fun at the wedding. "So, what do you like to do?"

A lump swelled up in my throat. It seemed like a trick question I couldn't answer right off the cuff like that. I didn't want to ruin what was one of the best conversations I had ever had with a girl by saying something stupid. So, I told her the truth. "I like to fish."

"Hmm," Just George said, taking another swig from her Pepsi.

"That's *really interesting*," Jack Francis smirked.

"Don't be smart," said George, poking her finger into her brother's chest.

"Well, it does sound boring, even to me," I said. "But it *is* a sport."

"Yeah, like raking leaves is a sport," said Jack-Francis.

"There's fishing and there's *fishing*. Daddy caught a blue marlin off Grand Bahama that was ten feet long and a thousand pounds," George said, tapping a foot to the band's beat.

"Yes, there's fishing and there's *fishing*," I said, leaving it at that, rather than bringing up my biggest catch, the leviathan from the Passaic River—the 15-inch brown trout that weighed two pounds or so. We stood watching the dance floor. Everyone was dressed up, couples sometimes dancing slow and sometimes fast. Then they got in a long line, single file, turning their bodies this way and that.

Just George yelled, "Conga!" and grabbed Jack Francis and me by the wrists, linking us to the line of people that coiled and uncoiled, each holding on to somebody and then raising their arms way over their heads and being rowdy, but in a good way. I held on to a pudgy lady's waist while I felt George's slender fingers around my own waist and we'd all let go at the same time, point to the ceiling, and yell "Conga!"

I didn't know what I was doing, shuffling my feet and stumbling occasionally. But I'd have to say it was just the best time ever and I never wanted it to end. I loved her, that was all there was to it. When all the shouting was over, and the band started playing slow music, we moved off the dance floor. George saw someone waving to her from her table.

"That's Mommy. Back to the salt mines," she said, her brother in tow. "It was fun meeting you, whatever your name is."

"His name's Billy and he's been drinking beer," said Francis.

Just George made a funny face, scrunched up her nose, and laughed. "Well, it's been fun meeting you, Billy."

She stuck out her hand and I shook it like a shy little kid might—the dead-fish handshake. I wished in the worst way for a do-over. I wanted to shake her hand in a manly but tender way that would have convinced her to stay. But the moment was already over.

"So, Sayonara, Billy!" she said.

I wanted to tell her that sayonara could mean several things, but it was too late. I watched them leave the dance floor and lost track of them as they disappeared among clusters of guests on the way to their faraway family table.

"So long, Georgette. Adios, Francis," I said to myself.

That was that. When I got back to our table, Grandma said, "You're just in time. They're about ready to cut the wedding cake. Look at your Uncle Don and Audrey. They look perfect together! From now on, don't forget, you'll be calling her *Aunt Audrey*. Isn't that nice?"

"Yes, indeedy," I said. Grandma gave me a funny look. The beer put weird words in my mouth.

I looked across the ballroom and saw Dad and Uncle Richard sitting at opposite ends of the wedding party's table. Richard was chattering away with the bridesmaids, while Dad sat drinking and scowling. I was relieved they weren't fighting. When the cake came, I couldn't eat any, feeling a little sick to my stomach. My family seemed small and far away from me. It was that feeling of seeing things through the wrong end of a telescope. I wondered if they saw me the same way. I got up from our table and walked around, looking for Georgette and Francis to say good-bye, but couldn't find them. Soon, the waiters started clearing the tables, the band stopped playing, and men helped ladies on with their coats as all the party magic drained out of the room.

When my grandparents and I walked out to the parking lot, Dad and Uncle Richard were at it again. Dad pointed to the curb and said he was going to stuff his head into the storm gutter, which Richard thought was just hilarious. I was scared by Dad's anger and Uncle Richard's weird laughter. It was a bit crazy. Grandpa told them to knock it off.

It was a long and silent ride home and chilly in the back seat because Dad's window was wide open, his head hanging out the side the whole way back, in case he threw up. Grandma was talking up front to Grandpa, saying that it was the army that changed Dad and ruined his future. Grandpa just drove and listened. As usual, he didn't have a lot to say about these matters. Grandma's complaint about the army was a familiar theme that I'd hear every so often. Sometimes she'd say it apropos of nothing—saying it more to herself than to me, not even looking up as she absentmindedly ironed Grandpa's dress shirts or tidied up after dinner. Whenever Grandma blamed the army, I thought that she considered my mother and me part of the same bundle of bad luck. I took the comment personally, as I did most things, but I kept it to myself. I didn't want to make a bigger deal about it than it was.

Occasionally, I'd catch glimpses of my mother out of the corner of my eye, but never the whole of her. For example, at a railroad crossing, watching train cars rumble by, passengers in the windows, their blurred faces in profile. I wondered if Mom, somewhere in Japan, might have seen a kid whizzing by on his bike, and thought it was me.

My grandparents murmured in the front seat and my father drooped his head out the window in the dark like a sick dog. I wondered about Just George and Jack-Francis. I leaned over Grandma's seat and asked her about them. "Grandma, do you know who the kids were that I was dancing with in the conga line? A tall girl with long brown hair and a little boy in a funny bowtie?"

"I haven't the foggiest," she said. "But you were dancing up a storm."

I wondered if I'd ever see them again. Those two were my kind, even if it was just for a little while. Georgette reminded me of Dallas, the saloon girl in *Stagecoach*, because she was so sassy. I wanted to swoop her up next to me onto the buckboard, tell the horses to *giddy up*.

> *Look how Georgette nuzzles closer to me as we cross the final rise to our house on the prairie, lazy smoke drifting from the chimney up to the forever azure sky.*

As if that would ever happen. It was painful, as most of the truly beautiful dreams are.

Chapter 24
BOOM

1960

After my grandfather retired, we moved sixty miles southeast to a stretch of farmland in Monmouth County known locally as Ardena. I was going on eleven years old in this summer before I'd start fifth grade.

City slickers might say Ardena was in the middle of nowhere. Although it had no official identity, it was conveniently located near places that earned designations as towns and villages. Ardena abutted Route 524, unofficially known as Adelphia-Ardena Road, which lay as straight as a plumb line between Adelphia to the west, a crossroad with a post office, firehouse, and funeral parlor, and Farmingdale to the east, a town with stores, restaurants, two doctors, a supermarket, and a pharmacy. Ardena, together with West Farms and Squantum, were constituent parts of Howell Township. But everywhere across the flat land, no matter how remote, you'd see the steeples of old churches pointing to the firmament above, their foundations rooted in the rich soil beneath, at least for the time being—before yet another housing development began to shove farming and worship into the past.

Our home was at the midpoint between Adelphia and Farmingdale. If you went six miles farther west beyond Adelphia, you'd reach Freehold, the seat of Monmouth County. If you went ten miles farther east beyond Farmingdale, you'd reach Asbury Park.

◈ ◆ ◈

Although he came uninvited, we had a guest from the first day we moved in—a stray cat, a youngster, with black and white markings which were smudged and matted by tough times from being scatted from barn-to-barn by humans or harassed by other farm animals. Because of his scruffy countenance, either Dad or Grandpa called him *The Scroot*, and the moniker stuck, even though after a few weeks of good meals and a barn he could sleep in without being harassed, he struck a dignified pose at rest, and when he was on the move, he was very fast and looked purposeful even when he was just showing off. As his kind know, looks are nothing without personality, which he had in spades. He won Grandma over by revealing himself as an accomplished mouser, leaving an occasional trophy on the back stoop for us, with its head chewed off. He wasn't just a stray, and he was mine really, and if asked what he was I'd say he was a tuxedo cat, which suited him perfectly. I thought he deserved a more dignified name than The Scroot, even though he didn't seem to mind. Most of the time, I called him Boy. Grandpa's vegetable garden, Grandma's flower beds, our backyard, and the expansive field of golden rye beyond it was our dominion for that summer and fall. He was my first friend in our new place, and I know it is true that we loved each other. There is no marker where he is buried, but for this, in memory:

The Boy and the Black-and-White

From the hedge row, the Black-and-White
bounded to the road as the boy yelled No!
but the deadly play was already done.

He was a tom, a stray. Though never given
a noble name, he had found a bed, a dish, and
the cooing affections of clumsy, larger creatures.

The car flung the Black-and-White to the shoulder
where he lay serenely, suggesting the way
his kind luxuriate on a Sunday porch.

But this is not leisure. The cat's head lolls,
its last breath of autumn is a wisp of steam
drifting toward the boy, then disappears

*Forever, like hope unhinged. He wants the day back
to what it was. He hates himself for time he wasted,
mindlessly waiting for a school bus.*

*His grandmother hangs clothes out to dry,
sees the boy, now lost, stumble as he cradles
the still-soft checkerboard of a cat.*

*She knows anguish; sees it coil around the boy
and grab his throat between sobs. She thinks
if only, then remembers, he must work through it.*

*Driving him to school, she tells him that when
he comes home, he should make a grave –
lay the Black-and-White under the red maple.*

*Later, raking leaves and acorns, she watches him
finish the burial. He drags a rusted spade behind him
drops it by the white barn; stalks to the far fence.*

*He rages, kicks clods of dirt in an empty field.
Moments ago, summer was a flying carpet—as real as
a boy and his cat who soared over a sea of golden rye.*

⋄ ◆ ⋄

For most of the next decade, Ardena would be the center of my universe. My first summer here splashed with gladioli, corn, wheat, and tomatoes, along with the sounds and smells of chickens, cows, and horses. Much of the open land was also hardscrabble country. From dawn to dusk, fields teemed with migrant workers and locals who tended to whatever crops were in season from June through September. Middle-class families lived either in town, or in one of the developments that had recently digested a meadow. Along the countryside, you'd see enclaves of Puerto Ricans, Blacks, Russians,

European Jews who had survived the Holocaust, and Kalmyk Mongols, an Asian people I had never heard of. It was hardly a melting pot. The new arrivals worshiped in different churches, synagogues, and mosques, lived in different neighborhoods, and married within their own kind. The saving grace was that most children attended the same schools and played together. If I felt a sense of *not* belonging, I knew at least that I had company.

Ardena Elementary was a large two-story building of red brick and white trim, capped off by a large cupola you could see from half a mile away, a presence that beckoned children from miles around to learn all things elementary, from kindergarten through the eighth grade. To the east of the school was Merrick's dairy farm, and to the west, Rapp's chicken farm. Behind the school, beyond its jungle gym, seesaws, and baseball field, were woods and the Manasquan River.

Before the school year began, Grandma reminded me that our move was yet another opportunity for me to start fresh. Her pep talk was short and familiar. Pay attention to my teacher and mind my own business. I wanted to put my past behind me, forget about my troubles in Liberty Corner and Basking Ridge, where I was the yellow worm in an otherwise fine white apple.

To augment my learning, Grandma gave me an almost complete set of the 1938 edition of *The American Standard Encyclopedia*, which she had bought at an auction. Grandma wanted to help me develop intellectual curiosity, but on a budget. It was easy to contain my excitement, because I had none. Grandma conceded that, "Well, it's not the *Encyclopedia Britannica*, but over time you'll find it useful." She was right about that. It would be useful, as long as the subject I was looking up wasn't in one of the three missing volumes, or if the subject I was looking up wasn't about the present-day world. She also gave me a copy of *Van Loon's Geography, The Story of the World*, a book that she had given to Dad when he was my age. It was still in good shape despite being published in 1940. I read and reread it many times, enthralled by the sense of places the book established, although again, its authority stopped two decades earlier. Thus, at the same time that I was forming my opinions about life in the present, I was developing a view of the world which was somewhat anachronistic—the past worlds that my grandmother and my father grew up in.

My grandparents were beginning a new adventure, too. They dedicated most of the first floor of our sturdy farmhouse to their long-held dream, now realized— their new enterprise, Homestead Antiques.

◈

In front of our class, Mrs. O'Brien began the air-raid drill with the zeal it deserved. Our lives might depend on it. She was obliged to teach us how to survive an atomic bomb attack and outlive the communists. Mrs. O'Brien yelled "Drop!" Then, after several beats, she screamed, "Cover!" We collapsed under our desks and wrapped our arms around our heads until she gave us the *all clear*.

At lunch time, my friend Orrin, the smartest kid in my class, summarized the rationale for drop and cover. "It's like this," he said. "Dropping protects you from the fireball, so you don't go blind. Covering your face and the back of your neck protects you from flying debris." He described how window glass would shatter, and how our desks, books, lunch boxes, chalk—all of it, and all of us, would be vaporized. He shrugged, mimicking Alfred E. Neuman's signature motto, and said, "What—Me Worry?" I choked on my straw, milk running out of my nose. It was hilarious to think that hiding under our flimsy classroom desks could shield us from atomic bombs. Did the adults in charge really believe it?

At home, my grandparents tuned in the evening news, and we saw fuzzy black-and-white footage of Khrushchev, a bald troll, replete with a prominent wart. He belched insults at the hapless delegates of the United Nations and menaced them by banging his shoe on a desk.

"So rude!" said Grandma.

"What you'd expect from a Bolshevik," said Grandpa.

The paranoid scenarios reflected in the news seemed to teeter between the edge of a dark fairy tale and insanity.

> *Even though we had no say in the matter, my contemporaries and I formed the vanguard of a generation anointed as baby boomers, the product of an orgasm of fertility between 1946 and 1964. In just 18 years, America's mothers spurted out 76 million children. The bonanza was worldwide, babies squirming all over the globe. One might have expected boomers to be beneficiaries of the free world's triumph over Japanese, German, and Italian fascists, but there was barely a moment to savor victory and peace. We braced ourselves for an attack by a new enemy, the Soviet Union, which had already enslaved much of Europe and Asia. Although the grown-ups worried about it, we found other issues more compelling—sex, for example, if only in the theoretical sense.*

One afternoon at his house, Orrin showed me a plastic model he had assembled called *Visible Man*, a figure with transparent skin whose insides—from skeleton, to musculature, to guts—were on view. He gave me a brief lecture. I regarded Orrin as a wise man, although his face reminded me of a chipmunk's. He pointed to Visible Man's body parts and identified the heart, lungs, stomach, liver, large and small intestines, and all the major organs. This model was serious business, a teaching tool that represented the male human with anatomical accuracy, with one glaring exception. Orrin noted the Visible Man's crotch and sighed, "And these are supposed to be his genitals."

"His what?" I asked.

"You know …. his dick and nuts!" he said.

"I see," I said, inspecting the model more closely. "Yes, he has no … gentles."

"Genitals, not gentles."

"That's what I said—gentles."

We concluded that Visible Man offered nothing new to our knowledge about sex. The representations of his scrotum and penis were just impressionistic bulges painted with hairline-thin blue veins and red capillaries. We scoffed and laughed at the Visible Man's shortcomings. Sadly, he had no signs of pubic hair, and he was a *grown man*. I wondered aloud if a version of *Visible Woman* existed. Wouldn't that be something! Orrin didn't know. We were both intrigued, however. Maybe it would clear up questions about the *sex thing*. We reckoned that if the Visible Woman existed, the model makers would make her *sex thing* as vague and disappointing as her male counterpart's.

Our knowledge about sex was riddled with information that was incomplete or grossly wrong. For example, Mike McNeil, my other best friend, told me that he got a boner while he showered. He confided to me in a newsworthy way that: "It's a handy place to hang your washcloth." Mike was a practical kind of guy. Why not? I experienced my boners as nuisances that arrived in my pants uninvited, but in a feel-good kind of way.

Hearsay was the primary source of information about sexuality. Even if the facts were all wrong, it was still news. Explanations from adults were so obscure that sex seemed as exciting as putting your socks on. While the velocity of human sexual activity in the mid-20th century must have exceeded that of all recorded history, sex was still a big secret. Outside the context of doctors' offices and general health, grown-ups avoided squirm-provoking talk about sex. In its proper perspective, intercourse was a medical condition.

Information about sex from morally dubious characters was the *crème de la crème* of all sources. Older kids smuggled pornography— what we called dirty pictures and adults called smut—onto the school playground. Smut came to us in the form of tattered folios made wretched and worn by hundreds of desperate thumbs and depthless lust. Their content featured blurry photographs of men and women in various poses of sexual ennui, or primitive line drawings that kidnapped characters from the benign worlds of *Peanuts* and *Lil' Abner* and posed them in horny and outrageous situations. It was awful. But it was impossible not to look.

Sammy Savante was our channel to dirty magazines. He leafed rapidly through the pages of smut, as six or seven of us crowded around him on the playground.

"Get a load of the masked man!" he crowed.

"Stop pushing, I can't see!" I yelled at the kid behind me.

"Keep your shirt on, Billy Boy!" said Sammy. "Don't have an orgasm! Keep your cool!"

"I'm keeping my cool," I said. "No orgasm here."

"Mrs. O'Brien's coming!" someone yelled. Like convicts in a prison yard, the group dispersed as the warden approached. After Mrs. O'Brien strolled past us, we spoke about sex in low, agitated voices, as if planning a break-out that would set us on a new course to freedom.

The playground roiled with interesting developments. Invariably, someone was chasing someone who was going to be separated from the herd, out of the sight of teachers who were jabbering in a huddle or sneaking a cigarette when they were supposed to check the mayhem of recess. That's when you'd see a lunch box drop-kicked, or overhear dirty jokes exchanged among the seventh- and eighth graders. Even if the jokes were beyond my understanding, I'd laugh in a wise, smug way.

The more I discovered how little I knew, the more I wanted to be regarded as knowing and interesting. I had impressive credentials. I was eleven, soon to graduate from the fifth grade, and considered my grandparents out of it. As we ate dinner, some news on the radio provoked my grandfather to comment on it.

"That's ridiculous!" he scoffed, agitated with the broadcaster's position.

"No sense having an orgasm!" I told Grandpa.

My grandparents, usually poker-faced, looked stunned. Grandma slowly set down her fork, wiped her mouth with her napkin, and said, "Billy, I want you to excuse yourself and look up the meaning of the word."

I knew what the word meant. It was an expression that meant you should keep cool like Sammy had said. Relax, don't get yourself worked up. I went into the living room and plucked the dictionary from a bookcase. O – R – G – A – S - M. *Orgasm*. Wait. This couldn't be right. I read the definition of orgasm several times, first in disbelief, then in sweltering denial that this couldn't be so! I had told my grandfather – in front of my grandmother – not to have a *sexual climax*!

It was awful enough to be ignorant about what *orgasm* meant. But what was worse, my own grandparents knew what it was, and it dawned on me that they had *practical knowledge of it!* They would now know that I knew they had had an experience, which, up to this point ... was unspeakable! My legs turned rubbery as I shoved the dictionary back onto the shelf. I slouched to the kitchen and wondered how my grandparents and I could ever look each other in the eye again. "I didn't know what it meant," I said, returning to my chair at the table.

Grandma picked at a string bean on her plate. "Apparently not. Don't use words you haven't the foggiest notion about," she said, smiling small, in a sort of a sad way.

"I'm sorry," I said.

"Apology accepted," said Grandpa.

He lifted a glass of lemonade to his lips, and before he took a sip, he looked me in the eye and added, "Don't have an *orgasm* over it."

❦ ♦ ❦

Our backyard abutted fields that rotated crops with corn, wheat, and winter rye, and beyond those fields there were woods and within them, a gravel pit. Beyond the fields, I'd play with kids in the neighborhood. For my eleventh birthday, Dad gave me a

.410 shotgun to hunt for rabbits, quail, and other small game. He taught me the fundamentals of hunting and gun safety, which I ignored as soon as I was on my own. I remember killing only two creatures in all my time toting that shotgun through the woods and meadows by our house. After I killed a rabbit, I dressed it so badly that I transformed a beautiful thing into a wretched pile of bloody fur and splayed limbs. I tried to remember how Dad skinned and dressed small game, but I failed miserably. I was a poacher for my next kill, shooting not at a game bird, but a downy woodpecker as it plucked insects high on a tree. Even the blast of a small-gauge shotgun is thunderous. Its report silenced the entire woods, which, just moments before, had chirped, buzzed, and rustled with life. The woodpecker tumbled soundlessly onto the loamy forest floor. After I picked up the soft bird, its limp neck hung over the palm of my murderous hand. It still felt warm. For the rest of my gun-toting life, I only shot at bottles and cans in an abandoned gravel pit beyond the woods, not counting the time Jimmy Oats and I chased each other in his basement and fired off a couple of rounds with his father's thirty-eight caliber revolver (we had pried the slugs out of the shells), or the time Sammy and I borrowed my father's .22 rifle and took shots at a helicopter flying in the wild blue yonder high above Ardena's cornfields. The possible consequences of these dangerous amusements were beyond a fool's consideration.

Chapter 25
MORTUARY RUMORS, DREAM GIRLS, AND GAMES OF CHANCE

If you went east fifteen miles from our house, you'd reach Asbury Park's boardwalk, which bulged with amusement rides that scared you and confirmed that you were truly alive. A hundred yards to the east of the boardwalk, the Atlantic Ocean crashed on the sand. If you went west from our house, you'd reach Route 9, which took you to Freehold to the north or Lakewood to the south. Once reaching those points, I believed I could find a road that could take me anywhere in the world.

A sign, "Homestead Antiques," hung in front of the hedges that separated our property from the road's shoulder. The shop was Grandma and Grandpa's dream come true. While it would never be a bustling destination, enough customers came and went to make the enterprise worthwhile, and probably more important, to make things more interesting. The shop was Grandma's bailiwick and her satisfaction.

Sometimes, if Grandma was indisposed, I'd answer the door, and on one of these occasions I greeted a rumply old antique hunter who asked if I was the house boy. Given the obvious circumstances, I said yes. I mean, I lived in the house, and I was a boy. Later that day I told Grandma about that encounter, and she looked up at the ceiling and said the man was an idiot.

In the meantime, Grandpa tended to a lush garden that each year offered strawberries, asparagus, string beans, cukes, tomatoes, and corn. Grandma took custody of the zinnias, snaps, roses, and peonies. Our driveway curled around the house in a semicircle between the back of the house and a white barn. On one of his weekends home, Dad built a backboard and hung a basketball hoop and net from the barn. I'd play one-on-one or h-o-r-s-e with my friends; play a country boy's version of jai-alai against the barn wall; or play stoopball on our back steps.

It was a predictable life. Intrigue had to be gleaned from elsewhere or invented from imagination.

Although we girded ourselves for an attack by bad actors like Khrushchev and Castro, we had local examples of conflict and bad behavior. Friends and classmates burped out local rumors that ranged from petty feuds to horror stories wrapped around the dead. For example, the Brandons poured kerosene on shrubs planted by the Whites, because the Brandons said the plants encroached on their property. These were minor departures from civility compared to rumors about the Johnsons' funeral parlor in Adelphia. The story was that George, the peculiar son of the morticians, arranged cadavers around a table and staged card games. What's worse, according to the story, he'd accuse the deceased of cheating, scold them, bang on the table, and throw the cards at them in an angry fit. The less spectacular rumors were about flirtations in the neighborhood, car wrecks, sex in unusual places, and how the barber got a black eye.

Back then, before playdates and GPS, friendships developed spontaneously. After school, we rode our bikes, trolled playgrounds, ball fields, and neighborhoods looking for our kind. The geography in my reach was what I could cover in half an hour. I could bike anywhere in a three-mile radius and get back home in time for dinner. Coasting downhill during these delicious afternoons after school, I had no worries or wishes.

Orrin's house was a magnet for kids, and his mother always kept the door open to her son's friends. Some days, I was the lone beneficiary of his insights and wisdom, which advanced my awareness of the world. I considered the *Hardy Boys* serious reading until he loaned me Ray Bradbury's *The Martian Chronicles*. Literally, it opened up a new world for me. If not for Orrin, I might never have read it. What else was I missing? He introduced me to great board games, like *Risk! War Between the States*, and *Clue*.

Meanwhile, being friends with Mike McNeil opened up new worlds in a different category. We'd play barn jai-alai, build forts made of pine boughs in the woods, build dams in the brooks, and traipse around the Patterson's' sprawling farm, teasing the cows and goats until they chased us. The bonus for being friends with Mike was that girls adored him. They could not resist his easy smile, dimples, and the cowlick that slipped into his eyes.

One summer afternoon we were at Karen Rose's house, *in her bedroom*, with her best friend, Linda, unhinged from adult supervision. She began to chase poor Mike around her room and smothered him with kisses when she caught him. Mike begged her to stop and shielded himself by draping his arms around his face. When he tried to make a run for it, she lunged to the doorway and blocked it. I was speechless. The suspense was excruciating. Karen had the noteworthy distinction of owning the largest breasts in the sixth grade at Ardena Elementary. She stood in front of that door panting, her entire body heaving. I never saw anything like it. Who knew what could happen next? I intended to stand there and gawk until the sensational attack was over. She closed the door and went after him. Mike's pleas became more urgent as he thrashed around the room, over her bed and under her vanity. As his face turned red and he gasped for breath, he blurted, "Get away from me!" He was scared, and his eyes teared up. He was *actually crying*. Rather than being a sympathetic friend, I was annoyed. I thought if that was happening to me, I'd be crying *for joy*. If only it was me under attack. I'd let Karen do whatever she wanted. But she was busy wrapping Mike up in her web. I glanced over at Linda and our eyes met. I had ideas. Hers darted away from mine, her face being the one you have when you smell something bad. Mike ran out of the house, wiping the sloppy vestiges of Karen's kisses off his face, and I trailed after him. We jumped onto our bikes and stopped a few blocks away, where a bunch of kids were lining up at a Good Humor truck. We sat on the curb sucking popsicles.

"What was that like?" I asked Mike.

"It was awful. Don't tell anyone."

"Of course, I won't—but it's such a good story!"

"Well, it *was* something different." Mike finished off his Bomb

Pop, then stuck out his blue tongue.

"How about I just tell some of it. And you correct it as I go along."

"Now that it's over, it *is* a pretty good story. But just leave out the part where I got scared."

"Sure, but how was it when she was climbing all over you and kissing you? She really *wanted it* I think."

"Well, imagine Big Luis Navarro—only he has boobs—and he's sitting on your chest going wild."

"OK," I said, "Let's forget the story."

We biked to his house and played barn jai-alai, bounced a rubber ball off barn doors the rest of the afternoon. Before that summer ended, Mike McNeil and his family moved away when his father, an army major stationed at Fort Monmouth, was sent to West Germany. It was sad, in a way, but I wouldn't dwell on it. He was gone, and that was that. But then again, I wouldn't forget him.

The school playground was a casino. You'd see eighth graders playing cards for money on the benches behind the infield backstop. The rest of us gambled by shooting marbles and flipping baseball cards. Over a week, I lost all my marbles—not those marbles—but cat's eyes, puries, and aggies, and most painful of all, some antique ceramic marbles that Grandpa had given me, which I was showing off. I lost all my baseball cards, mostly Red Sox players, to Jimmy Oats, a Yankee fan. After he won my cards, he rubbed several in the playground dirt, including Jackie Jensen and Frank Malzone, just to get my goat.

My gambling bug got more serious that summer when I went to the Adelphia Firemen's Carnival. I rode my bike the two miles there. I passed the familiar landmarks—Ardmore Estates, the new development, Ardena Baptist Church, Delilah Gladioli Farms, and then entered the center of Adelphia, which was the fire station, the post office, and Johnsons' Funeral Parlor.

As I coasted into the fire-station parking lot, the smell of burnt meat wafted from the carnival grills. The carnival was set up between the fire station and the Little League field. I planned to treat myself to a dog or burger, or both. Or some raw shucked clams or steamers and have some cotton candy for dessert. I followed the jangly music that poured out of the loudspeakers near the cheesy rides, like the giant teacups that could seat two people and you'd swirl round and round on a big saucer that would spin and slant on its axis. It was a borderline kiddie ride but if I didn't see anyone I knew, I'd try it. Most of the other rides were even more lame. For sure, this wasn't Asbury Park.

The excitement of the carnival hummed like one big engine, the steady noise pierced by yelling and screaming. A fat man in Bermuda shorts held three ice cream cones and bellowed, "Over here! Over here!" As chocolate and vanilla globs dripped on his forearm, he licked them off. High school girls squawked, "That's so gross!"

> *Look at the volunteer firemen and their wives rake hot dogs and flip burgers, roast corn, steam clams, and sweat over an arsenal of superheated charcoal. Feel the heat of grease flaring up like rocket fuel, and sputter and coalesce into oily blue clouds that give everybody under the canopy sore throats and burning eyes.*

I passed the Wheel of Chance, where I saw a guy wearing a fireman's cap exhorting passersby to bet on one of ten numbers on the wheel, for a quarter a spin. "All for a good cause, folks. Help out the Adelphia Volunteer Fire Department."

I started out with four bucks. I lost all but three quarters in minutes.

"Sorry, kid, you lose again," said Mr. Fireman for the umpteenth time.

In the meantime, there was this girl with long brown hair that cascaded from under her Mod-style cap that had a humped top and a short bill in the front. She wore it at a sassy tilt. Her blue jeans had a matching vest, and she licked a huge lollipop as she walked around. I didn't know who she was and thought that she might be younger than me. Still, she was tall and lanky in a peculiar way, sophisticated—or at least, as sophisticated as you could get at a fireman's carnival in the parking meadow of a hick town in the middle of nowhere. She piqued my interest because I pretended, even to myself, that our glancing at each other was the kind of thing I knew about. I could feel myself falling in love with her a quarter at a time. Nonchalantly, I tossed my last 25 cents on the counter and lost.

"Too bad, kiddo," said Mr. Fireman, flipping my quarter up in the air and catching it behind his back.

That was it for the money I brought. But back home, I had another four or five bucks of chore earnings I had saved over the last month. I told him I'd be back, saying it loud enough for the girl to hear it. I raced home, got the rest of my money and hurried back to the carnival, hoping I could get there before they shut down the Wheel of Chance. I got back in time for the Wheel, but the girl was gone. My quarters began disappearing in a flurry of spins. I was miserable but tantalized by the notion that I could win all my money back. Desperation and hope alternated in my gut—heart-banging feelings that spun frantically inside me with each last chance. As Mr. Fireman swept up my last quarter, I had hoped he might feel sorry for me, give me back my money, and tell me something like, "I hope you learned a lesson, son."

Then I'd say, "Oh, yes, I have, Mr. Fireman!" I imagined my pockets jangling with my recovered quarters as I pedaled home, having learned a valuable lesson.

That might happen on *The Andy Griffith Show*, but not in real life. I was not a cute All-American kid named Opie. The bike ride home in dusky twilight seemed all uphill as I ranted, "Fuck you, Mr. Fireman!" Only the tall green corn in the fields could hear me as I huffed past. I flipped the finger to the field of corn and told their deaf ears to go fuck themselves. I felt a new kind of shame as I pedaled home in the coalescing dark. It was a bad feeling, being a vulgar and angry loser.

Chapter 26
THINGS ARE TOUGH ALL OVER

When I complained, Dad might say, "Things are tough all over," or "That's the way the cookie crumbles," then get back to tinkering with his fishing gear or watching the ball game on TV. I knew I had it easy compared to some, but I didn't like the way he dismissed me, particularly considering all the carping *he* did.

Yes, things were tough all over, but kids understood that it was grown-ups who were often the source of most problems, or at least aggravated them and turned small problems into bigger ones. If you believed that parents always knew best, you probably still believed in Santa Claus. There was ample evidence of adult incompetence and worse, but you kept it to yourself.

One afternoon I went to play catch with a kid in the neighborhood, but his mother answered the door. Her eye was swollen, a purple and blue blotch that spread on her temple and cheek. I pretended not to notice. I heard that the kid's father had a temper. You learn from an early age, don't stare. She told me her son couldn't play because he had chores, then closed the door.

Not everyone was free to play after school. For example, Big Luis had to stay home to watch over his four younger brothers and sisters after school, until his mother or father came home from work. I went over to his house a few times to play or just hang out in his yard, but a kid would always interrupt, wanting something to eat or drink or needing to go *potty*. If his parents were home, they'd be constantly barking at Luis to do this thing or take care of that.

I could always count on Sammy to brighten a dull day. Before he unveiled his latest big idea, he'd comb his pompadour, and flash a mischievous grin. He was my high priest, a shaman of things your parents didn't want you to know or do. He was proud of announcing his ownership of a condom. The brand was Sphinx, and in pristine condition, bearing its eponymous image on the wrapper—an

Egyptian creature with the head of a man and body of a lion.

> *Watch Sammy present the condom ceremoniously, either in hushed reverence in the cafeteria as he slowly removed the artifact from his wallet—or in reckless celebration, at the back of the school bus. Look at Sammy waving the Sphinx in mid-air, grinning triumphantly, as if he had just unearthed the Rosetta Stone. I make it a point to tell others that Sammy and I are friends, thinking it will enhance my prestige. He's like a leader, but not the Boy Scout kind.*

When I first moved into the neighborhood, he introduced me as Ching to other kids. I had to put up with it for a while, but the novelty of the insulting nickname wore off and he called me Billy, then Bill, which felt like a promotion. Occasionally he called me Fells, which I considered a worthy nickname—the kind you might give to a sidekick, or an accomplice. He showed me how to shoplift, make small pipe bombs and rockets, and window-peep. Sammy was a self-taught genius in skills that straddled the space between naughty and criminal. He had the aptitude, the cool, and, most important, the drive, to be exceptionally good at doing bad things.

Eager to share his wisdom, he'd show me and other boys in the neighborhood the darker hues of our human nature. One afternoon he summoned us to the trash pit behind his parents' bar and restaurant to announce his new discovery. He said that there was nothing like it. We followed him behind a berm of scraggly shrubs that slanted into the pit and hid us from view. The ragged semicircle that we formed around him included his kid brother and several other losers from the neighborhood. He unzipped and started to strangle his penis. Nothing noteworthy happened.

"Don't look at me!" he scolded.

"Hey," said his kid brother. "You told us to watch!"

"No talking!" Sammy frowned and closed his eyes and tended

to the business at hand in an earnest, workman-like manner. After a few more minutes Sammy gave up, unable to sustain the concentration that was apparently needed to achieve the desired result. We dispersed from the pit, skulking away.

Despite Sammy's nonperformance, the genie was out of the bottle. Masturbation would become an enduring obsession that rewarded its practitioners with what seemed free and unbridled pleasure, but exacted exorbitant payments in terms of shame and self-disgust that followed. Although all things considered, jerking off was worth the price of admission.

"Everybody does it," Sammy said, and his logic was reasonable. "If it's so bad, God wouldn't have given us hands and a dick." According to him, denying that you ever jerked off was the worst thing. "Never trust guys who say they don't," he told me. "That's who the real pervs are."

He had an expansive range of interests and an inquiring mind. How many match heads will it take to fill an antenna tube and turn it into a pipe bomb? How baggy should your trousers be when you go shoplifting? Can you transform a toy cap pistol into a zip gun by condensing the cap powder? Sammy was the wafer-thin ice I skated on that kept me from thinking about life's little problems.

Most of the kids I played with came from homes that, at the least, provided shelter, food, clothing, and a reasonable chance to stay healthy and grow. Some came from families that were working poor, just making ends meet. A few were dirt poor, those whose treadmills moved in reverse. For example, there was the Venote family: a boy, his little sister, and an old woman. She was toothless and bent like a question mark. They lived in a shack with an outhouse, both structures set far back from the road. During the summer, the wheat, corn, or some other tall crop would obscure their ramshackle home. If you didn't walk off the road for shortcuts like I did, the house and the family were invisible. The boy was a couple of years older than me. The girl was five or so, always in the same soiled yellow cotton dress. I never saw either of them at school.

Their house was just one room. On one side was a kitchen area with a sink and a hand pump curled over it, a small wood stove, and a table with three unmatched chairs. In the other half of the room, two beds and a miserable couch lolled among the scattered debris—magazines, bottles, and parts of things that used to be something. The floor was dirt, packed hard. Instead of a bathroom, there was an outhouse, listing to one side, as if trying to escape into the cornfield next to it.

The irony was that the boy had a go-kart powered by a lawn-mower engine. I coveted that little car when he'd buzz around in his dusty yard. Occasionally, he'd let me drive. I asked the old lady how he was able to afford it. "He just saved his pennies," she told me. Whether she was the grandmother, mother, or aunt, I can't remember. Her humped back, wrinkled face, gnarled fingers, and raggedy clothes made her look not just middle-aged, but *from* the Middle Ages. Regardless, they were a kind family and seemed happy in their own way.

That made it more of a horror show when the town condemned their shack as a health hazard and burned it to the ground. I went to watch the burning, along with a crowd of eager spectators. I didn't recognize many of them, whose faces were contorted by the otherworldly light and crazy shadows cast by a giant torch, which, minutes before, had been the Venote's house.

> *Look at the crowd, wallowing in ghoulish fascination. Listen to us murmur as flames crackle and consume the shack. See us lurch back when the roof collapses and launches a swarm of blinking cinders to the night sky. Look at the toothless old hag weep, her grandchildren agape, their backs pressed against the red fire engine of the Farmingdale Volunteer Fire Department.*
>
> *My shadow mingled with others in that weird light. I couldn't stop gawking. Amid such tragedy, the go-kart*

whisked through my mind. Did the boy put it elsewhere for safekeeping? Maybe I should poke through the rubble the next day for salvageable remains. As the fire ebbed such selfish thoughts churned in my head. Soon, the hovel burned to the ground, the eyesore gone.

Sure, things were *tough all over*. I'd bike on back roads where hollow-eyed cars squatted in front and backyards, where errant cesspools stunk up the air next to a ghost house you hoped was abandoned. Out in the countryside, there were black poor, white poor, Puerto Rican poor, drunk poor, farmer poor, or out-of-work poor. Regardless, those who were not poor expected those who were to keep their poverty out of the road's sight lines or eventually get pushed out—or burned out, like the Venotes.

Chapter 27
ARTFUL FRIENDSHIP

Not long after the final day of school, my expectations about summer vacation collapsed under the weight of humidity and boredom. I was free, but I had no intentions. If I complained that there was nothing to do, that was Grandma's cue to tell me she'd find plenty of useful things for me to do. That was my cue to get on my bike and search for signs of life elsewhere.

After supper on one July evening, I spun west toward Ardmore Estates, a development of ranches and split-levels that continued their relentless march to flatten what were once meadows and woods. As I biked on Ardmore's interior streets, I heard the chatter and phony laugh-track guffaws of TV sitcoms tumbling out of open windows. From one house, I heard glass break, followed by shouts; from another, a woman washing pots and pans, banging them about like cymbals. From yet another, I heard a door slam, out of which streaked a blond twelve-year-old boy with a crew cut, Jimmy Oats, who raced past me on his bike. Gradually, I caught up only because he let me. We leapt off our bikes and let them clatter behind us where a wheat field abutted the development.

"I hate him," he said, wiping his glistening eyes. He meant his father, a once-promising minor-league baseball player, now a retired cop and stone-cold alcoholic. I picture him slouched in his easy chair, chain-smoking Salems, watching the Mets or Yankees and sipping a can of beer, the warm-up to shots of cheap rye he'd knock back later at the Blue Moon Tavern or Tom's Cabin in Farmingdale. Sometimes he'd squint at Jimmy and me as if measuring the distance between him and us. Although it never happened, I always kept beyond the reach of a slap on the face. "I hate him! Fuck him!" This time, Jimmy yelled it.

We flung stones into the field. "Fuck" had crept into our vocabulary, then began taking it over like the acne on our skin. Fuck this and fuck that. We spit a lot too, part of our general spewing.

I felt bad for Jimmy but didn't say so. No good would come of it. We were boys, men-in-training. who understood that when the boo-hooing began, you looked the other way. Hide what hurts and pretend it didn't happen. I was for him—as he was for me—a silent witness, not to judge or be judged. The friendship was simple but artful, sanctuary from the complexities swirling around us.

Jimmy was athletic and popular, a good-looking kid who wore cool madras shirts that his mother bought for him. Mrs. Oats drove a school bus part-time, but her real job was keeping a steady hand on the family's steering wheel, raising Jimmy and his older sister, Debbie. I thought Mrs. Oats sized me up as a bad influence.

"I saw you riding your bike with a cigarette hanging out of your mouth. Do you think you looked *sophisticated* or something? You looked ridiculous," she said. "You're too young to smoke." Ironically, the chances were good that the cigarette she saw me smoking was one of the *Salems* that Jimmy lifted from her pack. He and I shared cigarettes poached from his parents or from my grandfather. I told Mrs. Oats that I was just experimenting, that I found a butt on the shoulder of the road and didn't like it. I thought the repulsiveness of my lie made it that much more credible. I got that she liked me anyway.

Jimmy and I first became friends when we went to Sunday school at Ardena Baptist Church. I walked or biked the mile to and from church. I'd sit in those hard, butt-punishing pews each Sunday, sitting through mind-numbing lessons in the balcony of the church—a steam bath in summer and an icy tomb in winter. Our group was shepherded by Mrs. Donohue, a gentle and patient widow who gave us candy after we took Bible quizzes, regardless of whether our answers were right or not. Jimmy and I cheated anyway, just to break the monotony. After Mrs. Donohue moved, a new teacher with different ideas took her place. She would have none of our antics. Jimmy soon dropped out and I was left alone with a handful of younger geeks and a hissy young woman. I can't remember what I said or did, but I made her so livid she yelped that

I'd be going to hell. On the contrary, I thought to myself, I deserved at least some credit for just showing up.

When I told Grandma what happened, she left it up to me to continue or not with Sunday school. I said if I had my choice, I'd like to go to a church that served wine, not thimbles of grape juice at communion. After all, if Jesus had turned the water into grape juice, who would have stayed at the wedding? We had a quiet laugh over me going to hell. That was it for my formal religious training.

I felt lucky that Jimmy was my friend. He was an All-American kind of kid. I saw myself as *half-something else*, a loser with bad posture, a big mouth, and a dead front tooth (turned gray from an accidental baseball bat). I dressed in clothes that Grandma bought for me, which were sometimes suicide-inducing. For example, the bilious-green tennis sneakers she had plucked from Bamberger's clearance shelf, which I had to wear on gym days. They were bad attention grabbers, like pinkeye, warts, or a careless pee stain on your pants.

Jimmy and I sealed our friendship in recklessness. One afternoon, alone at his house, we played guns with a .38-caliber pistol that he took from a box of firearms secreted in his father's closet. We fired off a couple of thunderous rounds at tin cans in his backyard, but we were concerned about drawing neighbors' attention. We gravitated to his basement, pulled the slugs out of the remaining shells with pliers, and reloaded the gun. We turned off the lights in his basement and took turns stalking each other. We fired, deafened by the explosion, and amazed by the red-yellow bolt that flared out into the darkness. The risky madness of it was delightful, but once was enough.

We enjoyed more benign games, played Wiffle Ball, and swam in a neighbor's pool. We peeped through slivers of open curtains in the basement windows of older girls who had parties with high school friends. We'd glimpse them fast dancing to "The Loco-Motion," slow dancing to "Johnny Angel," and making out against a wall behind the pool table. The idea that I'd ever have a girl in my arms seemed impossible. *Not in a million years.*

We were on a mission. One afternoon in August, the sun blazing, we biked west five miles past Farmingdale to Collingswood Auction Market. Jimmy's friend Larry joined us. But there was no auction at Collingswood Auction Market. It was a fluorescent inner city of huddled kiosks conjoined to each other. These concerns sold mistakes at a discount—*irregulars*, they called them; shirts with pockets stitched at a slant, pants with double seams, upholstered furniture that looked good, but smelled as though it had been pulled out of a dump. Other booths sold used goods, lamps, toasters, furniture, and 8-track audio-tape cartridges. You'd find out soon enough whether they worked or not.

Our destination was a booth that Sammy had told me about, where there were used books and magazines, including *Playboy*. There were makeshift curtain walls all around the perimeter of the kiosk, except for the entrance. After hemming and hawing about who would go in first, we agreed to go together. A grubby guy trolled around his merchandise and greeted us, the unlit stub of a cigar soaking in a corner of his mouth.

"Hello, boys, what can I do for you today?" he said.

When I told him we were just looking, he warned us not to even *think* about ripping him off.

"And don't mess up anything. The girlie stuff is by the *National Geographics*." He hiked up the waist of his pants to his chest, to show us he was serious.

There—next to the *National Geographic* issues featuring the natives of Java, the migrating wildebeests of East Africa, and the pre-Columbian ruins dug up in Chaco Canyon—was the motherlode of visual source material, beautiful girls in panties and negligees, their breasts fully exposed. There were stacks and stacks of secondhand tattered *Playboy* magazines, many with centerfolds intact. At only 50 cents a copy, I bought three issues and a copy of *National Geographic*, one that had a cover story about wildebeests. I wanted the smut merchant to understand that I had interests that extended beyond girlie magazines. I was a refined perv.

Mission accomplished, we spun home, our tires humming on the hot summer macadam. I hid my harem in the barn. There are some things your grandmother ought never see.

Chapter 28
MAIL CALL FROM YOKOHAMA

It had been raining for several days, so when I came home from school, I was cooped up again. I complained to Grandma that I was bored and regretted it. She gave me three alternatives to break up the monotony: do my homework; continue reading *A Tale of Two Cities*; or clean my room. This was not the best of times nor was it the worst of times, just bad enough.

I went upstairs and spent a few minutes tidying up my closet, got distracted by an old issue of Mad magazine, and gravitated to Dad's part-time bedroom, which was next to mine. I rummaged through his desk and looked for a pen to replace the Bic that had leaked blue blobs on my hands. I nosed around in a drawer for things worth taking. I felt entitled to take something, just for spite. I doubted that Dad would notice anything missing. He hadn't been home for over a month, nor had he called. Each weekend that he missed was another cold step in his march away from me.

Earlier this day I had eavesdropped on my grandparents. Grandma said that she was *fit-to-be-tied* about Dad's unreliability. Grandpa said something like, *Let's not work ourselves into a tizzy.* Grandma rarely raised her voice other than occasional blurts of *Oh dear!* or on the most blasphemous of occasions, *What the H?* But Grandma's disposition was far from pacific. She was a ruminator. Grandma kept her worries coiled up, as if waiting for the dark messenger to knock on our front door and deliver terrible news. Grandpa, on the other hand, craved peace and quiet, except for tuning into the *Sturm und Drang* of Wagner operas on the radio. Otherwise, he turned a deaf ear to emotional turmoil.

I was familiar with their old-fashioned restraint and antique turns of phrase, having lived with them for half of my life. As for me, I was *royally pissed-off* at Dad for spurning us. I'd keep it to myself, just as the family creed dictated. But that didn't deter me from payback. To punish him, I grabbed more pens than I needed. They were inscribed *Courtesy of Time-Life Circulation, Newark, NJ*. That's where he sold magazine subscriptions over the phone. I was twelve, going on thirteen, now in the sixth grade—old enough to know that a job as a telephone salesman had to suck. The idea of Dad as a *loser* gurgled up from my throat. I almost said *loser* out loud, but a reflux of shame stopped me. I still wanted the soldier-hero to return, the one who had kept his word and brought me and my mother to America.

Snooping deeper into the desk, I pushed aside a stapler, paper clips, Scotch tape, and other office sundries. A fancy chrome pencil sharpener, crammed with wood shavings, got my attention. When I emptied the shavings into the wastebasket, the scent of cedar wafted up. It smelled good and reminded me of rituals that began school mornings. I'd sharpen a couple of Ticonderoga No. 2 pencils, then blow the sawdust off a perfect point. The cedar smelled of *fresh starts*. Those were the times I sat at my desk with conviction because I was prepared, having done my homework and poised to scribble a new sentence or divide mixed fractions with a pencil point as fine as a needle.

I tucked Dad's pencil sharpener into my pants pocket, and then poked farther into the desk, pushing aside a nest of past-due parking tickets and pawnshop receipts. Underneath an old *Life* magazine calendar, several packets slid out—at least a half-dozen Trojans. I recoiled from the shocking discovery. I knew what they were because Sammy had removed a condom from his wallet still good as new in its wrapper. With a knowing smirk, he told me all about *protection*, and said it was *better to be safe than sorry*. As if he really knew.

I glared at the dubious cache of rubbers in my father's desk. Although I had suspected that Dad was dating, I still held on to the possibility that he and my mother might magically reunite. Now I knew my old man was a *cheater* and that he was dating *sluts*. He needed to pay. I thought about poking holes in the condom packets. Instead, I snapped a couple of his pencils in half and tossed them across the room. I calmed down, picked up the broken pencils, and tidied up the desk drawer. I kept two Trojans—one for myself and one for Sammy, a token tribute for my high priest of the lower regions. I'd tell him that I shoplifted it from the Rexall drugstore in Farmingdale to impress him.

Excavating through another drawer, I found air-mail envelopes that were postmarked from Tokyo, with my mother's maiden name on the return address—*Sachiko Takano*. The postmark on the envelope was dated two years earlier. There were several photographs of my mother. She posed standing, upright as a statue. Her posture was perfect, so unlike my slouch. Her face was that of an Oriental doll's, lips pursed, neither smiling nor scowling. In one picture she wore a kimono that was draped three-quarters over a dress. Varied patterns graced the kimono and fabric underneath. She wore sandals. Although it was a black-and-white photograph, I imagined the kimono sparkling with brilliant hues of red, orange, and gold.

For all the color I imagined, I could not invent warmth in her. She seemed as indifferent as the studio props in the picture: there was the chair, the dressing table, the potted plant—and yes, there was the woman. A hole opened up inside me, as big as the day she left.

As I sat on my father's bed, I studied the envelope, which was addressed to Dad and to me, posted in care of my grandparents' old address in Millington. I shuffled through a few short notes she had written, all indecipherable except one that was written in pencil with sweeping cursive of exactly twenty would-be words that I counted, of which only five were intelligible. I struggled to untangle the message among the exaggerated swoops of script and crippled grammar. Was it her mind or the language that prevented her from making sense? Her closing was the only thing I understood, and I read it several times. *"Miss mach Billy-san, love you."*

That was a good thing, I supposed, that she missed me and loved me. I didn't want to make more of it than there was. No mysteries were solved. She had signed off with her American name, Sarah, the name conferred on her by my American family.

Since she left four years earlier, my mother had become abstracted to me, an idea of a flesh-and-blood presence, a poor substitute for the real thing. Evidence of her had gradually evaporated. For example, the signature artifact of my mother and father's first meeting in Japan—the ivory carving of the night soil collector and his oxcart—was now gone. Grandma had sold it in the shop. Although it was out of place among examples of early American antiques, it eventually caught somebody's eye. My grandmother sold it like it was just another knick-knack. You notice these things. It didn't feel right.

I heard the stairs creak. Grandma worked her slow passage upstairs, her polio-shortened left leg coercing her into a penguin's sway from step to step. I buried the correspondence—and my mother—back into the desk drawer.

Padding quietly back to my room, I lay on my bed, pretending to read *A Tale of Two Cities*—a dog-eared edition that had been Dad's when he was a boy. Though Grandma had handed it to me weeks earlier, I had progressed no further than the first sentence of the first page, a sentence that unfurled into what seemed to me the longest sentence ever written. It took all I had to finish just the first page, no less the entire book! I watched askance as the silver top of Grandma's head bobbed into view when she reached the second-floor landing.

She stepped into my room out of breath, and we chatted a minute about the book. Facilely, I quoted its famous opening words—*It was the best of times, it was the worst of times*—intending that Grandma infer that I was well into the story. The unintended consequence was that she recited another quote in the book, this one from a character she identified as Sydney Carton—*I care for no man on earth, and no man on earth cares for me*. I had no clue who he was or what it meant, but nodded, as if it meant something.

As she smoothed out the comforter that I had bunched up on my bed, Grandma said that Carton was an unlikely hero because he had such a dark view of himself *and* the world. "But it gives you faith that people *can* change. Don't you think?" I told her that I guessed so, and hastily changed the subject to the weather, which we commiserated about.

All the while, questions squirmed inside me. *Did you know about the letters, Grandma? Why didn't you tell me? What else didn't you or Dad tell me?* After Grandma left my room, I wondered about the current circumstances of my mother. *What kind of place did she live in, was it an apartment or a house? Did she have a job? What would it be like to spend a day with her?* Whether or not she may have started a new family was a thought I banished from further consideration.

I once asked Dad what Mom would say if we saw her again. He had replied, "She'd ask me for money." As I stood in front of him waiting for more, he said, "End of conversation." He didn't like talking about stuff that was complicated by what you felt.

Although I tried to convince myself it was no big deal, the mysterious letters preyed on me. At dinner, Grandma asked me if there was something wrong because I hadn't eaten or said much. I told her that my stomach didn't feel right, which was the truth. She rested her palm on my forehead for a moment and told me I didn't have a fever.

"Best thing is to call it a day and get a good night's sleep."

As I went upstairs to my room, I heard Grandpa murmur, "He doesn't know whether he's coming or going. Just like his old man."

For the umpteenth time, I heard Grandma say it was the army that changed Dad and ruined his future. "There she goes again," I said to myself. "On and on and on."

I lay in bed wondering about those letters. I figured I'd get back to them when my grandparents were both out of the house. I wondered if my mother wanted to come back. I wondered if she was sorry for deserting Dad and me. *Probably not.* What gnawed at me was my secret about Mom. Whispers inside my head still accused me of sending her away. My wish had come true. So there. The idea that I might be my own worst enemy had crossed my mind long before I had ever heard of Sydney Carton.

I now knew she was alive, at least up to two years ago. It didn't make it any easier to go to sleep.

◈◆◈

I made friendships that gave me a sense of belonging, but it didn't add up to a state of happiness. Rather, it was a lunatic's glee that came from doing things that were bad or, at least, objectionable. Glee was time off from the thing that scraped the inside of your stomach, aching to escape. Glee was a break from the whispering dark that knew you were the trouble and not worth the trouble at the same time. You couldn't remember hearing anything to the contrary. When glee evaporated—as it always did, and quickly—there was again the thing in the belly, the whispers, and now, an emptiness that swallowed itself, like a small shadow subsumed by larger shadows. I had unfinished business, which I kept secret. I got my shotgun out of my closet, sat on the bed. I could blow my brains out, if I so decided. When they found me dead, they'd be sorry. But what about the mess? Even I couldn't take me seriously. I put the gun away.

◈◆◈

Outside, the world expanded to make room for the boomers. Housing developments sprouted up, the cousins of Levitt homes and other residences built for the urban flight of white men in suits and their families fleeing the darker skin and weird accents of the changing neighborhoods in the north. They formed the beginning of the tidal swell of commuters, which included my grandfather, who, during the final year before his retirement, commuted two hours each way between New York City and Freehold, the county seat and the closest bus depot. There were others who prospered close to home, developing land, starting businesses that sprung up along Route 9 or off the Parkway—strip malls, lumberyards, drugstores, furniture stores, burger franchises, and restaurants. Families with more money didn't live inland like mine, but moved to tonier addresses in Rumson, Fairhaven, Manahawkin, and other upwardly mobile havens along the north Jersey coast. The smell of old money, and lots of it, ripened in the mansions of Deal and Elberon; to their immediate north was Long Branch and to their immediate south, Asbury Park and Neptune. Urban blight had crept into all three big towns. In any of these towns, as you headed west and crossed the first set of railroad tracks, you'd begin seeing run-down houses and abandoned buildings in neighborhoods where the smell of ocean mixed with the odor of poverty.

In my neck of the woods, families moved, class assignments changed from year to year, and friendships faded away of their own accord. Sometimes, a classmate died. During seventh grade, Michael, a popular boy I scarcely knew from another class, was killed on his bicycle in a hit-and-run accident, the driver's identity forever a mystery. While the girls wept openly in the halls, boys like me pushed and shoved their way to the end of the school day, as if it were the same as any other.

> *Our transgressions were small potatoes compared to those of the grownups who built families, clans, and civilizations, and destroyed them. For our part, we survived the exploding hearts and broken promises of our youth through friendships that were like comfort food, a break from the daily diet of course correction from parents, teachers, and other adults—their cross looks, wagging fingers, and, among the worst of them, their angry hands.*

Chapter 29
DAD'S GIRLFRIENDS

One Sunday afternoon in June, when my grandparents were away at an antique auction, Dad brought a woman home. Grandma had told me that he'd be spending the day with me and bringing a "friend." It had been awkward from the start when Dad introduced me to Cathy, first because I wasn't expecting an attractive Japanese American woman, and second because my memory flashed on the rubbers I had found in his desk. It was hard to look her in the eye. Despite that, we went through the typical how-do-you-dos and friendly chitchat, and she told me about what great things Dad said about me. She was quite the looker and had the longest and reddest fingernails I'd ever seen. I was about to make myself scarce and go up to my room when she gestured with an upright index finger for me to wait a moment. She rummaged through her purse, fished out a five-dollar bill, and gave it to me. I gladly accepted it, but wondered if it was a bribe to like her, which was fine with me. I mean, a couple of bucks would have done it.

"Do something fun with it," she said.

"That really isn't necessary," Dad said.

"I can tell Billy deserves it." Cathy winked.

I thought about saying, "Hell yes!" but instead, thanked her and went up to my room. I left them on the living-room couch leafing through Dad's scrapbooks from Japan. I crouched at the top of the stairs, straining to hear what they said. Every now and then, they burst out laughing. I stopped eavesdropping when it seemed unlikely that any monkey business was going on, thank goodness. After a while, Dad told me it was time for him to drive Cathy back into the city. She and I exchanged nice-to-meet-yous and hope-to-see-you-agains.

Dad told me, "I'll see you in a week or two," which was just vague enough for me to know it wasn't a commitment.

Later, Grandma had barely come through the door and taken

her coat off when she asked me, "So what did you think about Dad's friend?"

"She was fine," I said. "She seemed nice." It didn't matter one way or the other.

I would meet a new girlfriend in the fall. Dad took me to Bronx on the first day of October to see the Red Sox play the Yankees for the next-to-last game of the season. We got tickets for great box seats behind the visitor's dugout. Yankee Stadium could hold sixty thousand, but on this almost frigid day, attendance was announced as ten-thousand-something. Only die-hard baseball fans came out for a game that was meaningless in terms of the standings. New York had clinched the pennant a week earlier and Boston was at the end of another humiliating season, finishing 32 games behind the American League champ.

"At least we won't finish in the cellar, thanks to Kansas City," I said, rubbing my hands to keep them warm.

"I was hoping you'd get to see Ted Williams play," Dad said.

"I thought I saw him playing catch during the warm-ups."

"Maybe so. But he's not in today's lineup. He officially retires tomorrow. He's got too much dignity to be trotted out for a bow, just for showing up."

I bit into a cold hot dog and was happy to be where I was. It was good enough to be at the ballpark with the old man and sort of see *The Splendid Splinter, Teddy Ballgame, The Kid* — the legend himself shifting in the shadows of the visitor's dugout.

After the game, Dad and I went to a restaurant in the Yorkville neighborhood of the city. We sat at a table near the front window, waiting for his new girlfriend. Dad told me she was a singer at a café lounge nearby. The neighborhood had been called Little Germany, but less so after the war. Dad said something about German sympathizers. When he told me that his date's name was Lucy Twist, I asked him if that was a stage name. Show business had piqued my interest. I had recently got the lead in the seventh-grade class play and we were in rehearsals for it. It was changing my life.

"No, it's her real name." He ground out a cigarette in the ashtray, annoyed.

"I mean because of the Twist craze and all. The dance, I mean."

"Yeah, I know about the Twist. I get it."

I was working on my second Coke when an eye-poppingly gorgeous woman tapped on the restaurant window and waved at us. As she walked in, Dad spun from his chair and greeted the tall, curvaceous redhead, handing off her cashmere to the coat-check girl. Several people nodded to acknowledge her as she passed by their tables. She was a local celebrity. After Dad pulled out a chair to receive her lovely behind, Lucy sat across from me. We went through the usual introductory chitchat. She had a slight German accent.

"*Vell*, Billy, tell me all about you. *Vhat* do you like? I mean, *Vhat* are your favorite things?" She leaned toward me, asking me the question as if it were just between us.

I didn't expect to be put on the spot like that. Besides that, Dad narrowed his eyes at me. I got the message that he didn't like me being in the spotlight. I sputtered out a few lame aspects of my miserable little life and was saved by the waiter asking if we were ready to order. I had sauerbraten, potato balls, and red cabbage, with apple strudel and vanilla ice cream for dessert. Lucy asked me how I liked the meal, and I said it was great, like being back in the old country again. I thought it was pretty funny, but they didn't get it. When we were set to go, I had a fleeting notion of goose-stepping out the door but restrained myself. When we were outside, Lucy pecked me on the cheek, poked around in her purse, then pressed herself against me while she slipped a five-dollar bill into my sweaty hand. Dad's girlfriends really knew how to treat a guy. I said thank you, trying not to overthink matters.

Dad and I talked for a while on the long ride back to Ardena. How about those Red Sox? As we'd come to expect, their bullpen blew an early lead. How was I doing in school? I said I was getting honor-roll grades in all academic categories but said nothing about my poor grades in deportment keeping me off the honor roll. I did mention that I was more or less starring in the class play. I said maybe he could see it. He changed the subject. How did I like the Boy Scout troop I joined? I told him I was thinking about dropping out. All we did was show up in uniform at the Ardena Elementary School on Thursday nights, practice tying knots, and marching in step around the cafeteria.

I wondered why Dad had gone to the trouble of introducing me to his girlfriends. The idea popped into my head that maybe he was proud of me. Our conversation shut down when I asked him if he ever thought about Mom.

"No, I don't think about her. I try not to. Let's change the subject, eh?" he said.

Chapter 30
BROADWAY LEGEND IN MY OWN MIND

In between the mind-numbing doldrums of seventh grade, I had successes and failures, triumphs and humiliations. By the time the year was over, I'd wash out of honor roll because of my chronic character flaws, earn the enmity of a girl who liked me, get the lead in the class play, and for the *piece de resistance*, have my face slapped by a girl I was crazy about.

Meanwhile, in the big picture, grownups fretted because somebody said the nuclear destruction clock had ticked down to one minute before midnight. If that were true, why waste the last minute just doing the regular crap? School mornings began with the recitation of the Lord's Prayer, followed by the Pledge of Allegiance. Dully in unison we mumbled, "Our Father who art in Heaven," *yadda, yadda, yadda*, and then stood and swore our fidelity to "the flag and the country for which it stands," *et cetera, et cetera, et cetera*. After those rituals, it was off to the tortoise races, sitting on your ass and urging three o'clock to show up sooner. The primary directives were to stay seated, keep quiet, and appear to be attentive. There were times I couldn't abide.

For these infractions Mr. Moore, my seventh-grade teacher, meted out an escalating scale of punishments that began with copying a page of the dictionary, and, for more serious offenses, copying historical documents, *verbatim*. The scale began with Lincoln's Gettysburg Address, then advanced upward to the Preamble of the U.S. Constitution, the Declaration of Independence, and, ultimately, the entire Constitution, replete with the Bill of Rights. I doubt there was a student who was better acquainted with our nation's founding papers than me.

One day, out of the blue, Madelyn Beemer asked me to carry her books. We were walking single file out of the cafeteria. At first, I thought she was kidding. I didn't say anything, then she nudged a couple of books toward me and smiled. Maybe it was the hairs on Madelyn's arms that put me off. They were long, dark, and there were a lot of them.

"Why not?" Madelyn asked.

"I don't need the extra responsibility," I said, which was true.

Besides, I had a painful crush on Joanne Zuzzio. Imagine Annette Funicello and Sophia Loren rolled into one. I longed for her, even when she quipped, "You have a face that only a mother could love." Hah! I took it as a jokey insult, and laughed like I didn't care.

When I told Orrin I had a crush on her, he said, "Who doesn't? Forget about her, unless you want to be miserable."

"I'm already miserable, so big deal."

"Well, you have a point."

I was optimistic. I sensed an opportunity to improve my chances when Mr. Moore enthusiastically announced he'd begin casting for a class play, a show to be performed for the entire school. His tortoise shell glasses fogged up as he described the play and said that there'd be opportunities for everyone in our class to shine, either as actors, or working on the set. I wanted the lead role. Only Henry Grant (no relation to Cary) stood between me and a new career. He was smart and a high achiever, and everybody figured the part was his, including Henry. But I was motivated as never before. What better opportunity would I ever have to be the center of attention? I wasn't about to give in to the red-haired, chubby snob who thought he was better than me. In the days leading up to the audition, I practiced in front of my dresser mirror, determined to win the part, bury my dowdy thespian rival, and, in the process, win the affection of Joanne. After Henry and I read for the part, Moore told the class that both of us performed exceptionally well, but said I was better suited to play the sneaky, self-absorbed, and obnoxious Thomas T. Trouble. "Basically, you can just be yourself." I took it as compliment.

The play was a parody of old-time melodramas where the villain connives to foreclose on the mortgage of the farm owned by the hapless old folks who have custody of their orphaned and gorgeous granddaughter. The best part was that Joanne played the heroine, Penelope, the luscious granddaughter. If only there was a kissing scene.

I was on cloud nine. In the weeks leading up to the show we rehearsed in the classroom. There's a critical moment in the story when Trouble tries to steal a kiss from Penelope. She rebuffs him and says, "Lips that touch wine will never touch mine," and slaps him. During the first run-through, Joanne gave me a gentle tap on my cheek. Mr. Moore wanted more conviction from his leading lady.

"Look, Trouble is the creep who's going to take the deed from your family's farm and destroy everything you love. Is Penelope just going to pat him on the cheek?"

"No," Joanne said meekly.

"Then show us she means it!" Moore exhorted. He stood next to me, gripped my chin in his hand and tilted my cheek toward Joanne. "Let's see Penelope mean it!"

She said "Yes!" with religion in her voice, and let it fly.

Her palm hit my face like a twenty-pound Easter ham and sent me inside a fuzzy cloud beyond pain. I snapped out of it when I heard the class erupt in cheers and applause. My cheek was on fire and my eyes got watery, but these tears were tears of joy. I was living the dream. I was in show business!

Moore revised his earlier direction about the slap to Joanne. "Good job, but go a tad easier," he said. "We don't want Billy in a coma."

Our show was a grand success, as grand as it gets in a grammar school in the sticks of New Jersey. Grandma went to the show (there was only one performance) and said she was bowled over by it. Dad didn't make it, of course. The sound of applause reverberated in my head that night and I kept rewinding the experience. I was a star. The sky was the limit.

After the audience had cleared out, no one was on the set except Joanne and me. I said, "It was really something, wasn't it?"

She had stroked my cheek and sighed, "It doesn't hurt too much, does it?"

"Only when I smile," I said.

That's when we kissed, and I wrapped her in my arms. She kept saying I was magnificent, and if my skin was capable of it, I'd have blushed, deep red.

That's how it had been. Sort of. Not really.

Like they say, *Yeah, in your dreams.*

✥

It's true my star had risen, but only briefly. I entered eighth grade at the crest of my previous year's celebrity. I was elected vice president of my homeroom but removed within a month. A cabal of mouth breathers had complained to Mr. Eldred that I had been mean and rude to them. I explained that I was just kidding around, but not necessarily making fun of them.

"I didn't mean it personally. Anyway, they're idiots, just like everybody else."

He looked at me as if my screws were loose and said that I ought to be ashamed of myself, being entrusted with a leadership position by my peers and then abusing it. It was pointless to argue, but I did anyway. I mean, who said that being obnoxious and rude were impeachable offenses?

My fortunes continued to fall. I learned quickly that life in the theater is fickle. Mr. Eldred selected a corny piece of crap for our class play and cast me in a minor part. What a waste of talent! He gave the lead role to a nobody. I sulked through rehearsals, and when it was show time, I flubbed the few lines I had.

I had peaked too soon, and now, I was already a has-been.

During a fire drill, I was horsing around when Mr. Litowinski, the school principal, grabbed my arm and pulled me aside. He towered over students and most teachers. Whether or not it was true, it was accepted knowledge that he was in the Marines during the war. As he approached you, his steely eyes and set jaw were his advance troops, arriving a step before the rest of him did. When he wasn't in his office putting mischief makers in their place and recording misdeeds on their permanent record, Mr. Litowinski cruised through the hallways, poking his head into classrooms, reconning the cafeteria, and, in the process, paralyzing the flotsam and jetsam of small humans who lined up for lunch, fire drills, air-raid drills, and assemblies. He escorted me to an empty stairwell landing for a private chat.

I expected a blistering dressing down, but instead he told me he was disappointed that my misconduct had gotten me ousted as vice president of my home room. I was about to defend myself when he held up his hand, which was as big as a stop sign, and he told me to just listen. He said it was important to be proud of who I was and that I should live up to a higher standard, telling me about the 442nd Infantry Regiment, best known as the most decorated in U.S. military history. Almost all of the soldiers were second-generation American soldiers of Japanese ancestry who fought in Italy against the Nazis during World War II. It was all I could do to keep from blubbering, not because I felt kinship with those heroes, but because I didn't. They weren't my people. Their ilk had berated me and others like me when I was in Japan.

I pulled myself together and rejoined my class, where my people were—even though some detested me, if not for good reason. Orrin asked me, "What was that about with Litowinski?"

"Who knows?" It was too much to get into.

All these troubles paled by comparison to the big picture. Everybody had their bowels in an uproar about the Soviets building nuclear missiles in Cuba, just 90 miles south of Florida. We had practiced hiding under our desks at school and held drills to prepare for a nuclear attack since the fifth grade. Who could take it seriously? For instance, the civil defense preparations that were under way. First, you were supposed to stay alert for the warning sirens. Then, get yourself to the nearest air-raid shelter, which conveniently for us, was Ardena Elementary. If you didn't get baked instantly, you were supposed to monitor the radio news. In the event of an atomic blast, you were told to stay in place for two weeks before emerging from the shelter. If you had them (nobody did), you should take potassium iodide tablets to decrease the effects of radiation poisoning. Some people built their own private fallout shelters beneath their homes. We didn't know anyone who had one. If they did, they had the common sense not to tell anyone. Orrin said the saddest thing about nuclear war was that we'd die as virgins. What was the point of us being born in the first place? So true.

During an assembly at the end of the school year, a local evangelist presented the invocation, extolling the rewards of prayer. "Just ask the Lord and He will deliver. Bring Jesus Christ into your heart, your prayers will be answered," he promised. He gave a weird example of a prayer answered, about a boy whose jaw was locked wide open after he yawned. Imagine that! His parents didn't know what to do. The local doctor tried to force the jaw closed, but to no avail. Lucky for the boy that this evangelist was nearby. He led the boy and his parents in prayer, and wouldn't you know it, the kid's jaw snapped right back into place. You'd think that God had bigger fish to fry. No wonder my old man was an atheist.

An awards presentation followed the invocation. I didn't make honor roll. But even chronic bad behavior couldn't come between me and my certificate for perfect attendance. Grandma insisted that I catch the school bus whether I had a cold, a stomachache, or the bubonic plague. Jimmy thought it was hilarious when I slouched up to the stage and sidled up to a dozen or so pathetic losers who made it to school every day no matter what. It was not a heroic moment.

Part Three
Passions and Disappointments

Adolescence is enough suffering for anyone.
— *John Ciardi*

Chapter 31
JUNGLE INTRIGUES

September 1963

The evangelist's story about curing the kid of his lockjaw problem was about as cheesy a miracle as you could imagine, but maybe the take-away was that there's no matter too small to bring to the attention of the Big Man Upstairs. Although praying for help in getting a girlfriend was my true purpose, I opened my appeal by asking for His guidance in helping me become a better human being. That would establish me as a worthy supplicant, before I prayed for what he might consider just another self-serving request from yet another schlub from below. I also didn't bother Him with the transactional details, like enumerating the repulsive habits I would give up. I mean, He already knew everything. As a token of my good intentions, I recovered the *Playboy* magazines I had hidden in the barn, and burned them in our backyard incinerator, a sacrificial offering that I hoped would confirm my conviction to become good. Thus was the shape of my religious convictions—an alloy of Shintoism, Buddhism, Old Testament Yahweh, and New Testament Christianity, which when blended with adolescent superstitions, formed my pagan compass.

Beyond battling my demons, my life as a high school freshman was as redemptive as the fish sticks we ate every Friday night. We weren't Catholics, but Grandma abided by meatless Fridays anyway. Grandma said that it couldn't hurt, eating fish once a week, but you could tell Grandpa felt differently, sulkily impaling fish sticks on his fork. On schooldays, Grandpa woke me each morning at six. Now retired, Grandpa was a proud breakfast cook, despite his dubious skills. His undercooked, translucent bacon, accompanied by an overcooked fried egg that looked like a brown coaster with blisters, still sticks to my memory as firmly as it stuck to my ribs back then.

My first hurdle each weekday was the long bus ride to Freehold

High School, my destination for the year, until construction was complete for what would ultimately be named Howell High School, just outside of Farmingdale, a few miles from home. The bus seemed to take forever, hobbling forward like a wounded water buffalo, stopping every tenth of a mile to pick up a startled-looking lemur on a country back road, or a cluster of mopey sloths in front of a housing development. Keeping aware of what kind of creature was getting on the bus was important. I'd prepare myself accordingly. I avoided eye contact with short-tempered baboons who didn't like my face. Occasionally, I'd glare fiercely at clumsy rodents and other small fry who clambered aboard. At journey's end, the bus would converge with others that formed a yellow armada in front of the school, each bus unloading its unseemly freight.

Shuffling with hundreds of others in the rumbling, lowing herd that filled the hallways, I gravitated to the middle of the moving mass to blend in. This was a survival tactic of the migrating wildebeests of East Africa that I had read about in *National Geographic*. If you got separated from the herd, you were fair game for bored jocks or greasers, or freelance jackals. Yes, much about high school was a cliché, but day after day, there they were, predators, prowling the hallway savannah. The thinning of the herd was in full sway during the school day's open and close, and between periods. The fluorescent halls and the slam of locker doors accented the general nervousness that was normal for horny and often angry male teenagers. Angry because hardly anybody was getting what they wanted. The price the weak might pay was a sneer, a shove against a locker door, or a random slap on the back of the head.

Getting up early dulled my concentration. I panicked early in algebra, floundered in linear equations, and spent most of my time fantasizing about Sonya, a sophomore who sat on at the other side of the classroom, gracing me with a view of her long legs as I sketched pictures of them in my notebook. I regretted incinerating my dirty magazines, but it didn't take much to fire me up. Although my voyeur's rendering was hardly more than a stick figure, it was all the erotica I needed. It seemed that the good times happened only in my imagination, while the tortures and troubles occupied the otherwise empty space that was my real life.

I'd get drowsy in civics but snapped out of it when I got harassed by Phil, who sat behind me and flicked the back of my head with a pencil, a prelude to a knuckle swat that was to come. Phil wore his shirtsleeves rolled above his elbows; his muscular forearms crossed in front of him like pale clubs. I had gotten on his wrong side the first week of class because I had made him feel stupid, somewhat intentionally. Sometimes, you just can't help yourself.

Mr. Bartolo had asked, "What are the three branches of government as enumerated in the U.S. Constitution?" and pointed to Phil, taking him by surprise. Phil furrowed his brow and bit his lower lip, pretending that he was actually thinking. Mr. Bartolo went to the blackboard and said, "Let me give you a hint; two of them are the executive and legislative branches. What's the third?"

After squirming through a few other thinking poses, Phil had said, "I give up,"

I stifled a laugh, snorting through my nose. I raised my hand and smugly answered, "That would be the judicial branch."

On uttering the response, I could feel the heat from Phil raging behind me. As soon as Mr. Bartolo turned his back to write the "J" in judiciary on the blackboard, Phil gave me a knuckle swat behind my left ear. From then on, he'd alternate swats left and right.

"Fuck you, Sneak Attack," Phil had hissed. That was his nickname for me, as in sneak attack *à la* Pearl Harbor.

Now, whenever Mr. Bartolo turned his back to write something on the blackboard about how a bill becomes law, judicial review, or other civics tidbit, I'd lean as far forward as I could, out of Phil's reach. I guessed I had asked for it. I had to wonder, who's stupid now?

I faked my way through German. I spent a lot of extra time with Frau Munch, who was also my homeroom teacher. She gave me detention many times for neglecting homework assignments. I got a kick out of singing, "*O die Schonheit auf dem Wand, ist das nicht ein Schnitzelbank?*" It was a lunatic's song, as far as I could figure. I exchanged insults with other detention-bound classmates. "Fuck off, *Scheisskopf!*"

English and art classes were more forgiving. I liked Mrs. Grasso, a snappy dresser who wore her dark hair short and her dresses tight. She was a taskmaster, however. Though she rarely gave me the time of day in class, she wrote encouraging comments on my reports and compositions. I actually enjoyed our weekly vocabulary quizzes and looked for opportunities to use words like *redemptive*, *translucent*, *cliché*, *litigious*, *empathetic*, *clandestine*, and *egotistical*. Those new words got forever italicized in my mind, like news clippings you put in your wallet as souvenirs of something you don't want to forget. Some considered me obnoxious for using so-called big words. I wouldn't argue with them though—I'm not the *litigious* type.

I liked art class too, learned the vanishing point and how to manipulate perspective. I liked Miss Hurst, who, despite being large and out of breath, spent a lot of time looking at what we drew or painted and critiquing what we did. She gave me some tips on how to sketch the basic human form, very useful in drawing girls' legs and breasts, even if I did it *clandestinely*.

In November, our principal told us over the P.A. system that the President had been shot. Teachers slammed doors or buried their hands in their pockets. They snapped at us more than usual. Some girls sobbed hysterically. Even some guys got shiny-eyed and morose. Girls fell into boys' arms for consolation. I wanted them to come to me for an *empathetic* embrace, but for all the wrong reasons. The event was perplexing, *surrea*l. Though the President was shot and murdered, no one in charge could explain what happened, at least with the clarity you might expect during a crisis. The talking heads on news programs seemed at a loss. They were usually ready to interpret what we saw with our own eyes and heard with our own ears, but not now. Then another shooter, a big guy in a white cowboy hat, shot and killed the President's assassin, right in the middle of a scrum of sheriffs and deputies who were supposed to be protecting him. You saw the scene over and over. The whole country seemed to hold its breath because no one knew anything for sure anymore, including the new guy, who hardly seemed the part. Now it was revealed—the emperor had no clothes. Nobody was truly in charge or safe. The killings were retold and reconsidered day after day in the coming weeks and months, but without revealing any further truth. You get the idea that nobody really knows anything for sure, and maybe, even prefers it that way.

I tried out for the freshman baseball team and after practice one day, I came down with a bad headache. Grandma had to pick me up at school. My vision blurred. It hurt just to look into daylight. What I saw was like what you tried to see after a flashbulb went off. My head felt like it was splitting open. A migraine is what Grandma called it and said she got them now and then. I was out of it for that day and the next. From then on, the headaches would come in varying intensity, frequency, and circumstances. I was embarrassed, enfeebled by the same malady that beset a little old lady, and for no apparent reason.

Unrelated to the migraine, the coach cut me from the freshman squad—not even retained as a bench warmer. Jimmy made the team and midway through the season, got promoted to JV, and then spent the last several games with the varsity team.

The first time I saw *her* was in the library. She sat at a reading table several rows away, whispering to another girl. She looked like Nancy Kwan, the beautiful actress who starred in the all-Asian cast of *The Flower Drum Song*. Whatever my assignment was, I forgot it. I was lost to this girl with jet-black hair, huge almond eyes and skin that I knew smelled wonderful, even from that distance. I knew right off the bat. She was absolutely *The One*. I had prayed for a girlfriend, and there she was! God had delivered, or so it seemed.

At the same time, I thought, *Who am I to think I have a chance?* Despite my doubts, I walked past her table several times, pretending to search for books. She giggled, and I took that as a cue to say something moronic, which I did, and *The One* and her friend burst out laughing. My heart leapt. The librarian, bespectacled, thin, and prematurely old, shushed me. As I scuttled back to my table, I saw a tall guy sidle up to *The One*. As he murmured in her ear, he fingered several strands of hair and lifted them to his face, inhaling her very essence! I wanted to kill him, right after I humiliated him in front of *The One*.

Instead, as the bell for the next period rang, I skulked out of the library and moped through the halls on my way to gym, that separate purgatory in high school with its collective B.O., slimy showers, compulsory nudity, and occasional fist fight. So much for the power of prayer. The girl I thought was *The One* was just a head fake. I figured that God ought to have given me a break, just for trying to become better than I was. Now, with my chances for romance as bleak as ever, I blamed Him. I toyed with the idea of becoming an atheist. That might get His attention.

Approaching the gym locker room, I thought I heard someone call me. I turned around. No one there, but my stupid, lonely life, catching up to me.

Chapter 32
ON THE FARM

I was fifteen in the summer of 1963, counting on a season of leisure after freshman year. My grandparents had other ideas. Grandpa arranged for me to work at Adelphia Farm. He said it was *honest toil*. I was miffed but conceded to myself that it was time to graduate from Grandma's agenda of domestic chores. I pictured myself working in The World of Men where I belonged, *honestly toiling* for $1.05 an hour—*real* money, not the loose change Grandma paid me. I imagined a spending spree on Cokes, Italian subs, pinball arcades at Manasquan's beach, and an occasional secret pack of smokes. But Grandma decreed that all but five bucks a week was earmarked for college, which I argued was a paltry sum that made it hardly worth working for. Grandma finally relented and said I could have eight dollars a week to squander.

I felt good about my first paycheck. My pay after taxes for the 40-hour week was $40.00 on the nose. The two bucks the government plucked out of my weekly pay rankled me. Regardless, it was the most money I had ever earned. I considered the printed bank check with my name on it as evidence of accomplishment more credible than certificates for perfect attendance and honor roll.

Adelphia Farm was run by Cook College of Rutgers, 200 acres of fertile red Monmouth County soil dedicated to hybrid fruits and vegetables, champions of their kind. Grandpa would drop me off at eight-thirty and pick me up at five.

The farm's superintendent was Mr. Kaminski, a big guy with a flat-top crew cut and quick scowl. I worked with seven other guys—half of us were in high school, half in college. Because of a drought, we spent most of the summer hoisting heavy galvanized irrigation pipes from field to field. Otherwise, we'd paint fences, clean outbuildings, and often, be dropped off in the Land of Never-Ending Rows of Soybeans. This is when Chuck, our supervisor, would point to the leafy green sea, and say, "A good day for weeding. I got eyes everywhere, so don't fuck off." A few minutes after Chuck's red pickup truck vanished, Roy and Ted, the alphas of the Cook College boys, would drop their hoes and crawl into the miserly shade of soybeans. The rest of us followed their lead.

Besides the farmworkers, old men in safari hats trolled through the fields with clipboards in hand. The college boys were deferential and called them Doc or Doctor So-and-So because they were research professors who taught at Cook College. Here they tended to plots of new varieties of corn, tomatoes, and other vegetables and compared their genetic performance against the control plots where current champion seeds grew—for example, the world-famous Rutgers Tomato, a standout for its deliciousness and resistance to blight, beetles, and mercurial temperatures. I'd smell pipe tobacco wafting out of a corn plot and soon see a professor in a crisply ironed white shirt and khakis sucking on a pipe, inspecting an ear of corn, or jotting down the progress of a new hybrid. I fancied myself as an essential part of the legacy of Gregor Mendel and his peas. Yes, I was more than a mindless field hand in the boondocks of New Jersey—I was among the silent heroes who delivered life-sustaining water for the *Über* vegetables of tomorrow.

Some days we'd get individual assignments. After I cleaned out the loft of a huge barn during a steamy August day, Mr. Kaminski inspected the transformed space and said, "Great job." Then he chortled, "You'll make someone a good wife, *Hansy*." As for *Hansy*, that was the nickname Roy gave me after asking me what my story was, with a last name like mine. I said it came from the German side of my family, and that my mother was Japanese. Since then, they called me Hans or Hansy. That was Roy's idea of irony.

Sometimes I'd overhear Kaminski complaining about what the *coloreds* were doing down South when he was talking with one of his supervisors. The Mason-Dixon Line ran through the southernmost counties of New Jersey, and occasionally you'd hear the worst word along with *spook* and *spade*. You might have figured that it was time to change all that, but for others it would never be the time to change. Except for one half of me, all who worked on the farm were white men and boys.

What can you say? Politics wasn't topmost on the minds of anyone I worked with.

Toward summer's end, we'd be sent on day trips to pick blueberries or potatoes in one of Cook's farms in the Jersey Pine Barrens. It was hotter and dustier down there. That said, we had it pretty easy, compared to some. On the way, you'd see legions of black and brown migrant families, including children, toiling in the fields of privately owned farms. We'd knock off early for the long ride back to Adelphia, in time to return to our homes for dinner. The migrants would still be in the fields. It would be dark by the time they returned to their company bunkhouses to prepare their suppers over cookfires, and then turn in for the night. Soon after sunrise, they'd relive what was mostly the same day all over again.

Back at Adelphia, when we broke for lunch, we'd sit on the shady side of the main field house. I'd listen to the college boys talk about school, girls, and sometimes, what they planned to do after they graduated. Conversations often gravitated to sex. The college boys cracked jokes about getting sumpin'. The high school boys, including me, would laugh knowingly, as if we weren't virgins. I, however, had legit knowledge about sexuality from *credible sources*, not just locker-room blather. I had scoured the school library and researched the female anatomy. I'd be prepared when it happened. It would be beautiful. I was an optimist.

One day we were sitting by a cornfield waiting for Chuck to drive us to the field house for lunch break. Having apparently eavesdropped on our conversation, he foisted unsolicited observations on us about *intercourse*. Patiently, we listened. He had credentials. He was older, bald, a married man, and supposedly familiar with that kind of activity. He *had* to know something. Still, it was hard to take him seriously. Pensively, Chuck leaned against the pickup door and cleared his throat, his prominent Adam's apple bobbing like an elbow joint that might bust out of his neck. "The most sensitive area of a lady is…is the cl…the cl…is the clavicle, which, is like…" Nervously, he gestured with fluttering hands. "It's positioned like ten o'clock to the…the placenta. Touch it right, they lose their minds. I mean… whew."

There was some snickering. Chuck was in way over his head. The business about the clock just confused matters. Although I hadn't even seriously kissed a girl, I knew Chuck had no business directing traffic vis-a-vis the female anatomy. He might as well have been driving aimlessly on the New Jersey Turnpike in search of the Grand Canyon. I felt sorry for his wife, and for her collarbone.

I knew about sex the way one might study a map of France, yet never had the experience of being inside France. Still, I knew that the clavicle was nowhere near the erogenous zones I hoped one day to explore.

I took a step forward and was about to offer our supervisor some unsolicited course correction when Roy nudged me aside, turned to Chuck, and said, "Thanks, Boss. That's good to know," and then turned back to us and winked.

There are worse things than being mistaken about the facts, like making yourself look smart by making somebody else look dumb, especially when he's your boss. It was a merciful way to end a weird conversation.

Working in The World of Men wasn't so great after all. It felt better to go home and see my former boss, cooking up something magical in the kitchen. When Grandma asked me how the day went, I told her that Mr. Kaminski commended me for a job well done. That news made Grandma's eyes sparkle. Other than that, there wasn't much more to tell.

Chapter 33
A MANASQUAN KIND OF DAY

Sammy, my mentor and tormentor since the fifth grade, was still my off-and-on-again friend and bad influence. He had called me on a sunny Saturday morning in August and said, "Fells, it looks like a Manasquan kind of day. You in or not?"

Of course, I was in. Sammy already had his driver's license and drove a candy-apple-red Chevy Chevelle SS, which stood for Super Sport. It was magnificent. The Chevelle's throaty V-8 growled at red lights and stop signs. A grin widened across Sammy's face when he revved up the 325 horses under the hood, slammed the Hurst shifter into gear, and peeled out, leaving a trail of burnt rubber in our wake. I had no wheels—just my feet and, for long hauls, a bicycle—both embarrassing modes of transportation that branded me as a kid, even though I was poised to begin my sophomore year. Regardless, it was exhilarating being a passenger in a cool car without adult supervision. We cruised eastward to the ocean. Sammy frequently checked himself out in the rearview mirror, combing his pompadour and smiling brightly, quite pleased.

We preferred Manasquan over the more glamorous Asbury Park, which was farther away and charged more for a daily beach badge. Besides, there were too many old farts in Asbury, lolling on the sand like beached whales, their hideous white bellies and thunder thighs destroying the view. Manasquan offered better views of half-naked girls. We played pinball and skeet ball in the arcade, smoked cigarettes and crushed them under our sandals on the gritty wood floor. We jumped into the surf for an occasional dip, but most of the time we sat on our beach towels and leered discreetly at girls in bikinis.

Sammy tutored me in honing my skills as a voyeur. Our blackout sunglasses hid our intentions. Sammy told me, "Keep your face pointed straight ahead as if you're looking at the waves, the ocean, the sky, *et cetera, et cetera, et cetera,*" affecting Yul Brynner's accent from *The King and I*, just to annoy me.

"Watch and learn, Fells," he said, continuing my training session. "Because of the shades you can eye-ball chicks sideways. Let your eyeballs do their thing." We gazed at a girl in a fake leopard two-piece. We watched her spreading suntan lotion on her arms, belly, and thighs. Abruptly, Sammy rolled over on his stomach.

"I got to stop looking before something pops out of my trunks like a Jack-in-the-Box. And listen, Fells, while I'm resting, don't give us away. Keep your head straight like you're watching the waves, *et cetera, et cetera, et cetera*."

I kept my head posted discreetly on the Atlantic horizon, but my eyeballs began to ache from shifting them side to side, one extreme to the other. I accepted discomfort as an occupational hazard of the beach peeper. I didn't care that I was a *reprobate*. The word even sounded like what it was.

As the afternoon leaned toward supper time, we left Manasquan. Neither one of us had the nerve to try to engage in conversation with girls. It was safer to be an ogler. Still, it had been a productive day. I had harvested a fresh cornucopia of fantasies for future reference. I expected to have a hot date with one that very night. Who could ask for more?

Returning home, we drove through Farmingdale past the Food Town, Gibson's hardware store, Sherman's Sweet Shop, and Rexall Drugs. WABC blared on the radio. Bob Dayton, the DJ, cheerfully dedicated the next song, "Sixteen Candles" by the Crests, to the anniversary of Hiroshima. The song's lyrics opened with, "*Happy birthday, happy birthday, baby.*" It was August 6, 1965—the twentieth anniversary of the first atomic bomb. Dayton acted like it was all a big joke.

"What an asshole!" I yelled, slapping the face of the radio grill.

"Hey, easy on the merchandise!" said Sammy. "What's the big deal?"

"It burns me up, that's all. Even if dropping the bomb had to be done, the douche bag shouldn't be making fun of it," I said. "I wish he'd drop dead."

"Well, remember, you be half-Yankee boy, too. So solly, you too sensitive! *Et cetera, et cetera, et cetera*," he said.

"Screw you!" I said.

"Come on, Fells, don't have an orgasm!" He still liked saying it.

We cackled as we headed west out of town, which took you around Farmingdale's sharpest curve. Sammy downshifted into second gear, took his hands off the wheel, then stomped on the accelerator with his right foot, and steered with his left. He was a contortionist with a talented big toe, dexterous enough to stay on the road as we careened around the turn.

"Thank God for power steering," hooted Sammy. As he flashed his gone-crazy smile. I wondered if the stakes were getting too high to hang out with him. "I can't wait to get home and jerk off. Just remember Fells," he said, as if pondering a mystery, "if somebody tells you they've never done it, that's somebody you *can never, ever trust!*"

"You've told me that before. Why's that so important to you?"

"It tells you something about them …about what makes them tick. What's the word?"

"Character?"

"That's it! Yeah, it's something we're born to do, so why lie about it? If you lie about that, you'd lie about anything." Sammy paused then asked me, "So, do you beat your meat every day?"

"Of course not," I said. "Everybody should take Sundays off, *et cetera, et cetera, et cetera*."

After we finished snickering, I told him that seriously, I was trying to reduce my self-abuse time. I said that there was more to what I wanted than sex. Like finding the right girl who I would treat like gold. There would be sex, but it would be of an elevated sort, entwined with love. While I had hopes, they were dimmed because I lacked confidence in finding the right girl who would have me because of the *race thing*, the complications of being neither fish nor fowl. This was among the deepest conversations Sammy and I ever had.

Apropos of girls in general, I asked Sammy, "Do you think they do it?"

"Do what?"

"You know, um, pleasure themselves."

"Really, Fells?" Sammy seemed genuinely disappointed in me. "Don't be disgusting! Of course not!"

◈ ◆ ◈

Bob Dayton, the DJ who had wished Hiroshima a happy birthday, caused a minor scandal. Ironically, the wife of the network's chief executive had honored the "Hiroshima Maidens" at a reception that same day. They were a cohort of Japanese women who had been horribly burned in the bombing. Dayton was fired on the spot. I guess he got what he deserved. But I didn't celebrate his downfall. My grandmother said the troublemakers usually got their comeuppance. I had to wonder, when would I face my comeuppance?

Chapter 34
LEGION OF THE LONELY AND THE BITTER

Before the new school opened, I'd bike to the construction site of Southern Freehold Regional High to check it out. Temporary fencing still circled the main building, outbuildings, and athletic fields. The sun had baked everything dry and choky. It was August and just a few plugs of grass survived a month of drought. Mounds of dirt and gravel squatted next to the athletic field. Hot gusts blew dust devils across the grounds. The design aesthetic of the new school, like other public buildings of the day, was inspired by the mind of the lowest bidder. The school could have been mistaken for an upscale detention center. Regardless of the facility's lack of architectural character, I was excited about starting my sophomore year at the new school.

When school started, Jimmy Oats and I were still friends, but our friendship had changed. He was going with a snobby girl from Farmingdale, and played varsity baseball and basketball and enjoyed the perks shared by desirable jocks; invitations to parties and all that. Most of my evenings were spent with the Ancient Ones. After I said goodnight to Grandma and Grandpa I'd go to bed, turn on my transistor radio, a birthday gift from Dad, and listen to Jean Shepherd tell brilliant stories about himself and his childhood friends.

I did well in most of my subjects; surprised myself *and* Mrs. Monahan, I think, with an A in geometry. I had kind of a crush on her too, though she wasn't my type. But the way she explained things had an effect on me. She made Euclid's plane universe seem elegant, explaining his hypotheses and proofs in a way that made precise sense to me. Her smarts seemed to translate into a different kind of sexiness I couldn't quite figure out. Biology with Mr. Edmonds was interesting, too. For example, watching cells splitting and duplicating, amoeba and paramecia gyrating under the microscope. One day, he stopped in the middle of a lesson to share, apropos of nothing, an anecdote about him and his wife driving in the vast desert of the

Southwest. He had this far-away look in his eye as he recounted the scene: from out of nowhere, a flying saucer hovered over their car, then, in a split second, blipped beyond the vanishing point. "You don't have to believe me," he said, "But that's what happened."

I trudged through second-year German and achieved consistency, with D's most semesters, and occasionally a generous C from Mr. Antione lifting me into mediocrity. Although I received A's and B's on my assignments and tests in English, I couldn't break into Miss Santos's favored circle of high achievers who dwelt around her desk, apparently chatting it up about cool stuff. I made a couple of clumsy attempts to sidle into the repartee, but the blank looks and silence from the inner sanctum made it clear I wasn't welcome to join the ranks of those bound for the Honor Society. Fuck them.

I began reading serious books for pleasure, and eagerly accompanied my grandfather on his biweekly trips to the Freehold Public Library. Founded by a Carnegie grant in 1904 and housed in a robust, brick neoclassical-style building, the library and its collection dwarfed that of my high school. The place had a sobering effect on me. I wouldn't need to be hushed. It would have insulted the thousands of books and their authors that resided in the stacks. The hour or two I'd spend there quieted my mind. It distracted me from sulking about my otherwise impoverished life.

Except for my grandparents, I kept my new habit a secret pleasure. I mean, what kind of 15-year-old looks forward to spending an afternoon in a library with his ancient grandfather? A popular version of myself would have spent afternoons after school hanging out with friends at Connie's (also known as Sherman's) sweet shop, yakking it up over cheeseburgers and cherry vanilla Cokes. Instead, on my first library visit, I gorged myself on the short stories in Hemingway's *In Our Time* and Steinbeck's *The Red Pony*.

About this time, Grandma bought me my first typewriter, a vintage black Corona. I hunted-and-pecked the rest of my high school papers on that small keyboard, as well as the assignments in my junior and senior years as a reporter for the local weekly, *The Howell Booster*. Such were the circumstances of my moments of meager happiness.

Occasionally, there were still assholes who might blurt *chink*, or an equivalent insult at me in the hall or cafeteria. But now, new smears from Vietnam were importing their way into the racist lexicon. There was an asshole who harassed me for no reason I could discern. He camouflaged his bile, insulting me quietly as if he was telling me something in confidence, whispering "What's up, you stupid *slope*," and "You make me sick, *gook*." Although part of me wanted to belt him, I did not. I had practical experience that there was better than a fifty-fifty chance I'd get my face punched. Fuck him.

But racial insults were rare compared to your standard inventory of equal-opportunity taunts. More common than insults based on race and ethnicity were disparaging references to your intelligence and physical attributes—or your sexuality. In regard to the latter, insults like homo and queer were hurled compulsively in the boys' locker rooms, along with commands like blow me and kiss my ass. The insults were tedious and made no sense. Barking at your male classmates to perform these acts was a strange way of reinforcing your position as a regular heterosexual guy, but there it was. I don't remember any kid coming out of the closet, since it was still a place for brooms and coats. But looking back, I believe there were many classmates whose experiences of adolescence and coming of age were buried alive in those closets that didn't exist. Although Stonewall was just five years in the future and just 60 miles north in New York City; it was an eternity and light years out of reach.

Whether you were the object or purveyor of insults, most of the hostile dynamic was embedded in the male socialization process that featured monotonous name-calling that was indifferent to race or sexual orientation. You simply applied time-honored formulas to express disdain for the target of your scorn by compounding a foul word with an anatomical feature, producing monikers like *fucknuts*, or *shitforbrains*. The timeless and classic anatomical insult was then, and probably remains to this day, *asshole*, since all of us have one, and if we are honest, have been one.

In the spring, I played junior varsity baseball with would-be jocks like me, inferior versions of the athletic prototype due to flaws regarding anatomy, coordination, or psychology. Regardless, I was proud to have made the final cut to stay on the JV squad and even astonished, when Coach picked me to pitch on opening day. I was the losing pitcher that day and for the next seven games I pitched that season. I had a lively fast ball, but my control was erratic. For some reason I still can't figure, the local paper ran a photo of me in a sidebar of the sports page. You couldn't recognize me, because my face was in the shadows, but there I was on the mound, immortalized in post-delivery. The caption said, "Billy Fellenberg, a sophomore, shows winning form for Rebels' JV Nine." One might wonder how I showed winning form and yet lost all my games. Obviously, it was possible. I carried that news clip in my wallet until it eventually disintegrated.

By the season's end, my right arm felt like it was hanging by a thread. Coach had over-used me. I could barely grasp a No. 2 pencil. I had to ask my lab partner in biology, Laverne, for help in dissecting an earthworm. Incidentally, until then, I wasn't aware that the band around the worm was called the clitoris. I would have preferred never to know that. I felt at once nauseous and resentful, like when a colossal, iridescent fly lands on your cheeseburger, rubbing its bristly forelegs where you just took your delicious first bite.

Beyond insults, boys settled disputes on a spectrum that began with ambiguous slights, then escalated to sneers, feints of physical assault, shoves, or occasional elbow jabs to the ribs. If you wanted to take a gripe to an existential level, you got serious by scheduling your beef outside, in the parking lot. The build-up was usually lengthy and gossipy, but the actual fight was usually over in a blink, someone overmatched by a lot.

About girl fights—again, the expectation didn't reflect reality. It was rumored to be sexy, a torn blouse or disheveled skirt allowing a guilt-free peek at the contour of an ass cheek or brief flash of side boob. I heard about girl fights, but only witnessed one. Two girls stepped off our bus, screaming. As the bus sputtered away, we scrambled to the rear window to watch. They were still pulling hair, punching, slapping, and kicking as we passed the vanishing point. It was enough girl fight for a lifetime.

> *Did the cold-war paranoia compromise baby boomers' self-control? Did the "drop and cover" protocols of air-raid drills during our childhood stunt our judgment, make us paranoid? Or was it just me? Who really believed that high school was a crucible for intellectual, social, and moral development? Look past the drama club, the honor society, the big-game pep rallies, the yearbook, the seedy senior-class trip to the Poconos, the prescribed commencement homilies. This was a cauldron of humanoid trainees with half-formed brains and Zeppelin-size libidos. Baby boomers would be among tomorrow's psychos, agoraphobics, and depressives. Seventy-six million strong, we were queued up to lead America boldly into the future.*

As for me, I could've been a poster child for the Legion of the Lonely and the Bitter. Fuck me.

Chapter 35
DRIVING AMBITIONS

Out in the country without a car, you were as hopeless as a bird without wings. You were condemned to isolation. You were sentenced to be a virgin until you had wheels. In other words, you were nothing. I looked out the bus window into the parking lot and saw juniors and seniors getting into their cars to leave school. Some had hot cars, GTOs and the like. If you saw a souped-up classic like a '49 Ford, it was probably restored by one of the quietly brilliant guys who majored in shop. Others had dowdy hand-me-down sedans from their parents. One cool guy had a Citroen, an eccentric French automobile equipped with a chassis that could change elevation. I saw Joanne Zuzzio tucking herself into a snazzy green '53 MG TD. What a beauty! I mean, both the girl and the car. I heard that the driver was a college guy. I bet she never slapped him. The best part of the day was still ahead, at least for the *Ubermenschen* who mattered. They might head to Sherman's (also called Connie's) in Farmingdale for grilled cheese sandwiches and chocolate milkshakes after school. Hell, they might go to Federici's in Freehold or Longo's in Red Bank. My excitement at home was eating dinner, doing homework, and afterward, watching *Gunsmoke* or *Wagon Train* with Grandma and Grandpa. I ruminated about my lot in life. If I had a car, I'd escape the old folk's home, and everything else would fall into place.

Grandpa gave me driving lessons in our 1960 Nash Rambler American station wagon. It was a manual transmission, stick shift on the column. Mastering the clutch was tricky. Grandpa would sit stone-faced in the passenger seat, smoking an Old Gold. He taught me how to drive in the Ardena courthouse parking lot, which was adjacent to our house. It was the only government structure between Freehold and Farmingdale, other than Adelphia's post office. The building was small, but the lot was large and usually empty after hours. I alternately jerked to a start, jerked to a stop, stalled, and repeated the process.

I had my first opportunity to drive on the open road the day I passed the written test for my learner's permit at the nearest state licensing office. Because it was 15 miles away in Eatontown, Grandpa didn't let me get behind the wheel until we reached Farmingdale. The remainder of the ride was tense. I drove slowly and tentatively, just like an old man, for the last three miles of the trip. A line of cars formed behind us. Then the honking commenced. Approaching our house, I misjudged the sharp turn into our driveway, accidentally popped the clutch, and hit the massive oak that presided over our front yard. The Rambler ricocheted off the tree and sputtered to a stop in our neighbor's alfalfa field.

"What the deuce did you do that for?" Grandpa said, gripping the sides of his seat, an Old Gold dangling from his mouth. The driver-side front fender was dented, a headlight dangling out of its socket like a loose eyeball. Rather than be grateful that neither of my grandparents gave me grief for my bad driving, I saw the mishap as an opportunity to argue for a car of my own. I had saved what I considered a small fortune over the two summers working at Rutgers' farm. Grandma refused to let me withdraw some of my savings to buy a car.

"No way." she said, "That money is for college. You know that." she said.

"But it's money *I earned*! It's important for me to have a car!"

"Tell me why it's so important."

What was I supposed to say? *Well, Grandma, to be honest, I want a car because, ultimately, it may improve my chances of getting laid.* Instead, I said nothing. In fact, I said virtually nothing to her for more than a week. One night after dinner, she said:

"I don't understand you, Billy. You're just so different from my other boys." After she left the kitchen, she went outside to sweep the front porch. I heard her sniffling back tears. I should have felt bad. Instead, I felt the silent treatment was doing its job.

Scowling, Grandpa took me aside. "You've got Grandma worked

up in a tizzy," he said. "For the Christ's sake, stop whatever you're doing."

Regardless, I stuck to my guns. I mean, my future as a complete male was threatened. In the end, I got my way and Grandma relented. She'd let me withdraw up to $200 of my savings on a car. What caught my eye at the used car lot was a powder-blue Fiat Bianchina, a two-seater with a canvas sunroof and a 500-cc engine, more suited for a motorcycle than an automobile. Maybe I was bedazzled by the stick shift with a handle that looked like the silver hilt of a sword plunged into the floor. I had a discerning eye for shiny things.

"This isn't a real car, it's a clown car," said Grandpa. "You should keep looking." Driving up a hill or into a headwind, the Fiat's two cylinders were wheezing at 35 mph, exhaust seeping in through the floorboard. My car and my social life were in sync, both going nowhere. I kept it for a couple of months, then bought a 1954 Chevy Bel Air, a two-tone blue-and-white sedan, rust spots here and there, a lumbering automatic, a gas guzzler, homely, but generally reliable.

On the other side of the car planet, Jimmy was driving a 1960 Austin Healey 3000, a black convertible with red leather bucket seats. More good fortune for Jimmy that I coveted. Our friendship had been resurrected when his girlfriend's family moved to Rumson. Jimmy thought her parents had moved for two reasons: first, because they considered themselves better than those in humble Farmingdale; and second, increasing the distance between Jimmy and their daughter. The Austin Healey was beautiful, but was temperamental, afflicted by gas pump failures, electrical short-circuits, and other problems. But during the car's good spells, riding in it felt like a million dollars. One afternoon in Asbury Park, we drove past Steinbach's department store and Jimmy slowed the purring automobile to a crawl, pointing to a long row of display windows. He wasn't looking at the merchandise, but rather the reflection of himself ensconced in the magnificent sports car, a picture to behold.

When April arrived in my junior year, I was on the mound again for the JV baseball team. I pitched in our season opener, which was away at Shore Regional, which we won. Victory, unknown to me the previous year, was sweet. I responded to my first success with unwholesome vanity. I considered myself worthy of a nickname and suggested to my teammates that they might call me Billy the Kid or Fireball Fellenberg. I was open to suggestions. My catcher, Chuck, said, "How about Fuckhead Fellenberg?" His rudeness aside, the question of heroic nicknames I considered was moot because my pitching career would soon end on a perfect May afternoon.

Although I couldn't see it, I could *feel* it was a perfect day outside. I was locked up and resented that such perfection was going to waste. I sat at a table doodling in my notebook during the travesty called study hall. These were periods held in the cafeteria during non-service hours when it was used as a holding pen, a mass detention for students who had a void in their class schedules. Two teachers alternately kibbitzed with each other, separated, and independently scowled their way under the fluorescent lights in a room that throbbed with the repressed energy of teenagers compelled to sit still and shut up. I connived to slip out of study hall with another fugitive to enjoy the rest of the day and comb the beach in Point Pleasant. A few steps outside the cafeteria door, I was nailed by the girls' gym teacher, Mrs. Holmes, a she-bear in gray sweats. "You!" she yelped, giddy with glee, as happy as a prison matron who snared a would-be escapee. The principal suspended me for two days and barred me from extracurricular activities for the rest of the year. My undistinguished pitching career on a second-rate J.V. team at a high school in the boondocks of New Jersey was finished, and it hurt.

I expected Grandma to insist I stay home during my short suspension— do extra chores and consider the consequences of my foolishness for getting suspended. Instead, she was exasperated with the school's policy. "So preposterous to punish you for cutting classes by giving you more time off!" she scoffed. In some ways, Grandma was ahead of her time.

Chapter 36
WORK ETHIC

I was off to a job interview. Wes, a senior, told me that he had gotten a full-time spot at the Nescafe plant in Freehold. He gave me a heads-up about the job he was leaving, which would be up for grabs. He had put in a good word for me with Herb Z, the owner, so my chances were pretty good. I drove past woods, bogs, and a couple of abandoned farms and houses that were still occupied, despite their saggy roofs and cracked windows.

Mr. Z's plant, architecturally speaking, was a Quonset-like structure made of sheet metal that was weirdly grafted on to what looked to be converted chicken coops. I parked next to an old chevy flat-bed truck by the loading platform. Thick gray smoke churned out of a chimney into the blue June sky. A brisk breeze blew the smoke away and into the woods. Mr. Z stood by the main door and beckoned me. He was thin, tall, and had red hair and pale eyebrows that were barely visible. He wore a cardigan sweater and chino pants pocked with holes that were cleanly burned through, without any charred edges.

We talked about the job and the pay and after Mr. Z offered me the job and I accepted, I asked about the wooden plaque on the wall behind his desk that had lizards or dragons draped around a shield inscribed with Gothic-looking letters. It was his family crest. Asking Mr. Z about it animated him.

"Well, I come from Bavarian stock."

"Bavarian's the same as German, right?"

"Some similarities, but the same? A definite no," he began to say, then looked at his watch, excused himself and scampered out of the office. I sat in a chair in front of his messy desk. I looked up at his hoity-toity family crest, thinking it seemed out of place in such a dump. Papers and folders were scattered around a typewriter. Several file cabinets and a dozen or so carboys, 20-gallon containers of sulfuric acid and nitric acid, were pushed against a wall. Mr. Z came back, huffing and smelling of oily smoke. He told me he had to remove metal coils from an oven where grease on the materials was being burnt off. I asked him if you had to wear a gas mask for that, and he said it wasn't necessary, but you needed to hold your breath for two or three minutes while you were in the smoke room.

"Problem?" he asked.

"No problem." A buck seventy-five an hour was real money.

"And you can call me Herb."

In the meantime, I landed another interesting assignment. I got a job as a reporter for the Howell Township *Booster*, the local weekly. Even though its circulation was small, it was a real paper. The publisher, Mrs. Seligman, took a liking to me and hired me on a trial basis when I came poking around the office for a job and showed her samples from my journalism class and a recommendation from my teacher. Mrs. Seligman was also the *Booster's* editor, typesetter, printer, ad exec, and circulation GM. Her hair was graying, but she moved like a young woman, lifting several heavy trays of lead type off her desk as if they were nothing. She hired me to cover local sports, weekly proceedings of Ardena municipal court, and the monthly meetings of the board of education. Imagine, I just walked in and got the nod to cover *three different beats*. Mrs. Seligman also talked me into selling ad space on a commission basis and gave me a portfolio of ad cuts to present to local businesses. I said I'd do it, but my heart wasn't in it. In my lofty imaginings, I was starting a career in journalism, *à la* Hemingway. No, I wasn't covering the bloody Spanish Civil War for the *Toronto Star* as a foreign correspondent. But writing crisp declarative sentences for the *Booster* had its satisfactions, too. I got paid five bucks an article. My weekly reports covering municipal court and Howell High School sports, plus the monthly board meetings meant I'd be making $45 a month as a writer. Combined with my pay from Herb Z, I'd be grossing nearly $150 month. But the reporting was more than the money. I had my own byline.

I stood behind Mrs. Seligman in her office as she made final edits on my weekly submissions.

> Look at the two of us hovering over my copy, both of us chain-smoking, fluorescent lights buzzing overhead. Watch Mrs. Seligman quickly blue-pencil my story about a shoplifting incident at the Route 9 Seven-Eleven in Freewood Acres. On its face, it was a petty crime, but it involved a 16-year-old girl with the theft of several packs of cigarettes, cigars, and gum. I recognized her as one of kids in the special-ed class at school. The real crime was that two assholes, dropouts from Lakewood, had coerced her to stash the goods in her backpack. Judge Cavanaugh, Howell's sole municipal judge, ripped the boys a new one, but released them in their aunt's custody. Look at my face drop when Mrs. Seligman sighs and tells me we won't run the story. "It's Booster policy not to run stories about crimes by minors."

I considered myself a consummate professional and didn't make a stink. I put my angry energy into trying to massage a report on the latest Board of Ed meeting to make it interesting. What usually dominated the agenda were mundane items, like new office equipment, bus routes reconsidered, and so forth. Most controversial issues were discussed *in camera*. The press (meaning me) was excluded from those sessions, but I'd get wind of an occasional scandal. For example, the case of two teachers at Ardena Elementary who called in sick but were in fact, soaking in the Florida sun and consequently fired. I wanted to write that story, but Mrs. Seligman said it wouldn't be in the *Booster's* "spirit."

Once in a while, pissed-off taxpayers might show up at a board meeting to complain about the school budget, and demand more *accountability*. There'd be much hemming and hawing—irked residents on one side, and the defensive school superintendent and board members on the other. It rarely amounted to much. I'd cherry-pick verbatims from the opposing sides that each would consider inflammatory. I mean, what's wrong with some drama and conflict in a story? Mrs. Seligman would chasten me and remind me that we weren't a cheesy tabloid like the *National Enquirer,* and then delete my copy of unnecessary flame-throwing. Otherwise, there was rarely a pulse at those deadly meetings.

My wheel of fortune was spinning in a good direction. At the start of senior year, I was appointed sports editor of the *Accent,* my high school newspaper. How could the position not be conferred on me? After all, I was already a working journalist. Whenever an article appeared in the *Booster,* I'd run my fingertips across my byline. My soaring career was responsible for my growing confidence and optimism. I fancied myself an occasionally hard-drinking and chain-smoking journalist, although the kind who was not allowed to smoke in front of his grandmother, especially in the house.

"I can't force you to stop smoking, but I don't have to see it," she said.

I could live with that. I was discreet about two other habits she wouldn't approve of, involving alcohol and gambling, which I indulged in, usually independent of the other. I got the gambling bug at Freehold Raceway, betting on the trotters and pacers. I applied systems that involved math, prayer, omens, and mostly, the kind of desperate calculations that made me forget whatever else might be bugging me.

Generally speaking, my life was progressing, except I was still a virgin with no prospects. I still hadn't even kissed a girl, not in a meaningful way. I considered the ironies of my success. I had a car. I could go anyplace I wanted. My road trip adventures extended as far as Staten Island, 35 miles north, where the drinking age was 18 and I could buy Old Bohemian beer for $1.85 a six-pack. The irony was that I had the means to go to better places and do better things but couldn't identify what they were.

Tired of those trips to Staten Island, I forged my license and draft card to give myself a new birthdate that identified me as the 21-year-old Yuki Toyota. Although my sloppily doctored and laminated documents were not widely accepted, I canvassed liquor stores beyond our stomping grounds and eventually found one liquor store in Freewood Acres that served me. Initially the clerk challenged the veracity of my I.D. but came around when I expressed my outrage in a language of broken English you'd expect from a young immigrant fresh off the boat from the far, Far East.

Chapter 37
WHEN YOU HAVE IT MADE

I continued to work that summer at Z Refining. It was an unusual business, recovering the precious metals from gold- and silver-plated nickel coils that were valuable leftovers from the manufacture of watches, bracelets, necklaces, and other jewelry, as well as electronic components. I worked part-time with boys from school: Mark, John, and later on, Jimmy. The work exposed us to toxic fumes from smoke and corrosive acids and a workplace environment rife with physical hazards. Herb was too cheap to give us protective goggles and was reluctant to replace worn-out rubber gloves. I'd change from my school clothes into ratty jeans, sweatshirt, and sneakers that I kept there and then comb through a pile of rubber gloves searching for ones with the fewest holes. Whenever I told Herb we were running low and needed new ones, he'd get tense. He'd pinch the bridge of his nose between his eyebrows and bend his head down as if he had just gotten a telegram saying that his best friend was hit by a train.

Sometimes, we'd get a shipment of silver-plated nickel. The process to separate silver from nickel created silver nitrate, a by-product that caused our hands to turn blue. "Don't worry about the blue on your hands. It won't hurt you," he told me. "They use silver nitrate to swab the eyes of newborn babies, so it's basically harmless."

When I complained about my blue hands, he suggested I scrub them with a soap-bar size portion of cyanide to remove the stain.

"But scrub lightly and quickly. Otherwise, it'll get absorbed through your skin and compromise your lungs. One soap-bar size of cyanide dropped into a reservoir could kill a whole town."

He was thoughtful like that.

Herb's lack of regard for safety was consistent with his concern for disposing of waste. He hooked rubber hoses together and siphoned effluent from the tanks into the woods behind the plant. When I asked him about the waste leaching into the ground out back, he scoffed. "First of all, the solution is mostly water. There's nothing to worry about. No one lives close by, and there's not enough of it to do any damage."

Some weekends I'd work at Herb's house in Interlaken, a wealthy enclave north of Asbury Park. I felt good working outside, breathing fresh air and smelling the scent of ocean spray. It was a refreshing change from the witchy odors that wafted from the smoke room and from tubs of toxic broth at the plant that separated gold from the nickel it was plated on.

Mrs. Z was chubby and cheerful, the mother of two little girls. As I raked and groomed the spacious grounds, the girls followed me, scampering and dancing in the leaves. Mrs. Z walked out to the bluestone patio and brought me a glass of lemonade and a plate of cookies.

"I thought you'd enjoy some refreshments," she said. "I hope the girls aren't bothering you, scattering the leaves and all."

"If there's kids around, it's game on for every pile of leaves."

She smiled, and said it was bath time for the girls, and led them into the house.

I stretched out on a chaise lounge for a few minutes and considered the upper-crusty life that Herb enjoyed in Interlaken. The squalor of the gold refinery in the woods seemed a world away. From my perspective, Herb was living the American dream.

Several decades after that autumn day when Mrs. Z served me lemonade and cookies on the patio, her husband would be arrested for running a methamphetamine factory at that dilapidated plant in Howell. When Herb Z got busted, it made the front page of the Asbury Park Press. It wasn't just a side hustle for him. The enterprise was huge, supplying a network that stretched outward from Howell Township to Georgia and Kansas City. Instead of indicting him on narcotics charges, the Feds prosecuted him for multiple civil and criminal EPA violations—apparently, an effective strategy in prosecuting drug peddlers. Herb was put away for a long time.

Talk about art imitating life. His meth enterprise blossomed and blew up decades before *Breaking Bad*, the fine series about a chemistry teacher, Walter White, who pursues a second career manufacturing and dealing methamphetamines and accumulates a mountain of money. Herb, like Walter, probably yearned for one thing—More. Something you achieve, as William Blake wrote, only after you've had more than enough.

Chapter 38
HEART ON FIRE

The first day of senior year in the hubbub of homeroom, she walked in and dropped her books on the desk just two aisles away, the girl I had longed for from afar. Since I first saw her in the school library, I had discreetly inquired about her, even stalked her a little bit. Over the past three years I had eyed her in the halls during class changes, watched her laugh in the cafeteria, and seen her puzzle over and cheat on an English exam. I wouldn't classify it as stalking. I was no Boston Strangler, just a lonely dork entertaining fantasies about a high school girl, which sounds like how a weirdo starts out. It sounds worse than what it was. Whether it was fate, kismet, or the butterfly effect, some mystical clockwork brought her orbit into mine, this girl named Roxanne born to a Japanese mother and an American GI father of German descent. Just like me! You could say it was *providential*. While our racial recipe had ingredients in common, the outcomes differed in the baking. She was the perfect cake. In my movie, I saw her as the Eurasian beauty who would slide down the trunk of a coconut tree into my arms just as the closing credits rolled. On the other hand, I was the lopsided cake. The clumsy fellow with a Japanese face, a German body, and bad posture. But the girls typically were drawn to the *studly Nordic types*, as Jimmy Oats liked to describe himself.

I slogged my way through chemistry (which I was repeating because I failed it my junior year), English, German, journalism, phys. ed., and sociology. I daydreamed about Roxanne until I saw her in homeroom. I kept an eye on her without her knowing it. I was trained by Sammy, the best in the business for techniques in looking sideways at girls and sizing them up from top to bottom. This is not to say my intentions were anything less than honorable. Her every gesture was perfect. The way she exhaled between those full lips I'd die for. I felt her breath passing faintly by my face as she gossiped to the girl next to her. They were chatting about shopping. I joined in. In a fog, I began to have an actual conversation with her. I was intoxicated and I told my first lie to her. I said: "I like to shop, too."

"You do?"

"In fact, I *love* to shop!"

"You're a kind of odd, then."

"Very odd."

"In a kind of a peculiar way."

"Very peculiar."

"Really?" She cocked her head as if I might be a mistake.

"I think I meant particular." As in *discerning*.

Things happened so fast I couldn't keep track of the details of what we talked about. All I know is that the next day after school, I drove her to Monmouth Mall, where we shopped at Bamberger's. Although I was as excited as one of those over-amped crazy dogs that runs around in circles, yapping and slobbering, I kept myself under control. We stopped in Farmingdale to have a late lunch at Sherman's (also known as Connie's) Sweet Shop on the way home, Roxanne chattering away.

When I drove her home, she told me to park farther up the street. "That's my father's semi-truck in front of that green house," said Roxanne, ducking down into my shoulder. "He doesn't like me going out. If he knew I was with a boy, I'd be in trouble."

"But all we did was go shopping, right?"

"Still, he'd freak out."

"For real? Why?"

"You'll find out soon enough. It can wait."

Our shopping trip was an icebreaker and made it easier for me to ask Roxanne out for our first real date. I pulled out the stops, spending six bucks a ticket for a Four Seasons concert at Monmouth College. Why not? I was rolling in dough.

"The Four Seasons!" she shrieked. "I love them!"

My life became a dream. On a clear and starlit Saturday night in October, I picked up Roxanne in front of her house. She had a white uniform draped over her arm because she was working the midnight to 9 a.m. shift at Lakewood Hospital after the concert. She worked as a nurse's aide on alternating Friday and Saturday nights. Roxanne chattered on the drive to Long Branch, which made it easy for me not to have to make up things to say. There, in the college gym, Frankie Valli's falsetto transported us, exhorted me to *Walk Like a Man* and cautioned my date that *Big Girls Don't Cry*. And there we were, squished together in the bleachers with a thousand college *men and women*. Could it have been any cooler? In the back of my mind in all this bliss, I warned myself not to screw it up.

After the concert, Roxanne climbed into the back seat and took off her blouse and skirt.

"Now, you promised, no peeking!" she mock-scolded me.

"Of course not! I'm not that kind of guy," I said. But I was.

I watched her in my rearview mirror as she dropped her nurse's aide uniform over her head and squiggled into it. Roxanne seemed unaware as I watched her adjust her uniform and smile to herself. So, God had delivered on my prayers. Roxanne, the most beautiful girl in our senior class, became my girlfriend. I brought her home to meet my grandparents and Dad on one of the weekends he came home. They were all delighted with her, as I expected.

Roxanne introduced me to her mother soon after our first date but deferred telling her father about me.

"Why?" I asked.

"Lots of rules," said Roxanne. "No swearing, no taking the Lord's name in vain, no short skirts, no rock and roll, no coffee or tea. No cigarettes, liquor, or working on Saturdays."

"Why Saturdays?"

"He's a Seventh Day Adventist. They observe the Sabbath on Saturday, not Sunday. He's got problems with just about everybody."

"What about your Saturday-night job?"

"The job on Saturdays has Daddy's OK because it's in the worthy service of others."

"So, he's not a religious fanatic."

"He doesn't go to services or belong to the church. He had a falling-out with them, like he does with everybody else. Anyway, he's very strict. Keeps tabs on us, all the time."

"So, he has you, your mother, your three sisters and baby brother under his thumb. He sounds like *der Führer*."

"Who?"

"*Der Führer*. You know, Hitler."

"Well, that's a whole other story. If he knew about me having a boyfriend, he'd go ballistic. But enough about him."

Well, my heart almost exploded, being referred to as her boyfriend. *Der Führer* sounded like a prick to me, and I could wait until the Second Coming to meet him if need be. But I thought when I did, I could charm the family dictator with my good intentions, give him the impression that the last thing I wanted in the world was to get into his daughter's undies. Heavens, I'm not a complete *degenerate!*

Dating Roxanne on the sly was fine with me, although we had some anxious moments. I visited her at home only when *der Führer* was out. What made it riskier was that his schedule was inconsistent. He owned his own rig and contracted himself out to local trucking outfits on an on-call basis. One day her father came home earlier than expected. She and her sister hid me in their bedroom closet. An afternoon passed, and he was still in the house, and I was still hiding in the dark. I heard the refrigerator door opening and closing and imagined him goose-stepping between the kitchen and the living room with a knockwurst sandwich. To get him out of the house, Roxanne's mom told him that he'd need to go out to buy sanitary napkins.

"How could we run out so fast?" he complained.

"With three teenage girls, this is what *hoppens*," she said, her Japanese accent still lingering.

The girls looked out the living-room window as *der Führer* grumbled out on his errand. Roxanne opened the closet door, both she and her mother laughing. The coast was clear. I took off, a little scared, lucky to have dodged another bullet.

I took Roxanne to see *The Sound of Music* in the cavernous Paramount Theatre in Asbury Park. Once a regal art-deco palace, it was now decaying and smelling of mildew. The movie was boring. We didn't care. Like the Von Trapps who pranced their way around Nazi-dominated Europe, we, too, could overcome adversity. We made out for two hours in the deserted balcony. This was new to us both—or, at least, for me—the frantic kissing, the turning, and twisting, the rebuffs and reconnoitering. The godforsaken condition of what were formerly my testicles, now so achy and swollen they demanded to be memorialized in all caps as my BLUE BALLS.

We sat on the cold sand of Point Pleasant and watched the surf under a crescent moon in October. I felt worldly and insane with anticipation. I was prepared with a condom for the occasion. After I tore the wrapper with my shaky paws, I dropped the rubber on a blanket riddled with sand. If I remained a virgin for the rest of my life, I had no one to blame but myself.

But soon, we were on fire. We'd go out for drives after school to secluded off-road spots with enough cover that made my car invisible. I was drugged by the fragrances of her *Faberge*. I had doused myself with *Canoe*. I felt combustible, a prospect to which I would have happily sacrificed myself. Let my head blow off, who needed it? Our promises gushed like cream of wheat boiling over an untended pot. We kept our sex life secret. One Sunday when my grandparents were away at an antique auction, Roxanne and I were lost in an all-day marathon, which was interrupted by a visit from Jimmy. He came into the drive, got out of his car and knocked on the door.

"It's Jimmy. I'm not answering it," I said to Roxanne, beside me in bed.

"Bill … Bill, you home?" Jimmy persisted in going to different doors to beckon me. I didn't answer. Our situation was scandalous.

After all, nice girls didn't engage in sex; otherwise, they'd be considered sluts. Later that week, I confided to Jimmy that Roxanne and I were having sex and that it was the good and meaningful kind because our love drove us to it.

"Jesus, Bill, you think that's OK? I mean, fooling around is one thing, but this…is dangerous," Jimmy said.

"Are you judging me? Aren't you and Katy having sex?"

"No way! She wants to wait as far as going all the way goes."

Of course, his view may have been jaundiced because his older sister got pregnant when she was in high school. He took *that* as a personal injury to *his* reputation. After some more discussion, Jimmy admitted that he and Katy were having sex but that it was restricted to hand jobs and oral sex. I wondered to myself how good oral sex with Katy could be, considering her braces … all that jagged chrome.

When it came to sex, shame and pleasure were partners, like peanut butter and jelly. Jimmy told me that when Katy was plagued by guilt, he'd drive her to church for confession, and then wait in the car. He said that Katy would tell him that she didn't confess the actual truth to the priest. "She says that she'll confess something like, 'Forgive me Father for I have sinned. *I've let a boy take advantage of me.*' Then the priest will tell her to pray and ask for forgiveness. As far as God's concerned, her record's clean as a whistle."

"But she's not telling it like it is. I mean, as if you forced her or tricked her into it."

"Katy says all her Catholic girlfriends put it that way."

As far as *der Führer* knew, I didn't exist, until the school year was over. That was in June, right after commencement ceremonies at the high school gym, when Roxanne and I arranged to have my family meet her parents for cake and coffee at the Lakewood Diner. Roxanne sat between her father and mother. I sat across from them with Dad and Grandma and Grandpa. We let the family elders lead the awkward conversation. *Der Führer* only ordered a glass of water, which he sipped. It felt like he spent most of the time glaring at me.

I eventually met man-to-man with Roxanne's father in the comfort of his bunker. *Der Führer* was a Bible-thumping wannabe preacher. If he was home, I was obliged to sit and listen to him read his favorite Bible passages. I sat across from him at his dining-room table, where he had a Bible in front of him, opened to a favorite passage. I'd smile at him, and he'd force a smile back at me. I wanted him to see me as a harmless, sexless geek. As I sized him up, what I saw was a blunt instrument. If he knew I was having sex with Roxanne, he'd bash my head in and, for good measure, run his semi-truck back and forth over my body.

He was enthralled with the Book of Revelation, the grim hit parade featuring Armageddon, the End Times, the Four Horsemen of the Apocalypse, and the Number of the Beast, 666, *et cetera, et cetera, et cetera.*

"Do you see?" he asked. "Do you see that Satan is a real presence?"

I nodded pensively. I knew a thing or two about the end of the world and sin, having had a Sunday school teacher who told me I was going to hell.

"Do you see?" *der Führer* asked again. "Do you see that Satan is a real presence?" He repeated himself for emphasis, like a real preacher. "Do you see that Satan is a real presence?" Yes, I saw it, alright. And all too clearly. What I saw across the table was a massive round head full of crazy.

My English teacher allowed me to take study hall in the school library instead of the cafeteria, so I could research material for a report on *Leaves of Grass*. Though I toted around books about Walt Whitman, he was just my beard. My ulterior motive was to find out all I could about the female human's fertility cycle and determine, with scientific accuracy, the sweet spots in the menstrual calendar when ovulation was unlikely. Since *coitus interruptus* was our only form of birth control, I aimed to be expert at identifying what I logically calculated as the 27 out of 28 days that the egg was off duty. I mean, it worked like a charm for Catholics, right? I was trying to be responsible, but my confidence began to disintegrate when Roxanne's period was one week, two weeks, then three weeks overdue.

I was still working at the refinery and asked Herb Z for a raise. I told him my circumstances. He grimaced and pinched the bridge of his nose, which I took as judgment. But he came through with a token gesture. Instead of a raise, he gave me a check for fifty bucks and wished me luck.

The suspense was killing me until Roxanne called me over the weekend to report the wonderful news that her period arrived. Praise be! Sometime during the summer, Herb asked me about my girlfriend's condition. Although I told him she wasn't pregnant after all, I didn't offer to return the fifty bucks. He didn't ask for a refund, and I didn't offer. I wasn't proud of being that kind of guy, but I could live with it.

Senior year and the summer gave me a glimpse of the good life. I bought presents for Roxanne and took her and her sisters out for pizza. Instead of going to the senior prom, I took the girl I loved to New York City. We ordered dinner *and* drinks (whiskey sours) at the Tavern on the Green. Afterward, we strolled through Central Park, fantasizing about our future. Late that night, instead of driving Roxanne home, we took a romantic detour to my house where we rolled around on my grandparents' living-room rug. So cosmopolitan!

But as summer rolled forward, ennui insinuated itself into our relationship. After dates with Roxanne, I preferred the company of Jimmy and our mutual buddies. We drank and drove around the loop in Asbury Park in search of girls as witless as we. We strapped a surfboard atop the car we were in, although none of us were surfers. This extracurricular fun was harmless, but I began to consider what opportunities I was giving up. One night after we saw the incredibly boring *Dr. Zhivago* I told Roxanne: "I think I need some space. You know, to find myself."

When she replied, "Maybe I need some space, too," I was insulted and indignant. I promptly changed my mind.

"We can make this work," I said, wondering if either of us was convinced.

Chapter 39
LEAVING THE NEST

I left for Montclair State College on a windy day in September 1967. I had spent the morning packing my clothes and a few personal artifacts—a framed photograph of Roxanne, stationery supplies, and favored books. I folded my clothes into Grandma's nicked and bruised rush suitcase, which she had taken to Wells College when Woodrow Wilson was president. It was the same one I had taken to YMCA camp when I was a kid. There was no official family farewell. Dad was at work in the city. Grandpa was out doing errands. That left it up to Grandma and me to close out this chapter of our respective lives and begin the next.

I sat behind the wheel of my 1961 Plymouth Savoy, a lime green two-door sedan equipped with a slant-six engine and push button automatic trans, recently purchased for $190. A few acorns bounced off my roof—particularly irksome because I spent the previous afternoon hand-buffing my new car's finish to a satisfying luster. A few more acorns dropped harmlessly on the driveway from the ancient oak that was the sentry of my grandparent's house. Just two years earlier, I had plowed into that venerable tree the same day I had gotten my learners' permit. I couldn't begrudge the oak its revenge, if that's what the nuts were about. A lot had happened since.

This day had snuck up on me, its effect becoming more powerful as it approached. By that, I mean its effect, here and now inside of me, my heart thumping harder, my throat swelling up, my breathing labored, a sudden weight on my chest. I was parked in the driveway, going over my to-do list in my mind like a pilot checks his instruments, and tried to collect my thoughts as Ray Charles sang, "It's Crying Time Again." I turned it off, not wanting to be dewy-eyed and weepy as Grandma walked toward the car.

"Are you all right in there?" she asked.

I pulled myself together, rolled my window down, and said, "Everything's fine. I think I've got everything I need."

"Of course, you have," she said. Grandma had her hands clasped in front of her. The big farmhouse rose behind her. I thought life together had been good for me and for my grandparents the past eight years. Their vision for an antique shop and a big vegetable garden and flower beds in the country had all panned out. Surprisingly, my aspirations came true. I made it to college. I loved a girl, and she loved me back.

"Well, you're free, white, and 21 and you can do anything you put your mind to," Grandma said.

"I guess so," I said, concurring for her benefit. Although I appreciated her optimism, Grandma's description of me was somewhat *off* kilter, as she might say. I was only half white, 18 years old, and she overestimated the command that I had over my mind. When she said I was white, she took it for granted we were of the same mold, which was true, to an extent.

One day I had overheard Grandma asking Dad, *entre nous*, about the college application I had filled out—she was concerned I had checked the box "other" for race, since none of the categories applied to me. Though there was no accurate box for me other than *Other*, it should have annotated my response with a footnote: that part of Ida Elizabeth Kipp had flowed through my heart as soon as I began to evolve as a human being in my mother's womb.

Looking back, I wonder if my grandmother didn't think of this day as a passage for herself, as well. She had completed a mission that spanned a decade. It was a mission that she hadn't officially signed up for, nor one that anyone acknowledged, including me. After my mother quit on short notice, and my father downsized his role to part-time pretend father, Grandma assumed the role of both. She was more than a grandmother to me, but never quite mother. If we had talked about that, she might have said, "Yes, neither beast nor fowl." Her quaint clichés were proxies for moments like this. Reluctance to talk about our emotions was part of the family legacy. I saw how those dragons took my mother. The rest of us kept them chained up, good and tight. It had worked so far, hadn't it? As far as I knew, it was the American Way. A few more acorns fell through the shimmering light. This moment poured out with the life behind and the life ahead, too rich for me to describe no less fully comprehend. I wanted to tell her that I loved her, but instead, it went like this.

"So, I guess this is it."

"Write to us when you have the time. Let us know how your first week goes."

"Of course, I will. You can count on that."

We said good-bye and that was that. Such was our parting that day. I was on my own, and as she said, I could do anything I put my mind to. But it wasn't true. I couldn't even usurp the family code and tell her what I wanted to. It took more courage than I had to thank Grandma and tell her that I loved her.

Chapter 40
CARPE DIEM

I stopped by Jimmy's, my next-to-last stop before I headed north. We had a few laughs; told each other we'd keep in touch. He was getting a free ride to Monmouth College, a private school perched on the Jersey shore. His father recently retired as a cop, and now worked at the school as head of campus security, which came with a significant perk—free tuition for his college-bound son. Jimmy would commute from home, so he was all set.

For us, college now had an existential aspect to it. It shielded males from the military draft, at least temporarily, as long as they were enrolled as full-time students. In 1967, 228,000 men were conscripted, many sent to Vietnam.

My final stop to say good-bye was at Roxanne's house. She was leaving a week later to begin nursing school in Boston. We wouldn't see each other until Thanksgiving. We promised to love each other forever and to write or call at least once a week. She started crying. When I drove away from her house, I wiped tears from my eyes and snot from my nose, but I soon felt pretty damn good, poised for new adventures. I mean, I had heard that college girls were pretty wild. On the other hand, I wondered if Roxanne would recover from her sad feelings as quickly as I just did, when she left for school. That idea provoked a flurry of jealousy as I thought about her enjoying a liberated life in Boston. It just didn't seem fair.

I drove up Route 9 and the Garden State Parkway. Although it was only 70 miles to the school, it was my longest solo journey so far. I felt smugly independent. I was off to Montclair State College, where hoi polloi like me got their sheepskins. I was fine with that. My finances were in good order. Tuition was just $150 a year. Room and board and other expenses would cost about $2,000. Grandma had given me $500 she had saved for this day. I had more than a thousand bucks from my summer and after-school earnings. I'd make up the rest with student loans. Dad said he'd send me twenty-five bucks a week during the school year. Things were looking up. And incredibly, the Boston Red Sox were going to the World Series, for the first time since 1940-something. Dad told me not to get too excited. As I got closer to the college, I passed hill-top mansions with manicured lawns that cascaded toward the street below like waves of money. The houses became less grand closer to campus. I drove by multifamily houses, the make-ends-meet dwellings of the potbellied working-class stiffs who rented rooms out to students. When I reached the campus, many buildings seemed inspired by Mexican architecture, with stucco facades and terra-cotta roofs and trim, like the haciendas I had seen in the *The Magnificent Seven* and *The Alamo*.

Other buildings were newer, like my nondescript, two-story dormitory. I registered at the lobby, arriving earlier than most for freshman orientation weekend. The resident assistant gave me a folder fat with schedules, maps, rules, and policies, and a bag of orientation materials, including a red freshman beanie, emblazoned with Class of '71. He slid my room key across the counter to me.

"You're on the second floor … in the penthouse," he said. "Ha, ha, ha."

"Yeah, right," I said. "Ha, ha, ha." So far, I was getting along with everyone.

My room, like most, was a double, furnished with a pair of beds, small desks, chairs, chests, wastebaskets, lamps, and one closet. The décor was in various shades of neutral. There were community bathrooms on the floor with four sinks, four shower stalls, four urinals, and four toilets.

I unpacked my stuff and tossed two books on my desk that announced my edgy personality: *Naked Lunch*, for its shock value; and *The Sun Also Rises*, for its classic, but ambiguous manliness. My coarse summary of Hemingway's novel was, "I cried because I had no shoes, but then I met a man who had no penis." Actually, I was moved by the love story that could never be.

I was lounging on top of my spongy bed, staring at the ceiling and wondering if Roxanne was missing me yet, when my roommate came in with his parents. I hoisted myself up and introduced myself. There was a familiar pause, followed by a social stutter. We exchanged the usual pleasantries. During an awkward few minutes, I sat at my desk and pretended to read through orientation propaganda, as Jon's mother put her son's underwear and socks into his chest of drawers, like he was going to sleepaway camp for the first time.

I thought, *Jesus, even when I was a kid and went away to YMCA camp, I was able to unpack my crap all by myself!* Mr. Dad rummaged through Jon's orientation bag, pulled out a red beanie, and put it on his son's head.

"How do I look?" said Jon, as if modeling the cap. His folks had quite a hoot.

"Well, Bill, what do you think?" said Mrs. Mom.

"What can I say?"

Jon's old man slapped him on the back and said, "That's my boy!"

Meanwhile, his mother sat on her son's bed and buried her face in her palms. I sensed a pitiful good-bye. All that affection. To avoid it, I excused myself.

"Good meeting you," I said. "See you again."

I left the room and loitered near the door, listening to them speculate about the mismatch between my name and my looks.

"Maybe he's part Indian or Hawaiian?" said Mrs. Mom. "I was hoping for someone who had more in common with Jon."

"I bet Filipino," said Mr. Dad.

"Who cares?" said Jon. "He seems okay."

The geniuses in charge of dormitory pairings used the ethnicity implied by surnames to match up roommates. I heard a few muffled words, followed by Mrs. Mom's sobs. She wasn't crying because I wasn't the Bill Fellenberg she pictured. I suspected that it was from the pain of finally cutting off the umbilical cord that connected her to her son. I was touched, albeit briefly.

From the first, Jon was out late. He was rarely in our room. When I saw him, he seemed overly eager, or he'd be muttering to himself.

He began bragging that the most popular fraternity had asked him to pledge. "Just white boys only!" he chortled. "Just kidding! If it was up to me, I'd ask you in. One party after another. The girls!"

What an asshole. But wasn't it so unfair and ironic? Jon's night life was debauched and wild. Meanwhile, I was going to the clean-fun freshman programs in the cafeteria, where you drank soda and ate chips and listened to folksingers and clapped your hands. I was uncomfortable in my own skin, but this was my opportunity to reinvent myself. I'd be damned if I was going to wear a red beanie. I wanted to present myself as a young man blessed with wit, style, and a dash of insouciance; a poor man's George Sanders, that suicidal actor whose legendary final words were, "I'm bored." Asked what my major was, I'd reply, "English." Typically, the assumption was that I planned to teach. When I said I was in the liberal arts curriculum, some were incredulous and asked, "What can you do with that?" I said that you could learn to talk really good, for one thing.

After orientation ran its course with tours, events, and class registrations, I got a note in my mailbox to report to the dean of students. Jesus, I hardly had a chance to get into trouble. I couldn't discern what I had done. Nervously, I walked apace across campus to the administration building. His office was very imposing. I had spent a lot of time in principals' offices, but none had the gravitas of this one—instead of venetian blinds, floor-to-ceiling drapes; upholstered furniture; and the dean's big desk was polished, uncluttered, and ready for business.

"Good afternoon, William. Thank you for meeting me," he said, shaking my hand. He was tall, bald, and looked in charge. Instead of returning to his side of the desk, he sat next to me in the other chair for guests. The expression on his face was somber. Two creases across his forehead became half a dozen as he went through a litany of Jon's troubles. Apparently, my roommate wasn't enjoying himself at frat parties and cozying up to the ladies. In fact, what he was doing those late nights was lurking in the lobbies of the girls' dorms at the invitation of none. He was making them "uncomfortable." I wondered if the dean thought I had provoked Jon's meltdown.

"In sum, Jon is going home. His parents are, in fact, gathering his belongings as we speak. It's quite sad."

I thought to myself, *What a relief!* It was my roommate who was the subject of this visit, not me. The dean mistook my reaction, patting my shoulder in consolation.

"I can tell you're taking this hard, William. But in the long run, I'm sure Jon will be fine. Being away from home can be surprisingly difficult for some. And by the way, how are you doing?" He gave me a penetrating stare. I figured he was assessing me for signs of emotional frailty—maybe I'd be next. I told him I was getting accustomed to campus life, except for the cafeteria food—ha, ha, ha. He smiled perfunctorily, and shook my hand, and thanked me for my understanding. The following week, Vince, my new roommate moved in. He was a math major who played the trumpet. We bummed cigarettes off each other, discreetly ogled the co-eds, and got along fine.

I enrolled in Creative Writing, Comp and Lit I, Development of World Civilization I, and History of Early Drama in England. The class I enjoyed most was Creative Writing, which was relevant to what I wanted to learn about and get better at. My teacher was Mr. Roberts, who was bald, bespectacled, and seemed *oldish*, until he revealed the side of himself that was willing to be amused. When he found something funny his smile gave you a glimpse of his youth. Mr. Roberts said my work was promising and encouraged me to submit to *The Quarterly*, the college literary and arts magazine. The only other exceptional experience I had was in History of Early Drama in England, which was ridiculously *early*, held from 8:30 to 11:30 Saturday mornings, a freakish slot that seemed to be one of a kind. This meant that each weekend began with the cruel obligation of listening to my musty professor with the nicotine-stained teeth and double-bun hairdo wax on about the dawn of English drama, beginning with the medieval mystery dramas, Noah and the flood, and then the long slog onward to *comedies of manners*, which were deadly—the comedic timing off not by a beat, but by three centuries. Try that for a laugh.

I made dean's list, just barely, for the first and last time. I also made several friends, mostly other freshmen from the dorm. On weekends we'd go into the city where the drinking age was 18. We'd hit cheap bars along Times Square and then take a subway to the Village and try to be cool, as we hoped to mingle with hipsters around Bleecker and McDougal but ended up bumping into throngs of square undergrads from the suburbs and sticks who were just like us.

I saw Roxanne back home on Thanksgiving eve, and we stayed at The Moon Motel in Lakewood, spending a cozy night there like grownups, but probably with more enthusiasm than most of them. We celebrated Thanksgiving separately with our respective families. I felt truly full of thanks the next day, celebrating with the Ancient Ones and my Old Man at the homestead.

Roxanne and I returned to our respective schools and planned to reprise another holiday night at the Moon to kick off Christmas break. We could make it a Thanksgiving and Christmas tradition. But it wasn't to be. I had an opportunity to make a few bucks by delivering a shipment of processed nickel for Z Refining a few days before Christmas. The roundtrip to and from Attleboro, Massachusetts, took eight hours, not including loading and unloading time. It was well into the ink of December dark when I returned the truck to the plant. I was in no hurry, just glad to be back, and heading back home to hit the sack. It was drizzly and the roads were slick when a car ran a stop sign, forcing me to swerve into the woods and run a gauntlet of branches and scrub brush that thrashed the sides of my Plymouth until we bounced off a stump and finally jerked to stop, stranded over a cluster of deadfall. It was lucky I was unscathed, but my lovely Plymouth Savoy was totaled. The tow truck guy took it to a junk yard and we called it even. The asshole who ran the stop sign was long gone.

It took a few weeks to buy a so-called new car, which in fact, was much older—a '53 Dodge, a four-door sedan, with a dull black finish. Sal Russo, a dubious friend I made in the dorm, nicknamed my car the *Chan Mobile*, because it looked like the vehicle driven by Charlie Chan in the movies of thirties and forties—starring Sidney Toler, a white guy of course, playing the inscrutable, and unattractive Chinese American sleuth, who spoke with the standard accent.

I took on a more ambitious load of 16 credits for spring semester, but by mid-semester I slid down a rabbit hole of apathy which led to a D in German and an F in Earth Science. I blamed the Earth Science disaster on bad inside information I had received from a slacker who said the course was a piece of cake, perfect for non-science majors. I got a boiler-plate warning note from the registrar's office about my poor academic performance. But the bad news was somewhat redeemed by one of my poems and a short story which were published in *The Quarterly*. If Whitman failed earth science, would it have mattered to him? I ripped up the registrar's note.

The nadir of my freshman year happened in the final week. I was called into the dean's office, like a boy summoned to a principal's office. My dormitory's officious resident assistant, Dick Unger, had reported me for horsing around with a fire extinguisher. I expected the dean to be annoyed, not at me, but at Unger for bringing such a nuisance of a complaint to his attention. Furthermore, he'd probably cut me some slack, given my commendable behavior when my first roommate went around the bend.

But the dean didn't even remember meeting me. He told me I was being called to account for a very serious offense, and outlined several *what if* scenarios, all leading to tragic infernos. "Imagine a terrible fire unleashed through that dormitory," he said, shaking his head as if many had already died in a conflagration because of me. "An extinguisher is not a water pistol. It's not a toy. It's not your property to play with. I won't report you to the town fire marshal, even though there is a touch of criminality here."

"I'm not a criminal," I protested. I told him that I never intended to put anyone in danger. "We were in the lounge studying for finals. It was hot and I squirted a couple of blasts from the extinguisher to break the monotony."

This provoked the dean to repeat the same *blah blah blah blah blah* until he finally imposed sentence. Magisterially, he said, "You can stay at dorm for the remainder of the semester. After that, you are barred from on-campus housing for the rest of your academic career here. Mindless behavior. You're excused." The dean waved me off to send me back to the dark hole I had crawled out of.

That's how my freshman year ended in semi-ignominy. To myself, I cursed Dick, the compulsive-obsessive do-gooder who ratted on me. When I saw him back at the dorm, I tried to cast a look his way so menacing that he'd dream of criminals with shivs.

"You deserved it! I told you to stop it, Fellenberg," he blurted. "I meant business!" His hands were shaky, clumsily unlocking his door. Maybe he thought I was stalking him. Good.

Roxanne planned to return home for the summer, although our long-distance relationship had frayed during the last several months. I vaguely suspected her of seeing someone else when she missed a couple of my calls. Maybe my suspicions were provoked by misgivings about my own minor infidelities. First, a double date arranged by Sal Russo with two student nurses from a teaching hospital in East Orange. He knew his date from high school. The other girl, an attractive red-haired future nurse, was a stranger to me and remained so. We took them to see the rerelease of *Cool Hand Luke* at our campus auditorium. On the way back to the hospital, Sal and his date made out in the back seat, while my date chattered nonstop about Paul Newman. Those ice-blue eyes, oh God!

I had another date with a serious girl from my earth science class. She was obsessed with necessity of achieving ZPG (Zero Population Growth). There were too many human beings sapping limited resources and without reducing birth rates, we were doomed to die of starvation and thirst. In the meantime, I treated her to a jug-band performance in the college cafeteria, followed by cheeseburgers, fries, and milkshakes at a diner. That girl could really pack it away. That's irony for you. By the end of the evening, I had squandered eight bucks and she remained dour, not a smile to be seen. She even turned her head when I attempted a harmless goodnight peck. That was as below zero as you could get.

When the academic year ended, I was still feeling pangs of jealousy. Regardless, I drove into the city and met Roxanne at the Port Authority to drive us home to Jersey. She approached me from the Greyhound arrival gate wearing a miniskirt that was just a breeze below her awesome treasures. Although we were cool and indifferent to each other during the ride, by the following week, we responded to a passionate five-alarm fire, officially back together.

It was good returning to Ardena. I worked at Z Refining and lived at home with Grandma and Grandpa, just like the old days. Jimmy and I reconnected. He had finished his first year at the sparkly college on the Jersey shore. Although his girlfriend had broken up with him shortly after she started school in the Midwest, the rest of Jimmy's first year went well. He had been the starting second baseman for his college's varsity baseball team. Maybe pro ball was in his future.

My '53 Dodge died, and buying and selling cheap cars became an obsession. Although I intended to trade up, I slid down the used-car food chain. Rather than at dealerships, I preferred to troll through country roads and bargain hunt for cars perched on crabgrass-infested yards with scrawled cardboard "For Sale" signs slapped on their windshields. When I spent $30 for a '50 Pontiac Chieftain or $45 for a '57 Anglia (England's version of a compact Ford, a turd of an automobile), a full tank of gas was a prerequisite. I also owned, for one day, a '59 Nash Metropolitan, a two-seater convertible. I had stopped by Jimmy Oats' house, where we spent a couple of hours spiffing up the car, using Ajax to remove splotches of dulled, oxidized paint on the car. It looked damn good, and I felt great, until I discovered that the steering mechanism was severely corroded, barely able to make it to the previous owner and demand my money back.

That summer at home, I enjoyed the small town stuff, which if you have a girlfriend and a best friend, is about as good as it gets. Meanwhile, all hell had broken through in America, but only barely in Ardena—you got the gist of it through the pixilated screens of television sets.

Chapter 41
SOME CREATURES SHED THEIR SKIN

Passaic, August 1968

We had already seen the brutal passage of JFK into the afterlife five years ago. You might figure that one assassination would be enough for a generation, but there were more to come. MLK was assassinated in April 1968, followed by RFK in June. The three monograms together provided a shorthand convenience, a meme that memorialized the martyrs on an American triptych whose three panels were becoming unhinged by collective madness. Saggy-jawed senators blamed spoiled brats on drugs and said it was the end of something. During 1968, 360,000 men were drafted into military service. Racial animus had erupted in hundreds of cities between 1963 and 1968, coinciding with the tenure of President Lyndon Baines Johnson. He had anointed his administration as one that would launch "The Great Society."

A few weeks before school started, I went apartment hunting with Jake Cutter. He was another guy from the dorm who I made friends with. We both wanted the freedom that came with living off campus. When Jake called me and said, "It's time to live like adults, right?" I concurred. I wanted to be free of Dick Unger and others like him, anal-retentive resident assistants who were eager to prosecute me. Besides, the dean had excommunicated me from dormitory life. I looked forward to living with Jake, math major and semi-serious student, but not a fanatic.

The closest affordable place we found was on Broadway. No, not the Great White Way, but the one in Passaic, ten miles from campus. It was a one-bedroom apartment on the third floor, two dingy floors above Harry Platt's Bar & Grill, the landlord's eponymous watering hole. Harry sized us up during a brief interview in the bar. He chomped on a soggy cigar on one side of his mouth and talked through the other side, sort of like Edward G. Robinson, see?

It was Sunday before noon, and a few early arrivals had already grafted their asses onto their bar stools. They leaned into our conversation with Harry as he briefed us about the rules. He didn't want tenants involved in any *funny business*, which meant no cocaine, no heroin, no partying late at night, and no loud music.

When he seemed finished, he said, "Wait! Two other things … no spilling trash on the premises and no antiwar demonstrations!"

We agreed to abide by the house standards. The total rent including utilities was eighty-five bucks a month, the first month's rent and one month for security up front. As advertised in the classifieds, the place was *clean, safe and full of urban charm*—all that, and a view overlooking the Passaic freight yards—a screechy, chaotic tangle of electrified cables, rail tracks, switches, and idle train cars. As there was no lease, we accepted Harry's conditions with a handshake—not the thumbs-intertwined Bro handshake, but the firm-grip conventional eye-to-eye trust-me, I'm-an-American-guy handshake.

I enrolled in four courses: Intro to Poly Sci, American Lit, Intro to Visual Art, and Art of Poetry. I commuted in a homely 1954 Chevy, an incomplete restoration project, carelessly coated in dull gray primer. By October's end, I was struggling, money-wise and academically. I had lived large and burned through my cash and student loan. Dad's promise to send me a hundred bucks a month devolved into IOUs. After I paid my share of rent, I lived on chump change and bummed weed, Marlboros, and a few bucks from Jake. My Chevy was curled up in a fetal position on a side street, with electrical problems too mysterious and expensive to fix. Sometimes it started, other times it refused. I hitched rides with Jake when our schedules jibed.

I did the required reading for my classes, handed in most

assignments, and showed up for exams. I skipped a few classes. I mean, it was Montclair State, not Princeton. I spent languid afternoons in the student union playing hearts and Foosball. *The Quarterly* published another piece. I was a poet. When I wasn't writing, I was busy fending off my demons. Some professors expected their students to attend most, if not all, of their classes. As Bartleby said, "I prefer not to." I read Melville and Conrad like a good boy but wasted time on Bukowski and R. Crumb's *Zap Comix*.

After two recent checks from Dad bounced, the college revoked my check-cashing privileges for the year. I trudged to the teller's cage in the student union building to see if I could fix things. The girl in the cage said she was sorry, but it was college policy. She wasn't to blame. My father had let me down. The college now flagged me as a deadbeat, and if the dean had his way, it probably complemented my student record as a pyromaniac.

I called Dad at the Life Circulation Company in Newark, where he worked part-time, selling subscriptions for *Life* magazine over the phone.

"You sound agitated," he said. "What's up?"

"I'd rather talk to you in person, but it's about money."

"I can't hear you. Can you speak up?"

"Look, just meet me after you finish work!" I yelled to overcome the cacophony of a room erupting with sales pitches.

"I'll meet you at the Dubonnet."

"OK. The Dubonnet Lounge, then, at nine o'clock."

I took a bus to Newark with a few bucks in in my wallet and chump change in my pocket. Dad was sipping a drink when I arrived. He introduced me to Millie, the dancer who sat next to him in a skimpy outfit, a kid's onesie, with sequins. I guessed she was in her early twenties. She told me what a great guy he was, then squeezed his bearded cheeks between her palms, making him pucker up and squealed, "He's just so cute!" Her Jamaican accent completed her enthusiastic demeanor. We chatted before she excused herself for her set on the go-go platform. She shimmied and gyrated through an earnest and energetic set.

I was embarrassed, but not in a snooty way—rather, in the way I feel in a recurring dream, or some variation of it, where I'm on an unfamiliar campus, searching for the classroom where my final exam is scheduled, and for which I'm unprepared, then realize I'm naked from the waist down—that kind of embarrassed.

It's awkward. The Dubonnet's not an ideal setting to have a serious conversation. I had to yell in Dad's ear to tell him about the bad checks and their repercussions. After Millie completed her number, dancing to Archie Bells and the Drells' "Tighten Up," Dad and I were able to talk. He said he was sorry for the mix-up. He took out his wallet and handed me several twenties. He said he'd take care of the rest as soon as his next commission checks came through from *Life*. He said that he had had an exceptional month—*the best ever*. I had several beers and was no longer embarrassed, just drunk. I left without saying good-bye, in a rush to get the last bus to Passaic. I looked back and saw my old man chumming it up with his bar buddies, soaking in their stories about work, sports, or politics, and glancing absent-mindedly at the go-go girls.

❖ ◆ ❖

> *I take the back seat of a near-empty bus out of Newark, its poorest neighborhoods torched during last summer's national plague of race riots. It hasn't always been this way, has it? I'm hollow, looking out a window smudged by a child's greasy handprints.*
>
> *Thinking about the scene in the Dubonnet, I don't know whether I should laugh or cry. I don't know if I hate my father or love him. Like everything else, it vacillates somewhere in The In Between. The driver slows at a bus stop but changes his mind. A homeless nut runs beside us just long enough for us to make eye contact. An unbuttoned overcoat billows behind him like a ragged sail. I dub him the Flying Dutchman—the*

Flying Dutchman of Broad Street. Ahoy there! He gives me the thumbs up before sinking into the dark. The bus groans up Broad Street, roiling the flotsam and jetsam of trash in its wake. The bus driver grovels at every traffic light, refusing to accelerate through any yellow lights. This night shudders from red light to red light, as if conniving to cancel the rest of time.

◆

When I told Jake I planned to drop out, he said that yeah, it was the smartest thing to do, considering I had already failed *Supermarket 101*. He was snidely referring to the night I was escorted from the A&P by the seafood manager, after I had gotten soaked in the lobster tank, bobbing for lobsters. I blamed it on a Halloween party where the hosts injected grain alcohol into a watermelon.

The day before my twentieth birthday, I slouched to the college registrar's office and tendered my *withdrawal* from school. *Withdrawal*—it's the same nomenclature that applies to quitting addictions, or retreating from the battlefield, or *coitus interruptus*. This particular kind of withdrawal was drained of ceremony and devoid of emotion. I was handed a short form, which I completed standing up. There were no chairs. I figured it was intentional. Having a place to sit might encourage dropouts to indulge in long sob stories. I identified my reason for withdrawing as *financial*. There wasn't enough room on the form to describe the rabbit hole I had tumbled into.

◆

After I return to Passaic, I make two calls from the phone booth in Harry Platt's. I call Dad at his day job, intending to tell him I've dropped out. I'm uncertain whether to gently remind him about money he promised to send—or give him a double-barrel blast of shame, how he deserves an F for being a lousy father.

He picks up and says, "Hello, this is Bill Fellenberg, can I help you?"

It's very Twilight Zone to hear him say that. *Can I help you?* His voice sounds just like me. I hang up on me. After I take a breath, I drop seven quarters into the box to call Roxanne at her dorm pay phone. It pays for three minutes, then the machine asks for another quarter. We are high school sweethearts beyond our peak, stumbling from one long-distance call to the next. We decide to reunite after Thanksgiving break and stay at my place. Jake's going home to Toms River, so we'll have it to ourselves.

◆ ◆ ◆

After we spend the Thanksgiving down home with our respective families, Roxanne and I take slow, reluctant buses from Freehold to Newark, then to Passaic. We're busing it because my car is comatose on a side street by Harry Platt's. We stay together for a night and most of the next day. Like all doomed lovers, we speculate on the future. She can't keep up with the nursing program at Northeastern, and Boston's too cold. We're in a laundromat watching our clothes spin. Roxanne says that maybe we should get married. I present a litany of reasons why we shouldn't. There's the war on the other side of the world (again), the other one in our own cities, and there's the recession—good jobs are scarce. I'm a dropout with one year of college, and an English major, for Christ's sakes. I've got no prospects, hardly husband material. It's ironic, but Roxanne says she's dropping out, too.

Roxanne begins sorting clothes. "You're right. It was a childish thought." She looks at me with those dark, almond eyes so beautiful I could weep.

The clatter of empty train cars being shunted back and forth is the background music for this moment, when you know your first love can't be your last, and even though it's nobody's fault, it still feels like *somebody* should apologize. I know we've been cheated. I have it all figured out. Some creatures shed their skin to grow, but we'll shed each other.

"Bill?" Roxanne asks.

I know that she's addressing me, but I'm speechless.

The next day, I call Grandma to let her know I've dropped out. There's a silence so long I have to ask her if she's still there.

"Yes, I'm still here."

"So, it's a temporary thing. I just need some time to regroup."

"*Regroup?* With whom? It's an odd picture, one person regrouping with himself."

"What I mean is, I'll go back to school and finish."

"No, you won't," she says. "I've got to go. Supper's burning on the stove." As she hangs up, Grandma fumbles with the kitchen wall phone.

I hear Grandpa ask, "Who was that?"

"That was Bill. No, I mean that was Billy."

For her, it's déjà vu. I think she sees my father's failure and mine as conjoined.

Chapter 42
A HATCHLING POUNDS INSIDE MY HEAD

Dad said he got me a job where he worked. He said it's mine at least through February, probably longer if I wanted. He cut me short when I started to thank him. "It's *very* entry level," he cautioned, "but it'll get you by for now." This was nepotism at an embarrassingly low level, where I actually needed *inside pull* to get hired stocking shelves and making deliveries by bicycle. I reported to Feldman Stationers' warehouse on Second Avenue and 52nd Street, where my father managed commercial accounts and order fulfillment. From day one, two pretty Latinas in bookkeeping teased me, but in a good-natured way. I think they sensed my desperation. Although they spoke to me in English regarding most business, they would switch to Spanish in mid-sentence, roll their eyes, and start laughing. I sensed sympathy, but that unrewarding kind like when you approach a stray dog or cat to pet it, but on seeing its matted fur, and the yearning in its pathetic eyes, you decide you'd rather not.

Each morning begins with Dad giving me an itinerary and pointing to a stack of packages for delivery. I pedal an oversize bicycle that has two rear wheels and is outfitted in front with a metal storage box filled with bulky office goods.

It's like bicycling with a refrigerator on your handlebars. From Second Avenue, I inch west toward Madison and Fifth. It's the week between Christmas and New Year's. Horns blare, curses spit from taxis, trucks and cars jam up in a mass constipation of traffic that clogs Manhattan from the East River to the Hudson, from Harlem to Chinatown. Police cars and ambulances are paralyzed, their sirens crazy and impatient. Out-of-towners aggravate conditions by actually stopping at traffic lights when they're yellow. In theory, my bicycle is supposed to be able to navigate nimbly through traffic jams. In practice, it's a reluctant mule that I have to drag around mounds of gray slush and illegally parked cars. Rather than letting me maneuver past them, drivers shut me off. This is how it is in New York, recently coined by its feckless mayor as *Fun City*.

Most of my cargo requires me to enter service doors in the bowels of buildings, the dominion of resentful peons in shipping and receiving. I'm at their mercy. They take their sweet time doing nothing before signing off on my delivery. Occasionally, I deliver precious parcels directly to plush reception areas that lord over the foul streets below. Stepping off the elevator, I enter the light of executive success. Beautiful young women are ensconced behind glass walls. They greet advanced life forms, also known as men in suits, with convincing sparkle. For me, a lower life form, they do not sparkle. Despite their practiced restraint, their vibe rings like a gong. They skeeve me.

When my deliveries are done, I wend my way toward Feldman's tony retail store at 57th and Madison around lunchtime, grab a bite in the basement, restock shelves, break down empty cardboard boxes, and bring merchandise upstairs to the hubbub of cash registers cheerfully ringing up crystal paperweights, silver money clips, and *writing instruments* like Montblanc and ST DuPont. Some cost more than I make in a month.

Three partners own the business—two Daves and Anthony. Dad says their main job is to get new business, but they spend much of the day at the store. They often form a small huddle whispering, usually about money—specifically, cash. After these conferences, Dave with the goatee closes out one of the registers and divvies up the till in three manila envelopes…the partners' daily bonus.

Sam is the store's *major domo* and holds the place together. He's black, stocky, wears hornrims, a thin moustache, and is quick to smile. He and Dad are in constant phone contact, following up on orders from important accounts, or complaining that the partners are sucking cash from the store when they should be out developing new business. They scoff sardonically about their bosses' appointments with a Mrs. Colby, a "consultant" who visits privately and frequently with each partner in a remote cubby office in the basement, behind a row of file cabinets. The sign on the door says PRIVATE. I have enough sense not to investigate.

Sam invites Dad and me to his New Year's Eve party. I ask Sam if it's OK for me to bring my buddy Jimmy Oats along, and he says that's fine. We arrive at his home in Harlem and the party is full on, James Brown sending the night to the edges of delirium with "I Got the Feeling." We find Sam in his crowded man cave, where he's holding court with stories of hilarious predicaments, bad choices, and lunatic escapes. The affection and respect his guests have for him lift the party like it's being held on a cloud. When day breaks for the first time in 1969, we say farewell to Sam. James Brown accompanies our departure, with the poignant lament of "It's a Man's Man's World."

> *But it wouldn't be nothing, nothing,*
> *not one little thing, without a woman or a girl*
> *He's lost in the wilderness*
> *He's lost in bitterness, he's lost lost.*

◈ ◆ ◈

During this time, Dad and I carved a wide and rowdy path on both sides of the Hudson, our father-son bonding taking off on the wings of alcohol. For me, that toxic togetherness was a way to catch up for lost time. Sometimes these episodes spiraled downward when we drank too much. One Friday night Jimmy and I joined Dad at the lounge of the Embassy Hotel on Columbus Avenue. He had a thing going on with Kitty, a barmaid with credentials he was partial to. She had a German accent, copper hair, and youth. He was mesmerized by a beauty mark—more accurately, a mole—on that tender back part of the knee—just where it officially becomes part of a lady's thigh. Dad said that when he was unable to see it, it meant he had had too much to drink. I didn't know if they were dating, or just rolling around behind the bar after closing or whatever. Kitty worked the Embassy with Andrea, a big blonde with a southern accent. A piano man played on Fridays, cajoling patrons to sing along. On this night, a brittle old bird tottered to the piano, grabbed the mike, and said, "If you insist. Let's do 'People,' in the key of B-flat." She was tipsy and croaky from too many cigarettes but had oodles of self-confidence.

As she tortured the song, Jimmy sidled by and mimicked her, squawk-for-squawk and caw-for-caw, to the general amusement of the room, except for the bird-lady's enraged boyfriend who bull-rushed Jimmy but missed, then staggered into me instead, both of us crumbling to the floor. Though he had the wrong guy, he still tried to wring my neck. I shoved him off me. My recollection of the scrum is fuzzy, more acoustic than visual—the sound of breaking glass, bar stools toppling, shouts and yelps of dismay—like listening to a Wild West saloon brawl on the radio.

Kitty and Andrea quickly restored order. The old diva and her beau sloshed out, threatening to sue. Bar stools were made upright. Shattered glass swept away. Drinks refreshed. And the piano man played on, "People, people who need people, are the luckiest people in the world!" A crowd pleaser for slobbering sentimentalists like me. It doesn't take much for my eyes to get moisty.

We closed the Embassy, clinking glasses with Kitty as Dad presented the night's final toast, "Bombs away and good night!"

The last bus to Passaic was long gone. Instead of heading to the Port Authority, Jimmy and I crashed at Dad's place for the night. Dad forewarned me about the Capitol Hotel, an SRO at 81st Street and Amsterdam Avenue. It's a *shit hole* (his words), a stone's throw from Needle Park. His room wasn't that bad, with a full-size bed, mission-style chair, and below a pair of windows, a red banquette with a torn cushion sutured by duct tape. There was an easel with an unfinished charcoal of a dog, maybe a Great Dane. The room had a water closet with a sink and toilet, but no private shower.

Jimmy was already conked out on the banquette, his legs dangling beyond it. Dad and I politely debated who should sleep where. Dad was insisting that I take the bed and I was insisting that he should, when the benign banter swerved around a dangerous curve: "What happened Dad? I mean, living in a place like this?"

"I let things get out of hand. I got laid off from Acme Visible Files, like most of the sales force. It was losing out to companies like Burroughs. You know—automation, computers, that stuff. Acme was a dinosaur. I got into debt—over my head."

He told me a woman named Jill was in the picture, sort of an artist. I assumed that she's younger than Dad. Long story short, she started using. Dad tried to get her into rehab. She faked interest. At the end, she asked him for money to go back to her folks somewhere in Maryland, where she'd get straight. He gave her what he could, and then some. Dad knew it was a lie, that she didn't go back home. He saw her once, hanging out in Verdi Square outside the subway station at 72nd Street, a hangout for junkies, Needle Park.

"The worst part wasn't the lie. It was admitting to myself I had given up on her."

I'm rankled by Dad's crisis of conscience over this girl. I couldn't resist lashing out at him. The seven-year-old kid in me, the Sayonara Cowboy, has many grievances—especially when he's drunk here in The In Between, where thinking about saying something and actually saying it are indiscernible.

> *That was mighty white of you, Dad, feeling guilty about giving up on a junkie.*
> *It's not the first time you gave up on somebody. Let me jog your memory.*
> *After Mom left, you dumped me at Grandma and Grandpa's for the next twelve years.*
> *Do you think sacrificing your bed for a night makes up for being a piss-poor father?*

I forget how Dad responded. I don't know if I actually said those things. That's the ugly freedom of saying shit when you're that drunk.

By morning, the night's soaked up whatever was said. I wake up in Dad's bed. Jimmy's still conked out. Dad's in his *faux* antique chair, reading *The Goodbye Look*, Ross MacDonald's detective yarn featuring the imperfect, but indefatigable, Lew Archer. We're fans.

"What's new with Archer?" I ask.

"As usual, taking a savage beating in the service of saving gorgeous women."

That's how last night's bad karma between us gets resolved. Like it never happened. Everything's back to normal.

I ask Dad for a towel and some soap and for directions to the shower. He tries to discourage me, warning me that *it's not nice*. It's a single shower stall at the far end of the hall, shared with too many other so-called guests in this wing of the floor.

"As long as they aren't showering at the same time as me," I say.

"Yeah, well. You'll still have company."

I'm desperate to scrub the hangover off me. A hatchling pounds inside my head, fixing to spring from it. In the shower, there's no relief. And I *do* have company. Cockroaches idle on the ceiling, walls, and floor. Others skitter in and out of the cracked brown grout between once-pink floor tiles. It's the fastest shower I'll ever take.

I get dressed back in the wrinkled clothes I slept in. The collar of my winter jacket is ripped from the jerk who clawed me in the Embassy Lounge. I'm swollen with regret. Jimmy and I leave Dad's and begin a long walk to the Port Authority. I feel wobbly. We stop and eat breakfast near the park.

"Jim, did you hear Dad and me last night?"

"Hear what?"

"So, I guess nothing happened."

"I heard police sirens—then you and your old man bickering about who was going to take the bed. That's all."

Back on the street I feel better, coffee and an omelet settling my insides. But the healing's short-lived. As we resume our trek downtown, my stomach decides to reject breakfast. I seek a discreet spot to hurl, but I have to settle for a city trash can by a cross walk on Columbus Circle. I delude myself that purging into a trash can instead of on the curb or sidewalk provides me a curtain of privacy. I make a spectacle of myself. A couple makes a wide arc around me.

"Disgusting," mumbles the woman, sinking into her muffler as far as she can.

As her guy passes me, he snaps, "Dude, get a job!"

I want to say something civil, like "Don't judge me!" or clever, like "I'm pregnant, dude!" Instead, I flip him a double bird. Jimmy waits on the other side of the street, pretending he's studying the sky. I catch up as fast as my slouch-wise demeanor allows. I resist spasms to re-hurl. I imagine Dad sneaking up on me and giving me a slap between my shoulder blades, blurting his mantra, "Stand up straight, you look like you've got the weight of the world on your shoulders!"

Chapter 43
A BOUNCE OFF THE BOTTOM

March 1969

The memory of that hungover guy on Columbus Circle reasserted itself often enough that I was afraid I might get stuck in a Twilight Zone kind of loop, cursed to relive my public disgrace over and over.

I applied for readmission to Montclair State and received approval to resume studies in five months, when fall semester began. I went home that weekend, especially to tell Grandma in person about my plans to return to college. It was worth the trip. As I gave her details, the worry creases on her forehead began smoothing out. I could tell Grandpa approved, too. He was there on his couch in the living room, smoking a 100-millimeter Virginia Slim that looked as long as a chopstick. Dad also had good news. He told me he was moving out of the Capitol and to an apartment in Newark. He invited me to move in with him. When I offered to chip in on the rent, he dismissed the idea. "Never mind," he said. "It'll give you a kick start, saving for tuition." It felt good, Dad stepping up like that. It seemed a long time since we felt this good.

I moved from Passaic to Newark in March. I hoped, fingers crossed, that Dad and I living together would work out better this time. The last version of us as bachelor roommates was more than a decade earlier in Summit, a living arrangement that was cut short after my school's truant officer busted me for playing hooky. One aspect of the present situation echoed what it was then. That is, Dad insisted on giving me dibs on the only bedroom. He slept on the daybed in the living room. The Old Man wanted to make the place comfortable for me.

Our place was on the second floor of a four-story walk-up on Mount Prospect Avenue. Multifamily houses and prewar apartment buildings lined both sides of the avenue. The neighborhood was reasonably safe, meaning that you didn't have to be paranoid about being jumped—but it was wise, as with any street in Newark, to keep alert after the sun went down. We decorated the apartment in a style that might be called *bachelor cheesy*. The kitchenette was crammed in an alcove by the living room. Dad built a wet bar in the living room, replete with a vinyl alligator-skin countertop, lava lamp, and stereo. He liked to listen to Eddie Arnold, Rachmaninov, and Ravel. I played Dylan and Hendrix, which Dad asked me not to when he was home.

The location was convenient for the Old Man's commute to the city for his day job, as well as his evening part-time job in downtown Newark. There was street parking where I could park my new chariot, a '53 Oldsmobile I bought from one of my grandparents' friends. It was a Sherman tank of a car, a three-speed stick on the column, equipped with a radio that worked and had good rubber all around—a car befitting a man three times my age. My dream sports car would have to wait, probably forever.

I hadn't had a hangover since that blurry night at the Embassy Lounge. Although Dad and I might get together for a beer, the marathon drinking ceased. Besides, I was busy, cobbling together two jobs and saving for school.

I left Feldman Stationers on good terms and began working in East Orange for a home improvement outfit, mostly residential wall-to-wall carpeting. I was low man on the totem pole. When I wasn't making deliveries with the van, I cleaned the store's windows and bathrooms, got coffee for anyone that asked, and during down time kibbitzed with the carpet installer, bookkeeper, and ladies who handled the office paperwork. Though I didn't talk to him much, the boss seemed like a stand-up guy. My work was menial, the pay slightly better than at Feldman's, and the commute much shorter and less expensive than working in New York.

My other job was as a telephone rep at Life Circulation Company, the homely cousin of *Life* magazine, America's most popular weekly. Thanks again to Dad's connections, I worked two evenings and

Saturday mornings in the LCC boiler room in downtown Newark.

Dad shows me the ropes. Watch and learn," he says, dialing. "The secret is, never give up. That's Churchill. *Nevah* give up."

When a prospect tells Dad they're too busy to read the magazine, he says, "Perfect! That's the beauty of *Life*. The best-informed people like you don't have time to read. Do you think Nixon has time to read? You know what the secret is? He doesn't read, and neither do I! We just look at the pictures! And no other magazine does it better than *Life*! What a time-saver!"

In this case, the prospect hangs up. He turns to me and says, "Too bad, but it was fun while it lasted," then whispers another trade secret. "You don't have to make sense. Just *connect*."

This particular night he has a stack of leads in Belleville, many with Italian surnames. He's a chameleon on the phone, and becomes Italian-American, introduces himself as Joe Palumbo. He chats for a few minutes with his prospect and closes the sale. "*Grazie*, Mr. Gallucci, and Buonanotte!"

He hangs up the phone, grinds out a cigarette in his ashtray, rings the silver bell on his desk, saunters to a large corkboard, and with a flourish, sticks a small red plastic pennant next to his name. It's his eighth sale of the night, which is barely half over. He crows, "Joe Palumbo does it again! *Abbastanza bene!*"

The next call, he morphs into an Irishman. He chats it up with Mrs. Mahoney of Kearny. "Good evening to you, Mrs. Mahoney. My name is D'Arcy McGee. That's right, D'Arcy from *Life* magazine."

Don Armand, the manager, emerges from his office, a dead ringer for Jonathan Winters from the neck up. He's got a chubby head on an otherwise thin body. Don approaches Dad in a bobble-head-doll kind of way and says, "You're our super star!" and hands him a fresh batch of precious new leads, gold for top earners.

Vince DePalma, a desk sergeant with the Newark PD, and Ed Ruane, an insurance guy by day, stand up and start applauding slowly and accelerate it to a crescendo as other reps stand and clap. This was before the Slow Clap had a name. Dad gives the room a thumbs up, and muses, "That was different…but nice, the 'Slow Clap.'"

He then shuffles through his new leads. While Palumbo and McGee take a rest, his other alter egos, like Grabowski and Kousoulides, wait on the bench, eager to make a pitch when their neighborhoods are called. This was the night that my father gave the Slow Clap its name, on a spring night, 1969, in Newark, New Jersey. The term took a while to catch on.

Back in March when I first moved in with Dad, I had hunch-walked through Branch Brook Park during a cold drizzle, hardly the pastoral stroll I had hoped might brighten my outlook. A man chased a scruffy dog, a leash snaking behind it. An occasional gust tossed detritus across my path. An empty pizza box cartwheeled by. A plastic bottle bounced among the gnarly skeletons of cherry trees.

A month later I was walking in the same place, yet there was a world of difference. A bright sun blessed the park, its 400 acres exploding with pink and white cherry blossoms. True spring was possible even in this forsaken city. The day was strikingly brilliant. I wanted to make promises and swear to keep them, but I had no one to share promises with.

I began dating Natalie, a girl I had met three years earlier at Howell High, brief encounters that seemed inconsequential at the time. I was a senior and she was a junior. Occasionally, we sat at the same table during study hall. Our paths crossed again during a rainy halftime of a football game that I was covering for the Booster. We had run to my car for shelter from the rain. What I remember is the car heater warming us, the smell of damp wool, the innocent chitchat, and easy laughter. When halftime ended, Natalie went back to the bleachers to join her friends, and I went to the sidelines, scribbling damp notes about a forgettable game.

You could look at our recent reconnection as fate, but it was less mysterious. On a weekend back home, Jimmy had arranged for Natalie and me to join him and another girl on a double date. We were off to a great start. I let myself freefall into the new girl's smile. She was tall, with long brown hair and bright brown eyes to match. I liked the slight lisp that made her soft. I liked her casual ironic remarks, which further piqued my curiosity. Everything was going so right, I wondered if my life was occupied by an imposter.

Chapter 44
COLLEGE REDUX

I began my repeat sophomore year with lowered expectations, because my curiosity consistently ushered my attention elsewhere. Take for instance, my experience in Early American Lit. I was in the library researching Jonathan Edwards' sermon, *Sinners in the Hands of an Angry God*. Our assignment was to critique the work's influence on 18th century American culture. I spent an afternoon hunched in a library carrel scrolling through reels of microfiche for material about Edwards and the Puritans. I was about to call it quits, overcome by a gathering stupor of boredom, when lateral curiosity led me to entries about Jesuit missionaries in 17th-century Japan. That's how I time-traveled from colonial New England to Occupation Japan.

◈ ◆ ◈

From that incidental search, I gravitated to articles about postwar Japan. Some articles on the microfiche screen throbbed with words like *rape, mayhem, murder, G.I. riots*. These stories recounted incidents pursuant to Japan's surrender and the arrival of American soldiers. I read accounts about soldiers breaking into an Omori hospital, raping women and girls indiscriminately and murdering an infant. There were reports that in Nagoya, soldiers cut the phone lines and invaded homes, en masse, attacking women, old and young.

Questions lunged from the bilious tint of the microfiche screen. Where was Dad then? The theme of "Sinners in the Hands of an Angry God" bounced around in my head. The worse the secret, the more urgent the need to confess. To God, of course. Or else, according to Edwards, there's hell to pay. What did my father know about the criminality?

I asked Dad about it that night. He told me that he didn't get to Japan until 1947. He was still in high school when the G.I.s lost their minds in Omori and Nagoya. But during his first tour, he had heard rumors about it—references to *the spoils of war*, the veiled excuse for barbarism. The first soldiers assigned to the occupying force were veterans of the most vicious battles in the Pacific. Some arrived in Japan exhausted and paranoid, hardly fit to be peacekeepers.

He said, "It's an explanation, but it doesn't acquit anyone who did those things."

"I'm sorry. You weren't there, and I should've figured it out my own."

"Yeah, you should have."

◈ ◆ ◈

Dad and I don't talk much about the contemporary army, because it generally devolves into an argument about Vietnam. I'm not moved so much by the politics as I am concerned about Jimmy. He's at Fort Wolters, the army's central training center for helicopter flight school. He quit college the same semester I did, but instead of going back to school, decided to enlist before he was drafted. A smooth-talking recruiter talked him into enlisting and signing up for one of the army's most dangerous gigs. He said there'd be great opportunities for helicopter crewmen after the army. If he waited and got drafted, the recruiter told him, he wouldn't have any choices. That logic didn't sound right to me. I send Jimmy my version of a "CARE" package, not the candy-and-cookie, long-letter, and hugs kind, but material I figured he'd appreciate—porn magazines like *Hustler* and *Screw* that will lighten his load. Jimmy will tell me that he became instantly popular when he released custody of the magazines to the rest of the trainees in the barracks. I'll keep fingers crossed that he'll be okay, but he won't need the help. He's always been as good as Houdini getting out of dicey situations. Long story short, he'll wash out of helicopter training due to an ear infection, and ultimately serve the balance of his hitch in Washington, DC. He'll be ensconced in a nine to five desk job, date the beautiful daughter of his commanding officer (on the sly of course), and routinely get weekend passes to go home.

◈ ◆ ◈

I got an A on my assignment for Early American Lit., not bad for a sinner. However, my paper was returned with a firm, but civil note from my professor informing me that excessive absences could lead to a diminution of my final grade. Class participation would be a factor. I liked that he addressed me as *Mr. Fellenberg* in the salutation of his brief message. Despite his warning, my attendance continued to be spotty, and he was true to his word, giving me a C for the course, which could have been an A. I thought he'd give me a mulligan because I was so smart. Yeah, too smart for my own good.

I found a creative outlet at the office of *The Quarterly*, where I loitered, smoked Marlboros and weed, and made sort-of writerly conversation with others of my kind. I enjoyed the atmosphere of hanging out with ne'er-do-wells talking about big ideas, even though our conversations were often superficial—the term *sophomoric* being what it is for a reason. It was an anemic looking group, pale and thin, either from chain-smoking or not getting enough sunlight. Before the semester ended, I'd be appointed submissions editor by the editor-in-chief, which surprised me. I didn't get the vibe that she even liked me—I mean, as a colleague. Tracking submissions required more clerical than creative skills, filing and logging work submitted by eager undergrads who wanted to express themselves but weren't overly conscientious about writing well. The submissions were generally sincere, but often cringe-worthy.

Regardless, I felt good being on the inside, instead of the outside looking in. You could call it a clique, though it was hardly an exclusive one. In fact, those of us on the inside were always eager for company, maybe too much so, because visitors who entered the office often reversed course—hastily, like when you unintentionally barge in on somebody taking a crap.

I made friends with guys who had one-syllable names like Mike, Rog, James, Bob, Ron, Harts, and there was another Bill. I wondered about poet girls who seemed mysterious—or maybe they were just nervous. Or maybe I was the one who was nervous, not having been around girls in numbers, outside of class, for a while. They seemed more complicated than the guys and none had one syllable names, for example: Donna Lynn, Charlene, Elizabeth, Mary Jane, Mercedes,

Candice, and Lulu.

Occasionally, someone would write a poem that truly shined. When others wrote exceptional pieces, I'd pretend to rejoice in their triumph, even though every beat in my tiny black heart clanged with envy.

Talk was cheap, and we talked at length, taking it on faith that whoever appeared to be listening was actually doing so. As we sat in *The Quarterly* office and let another day swoon, James's what-if reincarnation theory resonated for me. He struck me as a fine poet and a complex guy. He had a good sense of humor and bags under his hound-dog eyes--an ironic pairing of characteristics. I had the notion there was a crucifix in his past, and sure enough, he once remarked that he had been an altar boy.

But I digress.

James had a theory in which each person would be destined to live the life of every person he or she had made eye contact with, no matter how brief or incidental. So much as a blink of the eye-to-eye—in the street; in the classroom; at a crosswalk; on horseback; in a bar; or in a hospital emergency room—and after you died, you'd be reborn and consigned to live the life of that person from beginning to end. Vice versa, for the recipient of your blink—*they'd be reborn as you*. It was tacitly understood that James's theory was appropriated, with a twist, from reincarnation beliefs with pedigrees centuries old, but the chatter, boosted by the weed *du jour*, was interesting enough to skip a class and continue bullshitting about the possibilities. When I considered that his reincarnation theory would apply to everyone that I made eye contact with on campus, the idea lost its luster. Living my one life as an ordinary schlub was more than enough, no less living out the lives of a multitude of ordinary schlubs. On the positive side, James's theory might make you more compassionate about the next ordinary schlub you were looking down your nose at. That schlub could have been you in a previous go-round. Considerations like these were elastic and expanded the mind's real estate—like anything else that invoked imagination. You'd get pulled back into reality when someone barked, *Hey, don't Bogart that joint!*

Other deep thoughts from the *Quarterly* office. My friend and fellow poet Bob insisted that in every romantic relationship, one partner had *the Upper Hand*. I admired and envied his poetic skills, but I was skeptical about his advice about romantic relationships, since he confessed that all of his had ended bitterly. I remember his poem that began, "I have a bloody nose from the fist of love." It had good imagery, the clang of oppositional analogy, and just the right touch of humor. Bob's zero-sum game theory of love seemed harsh to me, but then again, when you observed most couples, you could tell pretty easily who held the power. Regardless, wouldn't most prefer to have *the Upper Hand*, rather than having it tied behind their back? In the Good World, we should all aspire to achieve equilibrium in our relationships. But if push came to shove in the Real World, wouldn't most couples say the fifty-fifty proposition was best, but in their heart of hearts prefer to have one percent more?

Although I suffered general ennui—if not stupefaction—from lectures about poets and novelists of yesteryear, *The Quarterly* sponsored opportunities to meet writers who still walked the earth, for example, Hugh Selby, who read passages from *Last Exit to Brooklyn*. I expected a ruddy, blustery in-your-face author that matched the muscular squalor of the characters in his novel. But Selby was bespectacled, quiet and unassuming, almost frail. He came with several guests; family, I thought. During the Q and A after he read, Selby spoke about men and women he based his characters on in *Last Exit*, about their addictions, dreams, and failures. What they hungered for, he said, was basically one thing—and that was MORE. What came to mind was from William Blake's *The Marriage of Heaven and Hell*, where excesses lead to the "palace of wisdom." For me, it felt like sorcery, that an evening with a contemporary writer evoked for me a mystical poet from two centuries past.

Part Four
Love and Other Ephemera

After it has dropped,
the image of a peony
haunts me.
— *Buson*

Chapter 45
WHEN WE WERE BEAUTIFUL

After finishing her freshman year at Glassboro State, Natalie had returned to her family's home in Freehold for the summer. Most weekends, I'd drive home to my grandparents, just minutes from Natalie's. During that summer of 1969, we celebrated at the Blue Moon Tavern, which, until recently, had been a morose and dwindling watering hole for middle-aged men with rheumy eyes and high-mileage livers. Charlie, the owner/bartender, must have had a fuck-it-all moment when he decided to open his doors to anyone who reached puberty. Soon after, the Blue Moon became an ecstatic beehive of emancipation for underage drinkers. Natalie and I were senior citizens compared with some, who may have been hoisting a drink with their babysitters. I was twenty and Natalie was nineteen.

I imagined how it might have been during the old days of speakeasies and Prohibition—drinking illegally and to excess if we so desired. We were high—as much, if not more, from the glee of freedom than from alcohol. But the revelry was short-lived. The cops and the liquor authorities soon padlocked the Blue Moon's doors and put Charlie out of business. It was fun while it lasted.

When September came, we went to our respective schools at opposite ends of New Jersey. We saw each other most weekends. One of the first times I visited her on campus, Natalie got tickets to a Chambers Brothers concert in the college gymnasium. Afterward, we spent the night by a campus pond, melding anonymously into a landscape of undulating sleeping bags, like a field of giant squirming caterpillars. This was a month after Woodstock. Natalie considered the rock festival as historic—more than 400,000 so-called young people crammed together and stranded in the Catskills, convening peacefully while battling adversity in the mud and rain. Getting stoned, naked, and screwing your brains out was excellent karma, but I scoffed that there was social merit in it. Natalie frowned, and I could tell that I disappointed her. I said I was sorry.

The way we had effortlessly achieved agency over our lives seemed magical to me. We wore the mantle of adulthood without suffering the real thing.

When she visited her grandparents in north Jersey, Natalie took me to see a Claes Oldenburg exhibit at MoMA. It was part of the museum's first Pop Art show. I scoffed, couldn't see the point in making a sculpture of a slice of chocolate cake that was as big as a couch, or a hamburger as big as a Volkswagen. Natalie, an art major, said that Oldenburg was making familiar objects strange, provocative, and even funny. Although she explained in a matter-of-fact way, I felt like a giant asshole for having mocked what I didn't understand.

Natalie stayed with me for part of winter break. We went to the movies at the Paramount Theater in Newark, another iconic art-deco theater still barely in business. Just a few patrons were scattered among the Paramount's two thousand seats. We saw George Lazenby in his first and last appearance as Bond—James Bond—Agent 007 in *On Her Majesty's Secret Service*. We sat in the smoking loge in the balcony, because I still smoked. So did James Bond. Natalie and I snuggled, more for body heat than affection, the scant heat only offering an occasional wisp of passing warmth. A few sections away, a clutch of black and brown mothers hung laundry over the railings to dry. They gossiped while they kept an eye on their kids, who scampered up and down the threadbare carpeted aisles. When the credits rolled, the mothers folded their laundry and collected their kids. Natalie and I walked to my car, on a side street off Broad and Market. The area was once the heart of the city, when it had one. Though it was still the jolly season between Christmas and New Year's, there were no merrymakers. Regardless, I felt optimistic, because we spent the first day of 1970 together. I felt that we had opened a portal from what was, to what could be.

Back at Glassboro, Natalie had moved out of the girls' dormitory and into an apartment with two other co-eds. She had a room of her own, which added more glitter to our already sparkly lives. In the spring, we went to the Philadelphia Art Museum to see a retrospective of Matisse's works. She told me that looking at his paintings was like seeing true colors for the first time. I thought, wouldn't it be lovely if Natalie and I always saw each other as if it were for that first time? Going from the sublime to the ridiculously maudlin, we saw *Love Story*, a tearjerker in which the beautiful Ali McGraw dies and utters the iconic line, "Love means never having to say you're sorry." By contrast, it seemed as though I had been born to say I'm sorry. McGraw won an Oscar for it. She had me convinced. *Please, Jenny, don't die*. I sobbed silently.

Although it was nothing to be proud of, I met the standard of mediocrity I set for myself in terms of academic performance, maintaining a cumulative grade average just a notch above a flat C. The saving grace was that I was elected as editor-in-chief of *The Quarterly*, boosting my ego, which may have been too much of a good thing.

Speaking of egos, Gregory Corso was our guest artist that year. He presented his work, or more accurately, a short sample of it. He led off with "Marriage," the crowd-pleasing chestnut that was a ubiquitous entry in anthologies of modern poetry, from which Corso himself said he had made more royalties than anything else he had written. He seemed agitated, as though he wanted to get his reading over with. He loosened up at a post-reading reception at Mike and Rog's apartment. The celebrated poet and his androgynous date shared entre-nous moments with each other, at the exclusion of the rest of us. The couple chuckled, chain-smoked and let their ashes drop on the floor. Regardless of Corso's aloofness and lack of manners, we were enthralled to be in the same room drinking Mateus and smoking weed with a figure who had rubbed shoulders and probably other body parts with Beats like Ginsberg, Kerouac, Burroughs, and others. There was an awkward moment when one of our English professors recounted a story to our guest, apropos of nothing, that when he was a boy, he had skated on a pond in Paterson with Allen Ginsberg. Corso let the professor wax on about that encounter, until he squelched what was becoming a saga and said, "Isn't that *something*," allowing an icy smirk to float from his face before he turned his back. I felt bad for the teacher who had done a fine job energetically teaching "The Art of Poetry," a survey course I had taken. He deserved at least some respect from Corso.

⋄ ♦ ⋄

I had silent and unconsummated crushes on the poet girls who floated by *The Quarterly*, as well as others whose names I never knew—the girl with huge blue eyes who worked the ticket booth in the student union building, the skinny senior who wore bells around her neck, waist, and ankles, and other co-eds. They formed the ephemera of my alternate fantasy life as I dozed with eyes half open in intermediate German, Victorian Lit., and physical anthropology. This didn't mean I loved Natalie less. That said, there was another passage in Blake's *Marriage of Heaven and Hell* that I wondered about: "He who desires but acts not, breeds pestilence." I mean, was that the mystic poet's green light for fooling around?

In my *real* life, I sent Natalie letters and poetry. She illustrated one of my poems and bound it into a book, calligraphed the words, and adorned it with watercolors, line drawings, and collage. It was beautiful, the book jacket made of purple linen, her favorite color. Natalie's clothes, accessories, and decorative sensibilities spoke purple. She even arranged for students from her college's industrial arts program to repaint, in purple, her 1960-something Plymouth Valiant. I recognized that *The Purple Book* commemorated us. It was the Lascaux cave painting of our adventure from the very beginning. I kept it close by, even after I pushed our relationship off a cliff. Maybe what we had was too good for me.

I had my reasons. The bedrock certainty of the love I felt for Natalie was shaken by tremors of slights and betrayals, real and imagined. There was the time my car broke down, and I thumbed rides to Glassboro, mostly in the rain. It took me half the day to get ten miles from Natalie's place. I called and asked her to pick me up, but instead of eagerly saying yes, she said, "Couldn't you hitchhike the rest of the way?" I did that, then put it in my museum of grudges. Why didn't she pick me up? I don't remember what she said. It made sense and I didn't make a big deal about it, but it dug into me like an earwig. My suspicious mind created dots and connected them.

Then there was the time Natalie went to a pool party in her apartment complex. I passed on going to it, having just arrived after the long drive. I could have been hung over. When she returned, her long hair still wet, Natalie regaled me with how much fun the party was and how she swam *topless* and how it was such a *liberating* feeling! Well, I had a feeling, too, and, in fact several of them. First, one of Grandma's sarcastic expressions bounced around in my head—*Well, isn't that just dandy!* Disturbing images flickered in my mind's eye—Natalie stepping out of the pool, her righteous white globes bobbing to the cheers of horny campus geeks from the apartment complex and from the surrounding hick towns and villages in south Jersey.

I could say to myself, that it was betrayal, clear and simple—Natalie and her breasts had cheated on me! Jealousy, the green-eyed monster, could mess up a good thing. But the complaints I harbored were pretexts for what was the underlying truth.

Natalie had been my bridge out of boyhood that connected to a promising life together that came next. But it started to come apart when the certainty of the love I felt was changed, like a shape shifter. When I became editor-in-chief of the college literary magazine, my head began to swell with writerly self-importance. I met the New Girl about that time in my senior year. I broke up with Natalie at Christmas after she flew home to her family, who had recently moved to Houston. Instead of a present, I sent her a letter telling her that we were done. It would be easier on her that way, I told myself. She wrote back, desperate and sad, scoffing at the notion that a math major and I could ever be well suited for each other. Looking back, how could I not be ashamed? Although I hadn't abandoned a sinking boat full of women and children like Lord Jim, my betrayal and failure to do the right thing seemed cast of similar cowardice.

I ended up marrying the new girl, Lorraine. Natalie had asked me to return *The Purple Book* after our breakup, but I had declined—thoughtlessly rubbing salt into a fresh wound. I held on to the book through years of bad behavior in two marriages and the time in between.

Chapter 46
NOTHING LASTS FOREVER, MUCH LESS LOVE

Each time the New Girl came into my life, the rush I got was like betting everything on the longest shot in the race and then watching it romp past the finish line like a sure thing. The threat of desperation, combined with a chance at redemption, hummed inside me as if I had chugged a tall cocktail of adrenaline with a splash of holy water. For me, the all-in part of new love was like a seductive noose. I swung in the air blindly feeling the euphoria and exaltation of emerging love, endorphins in my brain setting off fireworks of pleasure and happiness. It felt as close to immortality as you can get, a touch of eternity. It didn't matter that I would die someday—just like every other human and living thing. Under the circumstances of emergent love, it was just a detail.

I met Lorraine when she occasionally stopped by *The Quarterly* office to hang out with the art editor, Mary Jane. They were both attractive, but Lorraine had that certain something, that *je ne sais quoi*, that made me crazy about her from the word go. Yes, she was a math major, but there was an artistic pulse there, and I wanted to find out about all her pulses. Lorraine, with her blue eyes and long chestnut hair and perfectly proportioned body, reminded me of Michelle Philips, flowerchild of the Mamas and Papas, ethereal counterpart to Mama Cass.

Within a month I was writing poems for and about her, and when a chapbook of my poems was published, I dedicated it to her. For my birthday, she gave me two books, a copy of the *I Ching* and the just released new edition of *The Yale Series of Younger Poets*. How cool was that? It was a delicious time for us—a confection. I finished my senior year four credits shy of graduation, which I'd make up for in the coming year. Despite that shortfall, I got hired as a copywriter, right off the bat, for a small editorial company in Bloomfield. Their principal client was a travel guide distributed nationally for the vacationing public who traveled by automobile. Six volumes, each representing a different region of the country, were published annually, and featured ratings of restaurants and hotels, as well as write-ups about attractions worthy of visiting. It wasn't poetry, but it was writing, even if it was swill. After living together in a cozy apartment for nearly a year, we were married the day after Thanksgiving in 1973, a civil ceremony performed by a judge in Bloomfield, New Jersey. It was thumbs up from every perspective.

◈ ◆ ◈

That was then, and three years later, this is how bad it gets. Because of my marital transgressions, Lorraine began to amputate me from her life in decisive cuts, the way a confident surgeon removes a tumor. The procedure began when she asked me to leave our beach cottage in Bradley Beach, just south of Asbury Park. We had moved from Montclair in July to save our marriage and make a *fresh start*.

I don't remember the details of how she broke up with me, but I was under the mistaken impression that it was temporary. I think Lorraine said that she needed "time and space to think," which to me, meant a week or so. I replied that I appreciated her need for alone time, but my motives were mixed. It would be a welcome break *for me*—a vacation opportunity, if you will, from the rigors of pretending I was doing something productive. I no longer had a job, because I was ostensibly a full-time writer—unpublished, but working hard on my craft. Given the opportunity for a few days of leisure on my own, I fantasized about laughs at the bars, fun at the races, fishing, and general goofing off. I said I'd give Jimmy a call and ask if I could crash at his place for a few nights. She said that would work for her.

A few days later, she visited me at Jimmy's to tell me it was over. She described a relationship she had formed with a colleague at her high school as an *emotional* connection. Mr. Lover Boy, like her, was a math teacher, and they were doing a number on me. She wanted a divorce. It took me a while to wrap my head around the news, but now that Lorraine was fixing to dump me, I felt betrayed and hurt, yet numb at the same time—like being embalmed alive, just conscious enough to wish I were dead. I was righteously indignant.

I overheard noisy chatter from a mocking voice, as the word divorce ricocheted inside my head and crowed, *What happened to you having the so-called upper hand?*

"I said divorce." said Lorraine, "Aren't you listening?"

"What?" I blurted. "We're supposed to be life partners! Wait! Did you have sex with him?"

"No," she said.

"Have you kissed him?"

"Yes," she admitted.

"Oh, Christ!" I cried. "How could you do this … to us?"

"Bill, enough is enough. There's more to a marriage than … this. I want something more."

More. There it was again, for crying out loud. How ironic, I thought, I was the one who longed for more, who mutated William Blake's counsel, as if he really meant that *the road of alcoholism, adultery, and general malingering leads to the palace of wisdom.*

"More? Not enough? Was it the sex?"

"That's got nothing to do with this."

"Wait! One more question. Who was better, him or me?"

She shook her head, exasperated, well past the last straw.

⁂

Although I felt betrayed, in my heart of hearts I knew in some twisted and clumsy way I engineered the ruin of us. I couldn't blame Lorraine for wanting out. How could she not, considering my behavior? But I balked when she said I'd soon be served with papers accusing me of *extreme mental cruelty.*

"But what about irreconcilable differences? That's how normal estranged couples divorce," I said.

"Because it takes a year's separation before a divorce can be considered due to irreconcilable differences—three months for extreme mental cruelty."

She wanted to make me a stranger, practically overnight. I thought, gee whiz, who's being extremely cruel now? Lorraine crossed her arms and scowled, her face twisting into a flinty aspect I hadn't seen before. I relented and said I wouldn't contest the grounds for divorce.

However, I had one condition, that when it was final, Lorraine would write me a letter that testified that I wasn't a *monster*.

The thing was, I wasn't so sure myself. I mean, that I wasn't extremely cruel. I had draped myself in the vices enjoyed by your common reprobate husbands—drinking, gambling, cheating, and mistreating her on the *slant*, cloaking my meanness in offhand comments or gestures that provided me the benefit of *credible deniability*. Mental cruelty was apt nomenclature for my behavior. No, I wasn't Jack the Ripper or your neighborhood wife beater, rather just your run-of-the-mill dumb fuck and occasional nasty prick. For a fleeting moment, I thought she might agree to moderate mental cruelty, if there was such a thing.

"I'm not a monster," I said to Lorraine, trying to convince myself, as well as her. Yes, I was the dumb fuck and occasional nasty prick who had squandered the second chance that she had generously offered to me, the second chance that was going to save our marriage.

◆◆◆

During our last wobbly year, I was all in on making a fresh start after I blubbered, in a drunken jag, that I had had an *affair*. It was a cringe-worthy confession. I asked Lorraine to forgive me, which she did. After several intense conversations, we were committed to starting over. We'd move to the Jersey Shore, near my old stomping grounds. I'd quit my job as an assistant copy editor and apply for unemployment. Lorraine would work full-time as a teacher, which would free me to write short stories, maybe a chapbook of poetry, or better yet, a novel. The fresh start was full of promise, but I did what assholes usually do with second chances.

I worked honestly at the writing, but it was hard. My prospects seemed hopeless. The rejection letters, first from such august titles as *the Atlantic* and *the New Yorker*, were now spiraling down the food chain to the bottom-feeders. Romance rags, third-tier soft-porn magazines, and self-described avant-garde little magazines spurned my work. After a couple of months of rejections, I abandoned the labors of writing and turned instead to the pretense of writing, which is harder than you might think. After Lorraine left home for school, I'd sit at my desk and furiously type whatever came into my head. It was good enough for Andre Breton, Virginia Wolfe, James Joyce, and other modernists, wasn't it? My dive into the so-called stream of consciousness was a bastardization of the real thing. I raced into flurries of automatic writing and littered the area around my desk with crumpled-up balls of copy, evidence of a day's work. By noon, I'd be free to malinger the day away, betting on the ponies, or dowsing at the bars or smoking weed with my cronies. When Lorraine came home from school, I planned to be at my desk so she would find me looking writerly, hunched over my typewriter, ashtray full, crumpled balls of ersatz prose and poetry scuttling about the spare-room floor.

Even the pretense of being a writer was eventually beyond my reach. Such was the coup disgrace of my marriage. Such was my self-loathing that I would have divorced myself if there was legal remedy.

The road to excess leads to the palace of wisdom. I dropped a tab of acid on one of the last nights I stayed at the cottage. Not much was happening. I examined The Face in the bathroom mirror. Fascinated, I watched The Face age fast-forward—creases hatching on my skin, hair whitening and thinning, the eyes turning rheumy and lost into those of an old man's. I had the sense to turn away. I didn't want to partner with my corpse, just to get a glimpse of The Undiscovered Land. I didn't want to die, not yet.

Now, our marriage is over, and I am drunk, and my heart is broken, just the way I like it. I was feeling sorry for myself at a college bar in Long Branch, thinking about horning into a conversation that three girls and a guy were having in a booth across from me. They were waxing on about the nature of love, massaging the subject like it was a prized Kobe steer on its final stop before the slaughterhouse. How many times have I heard the tired argument about the difference between being *in love* and *loving* someone? Blah, bah, blah. It's a difference without a distinction. You could split hairs like this all night long with lugubrious deep thinkers, one pitcher of beer after the next, and be no wiser for it.

I leaned in toward the booth and cleverly interjected. I said that I was perfectly capable of being *in love* with *love*, and *loving love* all at the same time. I smiled, but apparently it came across as a leer, judging from the collective revulsion from the booth. I was the source of one cringe-worthy moment after the other. I heard one of the girls ask her friends something like, "Do you know the old guy?"

Old guy? Just for the record, for Christ's sake, I considered telling them I was barely 28, still in my prime, but thought the better of it. I waited a minute or two before I attempted a graceful, or at least invisible, exit from the bar. I did the loser shuffle in the wake of their murmurs and nasally repressed chuckles.

I forgot to mention that I finally got my sports car. It was a 1968 yellow Triumph TR250, with a black racing stripe on the hood. I liked looking at it, but only from a distance. Up close, not so much. Frankly, it was kind of a mess. I sold it for three hundred bucks.

❦ ◆ ❦

I vowed to build a new life. I had my freedom and my wits. As my grandmother once said, "You're free, white, and 21, you can do anything." Not exactly, but at least I was free.

Now, I vowed to find a new job, get in shape, and fly straight. My conditioning came as I pedaled my bike the 30-mile round-trip to Freehold Raceway several times a week, fueled by fantasies of big winnings on the way there, and grinding out the grim trip back full of beer, smoke, and rage.

> Dear Bill, October 1976
>
> Last Friday I sat in a courtroom and heard a totally disjointed description of our marriage. The lawyer speaks of an "incident" that occurred in summer of '73 and then ties this to others in the winter of '73 and spring '75. The drinking incidents and the humiliation involved constitute mental cruelty he maintains and when the judge agrees I am granted a divorce.
>
> The day has quite an effect on me. For two days prior I have had a terrific headache, and I'm having trouble with my eyes. In fact, I see an ophthalmologist immediately following the court appearance. (He finds only a slight disorder.) My thoughts keep returning to this day because it is such an unfair way to look at a marriage. Although the incidents occurred, I know that you had no intention of hurting or embarrassing me. These were isolated incidents which hurt deeply, but which were in no way characteristic of our entire marriage. You were always good to me and very considerate, I will always maintain that.
>
> The problems we had I think related to communication and the lack of depth in our relationship. We each prided ourselves in how much we left the other alone, to be their own individual, without ever realizing how much we deprived each other of possible growth. Individuals grow strong while the bond deepens in a truly communicative relationship. I know that I was particularly deficient in this area. I really thought I was doing the right thing by leaving you alone to be a creative artist. But I know now, in the end, that I was only hurting myself and our relationship.

I hope you understand, Bill. It's taken me a long time to understand myself and I'm truly sorry that I never knew you better. I loved you very much, but now I know that there must have been so much more for me to love.

Always, Lorraine

Chapter 47
WALKING WOUNDED

Although I was still among the walking wounded, I made a date with a lovely girl I used to work with, only to bail out painfully late. I probably sounded drunk, which I was. I called from a phone booth inside Tierney's Bar. Rod Stewart wailed "Maggie Mae" in the background, as I claimed I was coming down with a bug.

This is how you do things when you're an asshole.

Sorry.

The next call I made was to Donna, and I made a new date for that very night. I knew through the grapevine that she was single again. We were friends in college. We had worked together on *The Quarterly* when I was editor-in-chief, and she was poetry editor. Although she had had a crush on me, I didn't think of her romantically. At the time, I was going with my second Forever Girl.

The way I remembered it, Donna and I had shared a comfort zone, warm and well-lit by laughter and mischief. After a raucous staff dinner for *The Quarterly* that celebrated a milestone, a milestone which I've since forgotten, we walked out of the restaurant together in a recklessly cheerful state. Apropos of nothing, I hoisted Donna over my head, then spun the little thing around, her arms and legs splaying apart like helicopter blades. After a couple of turns, I gently set her back on her feet. I think our pas de deux surprised us both. As Donna staggered to straighten out her skirt and blouse, we laughed and went our separate ways.

Did it happen like that? Had I been endowed with superpowers, albeit temporarily?

That was when we were in the salad days of our twenties. Since then, she had married and divorced, just like me. Did she remember that night? I wanted to reconnect with Donna right then and there. On the rebound from a month-old marriage breakup, I worried that she'd perceive my enthusiasm as the desperation it was. But it was just a date, not a big deal. Besides, she had quickly said yes.

The date evolved as a mini reunion with half a dozen mutual friends from school.

Neglecting them, Donna and I caught up. We engaged briefly in the forgivable sport of turning our ex-spouses into caricatures, sharing the CliffsNotes version of our failed marriages. Her ex-husband was a jerk. My ex-wife didn't understand me. I was grateful that Donna and I avoided a lengthy postmortem of our respective deceased relationships, although it had a morbidly seductive appeal.

We kept the autopsy brief and moved on. Much had happened since I last saw Donna. She had taught eighth grade English in a public school for a year, followed by another year teaching modern dance in a tony private school for girls. After an inner voice told her to become a rock star, she joined a band and reinvented herself as Ruby Dubois, writing lyrics and performing in an otherwise all-male band called Ruby and Dykes, a handle appropriated from R Crumb's Zap Comix. Briefly, the band soared with promise, secured gigs in semi-famous venues in the Village, then imploded and fell back to Earth.

Apropos of music, Woodstock poked into the conversation. I expected to hear the familiar trope again about how the festival changed the world, if not saved it, with three days of peace, love, and music, *et cetera, et cetera, et cetera*. But wait! She was actually there! What I remember most was the anecdote Donna told me about her departure from the festival. For some reason, she had to leave a day before the festival ended. Donna had come with her kid sister, Jilda, who brought one of her friends.

After they packed their gear, she slowly nosed her parent's car through a hundred acres of farmland that had vecome a trough of sodden mud. She zig-zagged the Chrysler between collapsed tents, abandoned cars, stoned music lovers, and scattered debris. At times, all seemed lost, the rear tires spinning vainly in the muck, going nowhere. It did not deter her, and Donna persevered. Far on the hill above them, Donna had seen a solitary figure from the very start of her journey, who like a sentry, seemed to be assessing the car's progress through the long, arduous pilgrimage. As they reached the top of the hill, the long-haired watchman, jeans splashed with mud, approached her car and gave her a signal to roll down her window. He shook his head, as if he had just watched a meteor crossing the sky, and said, "Baby, I don't know what you're on. But whatever it is, it's beautiful!"

This was the emblematic take-away I got from my first date with Donna.

After a short career teaching, and an exciting, but brief fling in show business, Ruby was now sweeping floors in a beauty parlor. I was back to my old job writing blurbs for a travel guide and among other responsibilities, inspecting and rating motel bathrooms, checking out toilets for cleanliness. I said something to Donna about broken dreams. She smiled wistfully and said she had no complaints and why should she?

After our dinner party ended, I walked her home.

"So, what do you want?" she asked, "I mean, from your life."

"That's a good question." I said, seriously considering it.

In that moment, I remembered being touched by profound happiness when I was a kid.

After a long, anxious separation my family was reunited—the Japanese shopgirl, the American soldier, and me. That pier in Seattle. The rollicking plane ride in a storm. The perfect sky the next day. We started out fresh in America. I didn't know what would happen next. But rather than fearing uncertainty, I sensed adventure and welcomed it. Maybe that's what I wanted now—to recover that fearlessness, that pluck, that chutzpah. I couldn't describe it to Donna. Anything I said would fall short of what I meant. You'd have to write a book to tell it right. Instead, because I didn't answer, the long silence struck both of us as comical. Maybe it was from the giddiness of a first date, and I croaked out a series of funny things that made her laugh so hard, she told me to stop, because she'd pee in her pants. I felt like a god. The feeling was rare and silly, like lightning bolts bursting from my inside out. Fireworks. Donna's eyes shimmered like two blue planets. I resisted the impulse to tell her everything I knew, funny or not.

In fact, I considered saying that I was sorry, not for anything I had done—yet. We had been dating for all of three hours. I thought I might apologize—in advance—for what I was bound to do sooner or later. The idea of preemptive apologies seemed brilliant, if just for an instant. Instead, I decided to wait until I actually did or said something reprehensible. It never took long.

I took Donna's hand. She didn't resist. Who was holding on tighter? I couldn't say.

"You didn't tell me what you wanted," she said.

"You go first. Tell me what you want," I said.

She was mulling it over when I began to hear a faint, but familiar rumbling in the distance— like a typhoon or a runaway train. It was a warning, but still far away.

"Did you hear that?" I asked.

But she was still pondering the previous question.

"Hmm. What do I want? I know it sounds crazy," she said, "but I could really go for some Japanese."

What did she mean? Or did I just imagine it? Regardless, I felt grateful, because, as peculiar as the night was, it felt promising, and there was no deadline to declare what we wanted. Besides, Donna seemed to know her way around.

Chapter 48
MARRIAGE PROPOSAL, THE HARD WAY

I had notions of being suited for more and bigger things than marriage. Besides, I already had had a marriage that crashed and burned, and so had Donna. But in my less grandiose mind, I suspected that fantasies of greatness (or at least better deals), rarely ended on a mountain top, but more likely wound up on a sour couch with a lonely beer. You could verify that destiny by a brief survey of the midnight barstools of America.

On a lovely July day in 1978, we were driving from a happy weekend in Vermont, returning to New Jersey. We had begun living together soon after our first date two years earlier. Recently, we were having more and frequent conversations about marriage, all of which were initiated by Donna. When I said I was perfectly happy with the way things were, she began a full-court press of arguments for getting married, a probing interrogation of why I resisted the idea. I pulled into a rest area off the Interstate, just to catch my breath. I was having an anxiety attack.

"I don't understand. What's the problem? This is what people do," she said.

I invoked the time-worn *love-doesn't-need-a-piece-of-paper* defense. "Aren't we doing fine, the way things are now? I mean, we're happy and great together. We don't need a piece of paper to make it official. Our love stands on its own merits, right?"

"I haven't got the time you're wasting. You don't get it. This is your relationship, this is it. I am it. It's not about something or someone else you imagine is out there. This is about us. Marry me."

After several iterations of the same logic, it took me by surprise, the clarity of why I should take this girl—and forever. Sure, there was an element of *or else* in the argument for marriage, but sometimes, you need that kind of feminine motivation.

For most of us, the sum of our lives will not hinge on a righteous act of courage, an opportunity to evacuate children from a sinking ship, or a single stroke of brilliance that in a moment, will save thousands of lives. Except for a handful, there is no kingdom to save, and no heinous wrong to right. For most of us, our tests will come from making a vow, and keeping our word, and doing consistently what has to be done, whether bathing a child, facing someone else's bully, consoling an elder, or having the conviction to stand up to a man who does not trust himself and make him understand you mean it when you say, "Choose me, choose me now. We'll have no regrets."

Chapter 49
SOULS OLD AND NEW

Today began innocently enough in the garden, the place where things have gone bad for men since the beginning. There's a snake in here, too. He was probably here first.

A passing thunderstorm's effect has been a painterly one, burnishing the landscape with an other-worldly sheen. We were gathering small branches and debris that had fallen into the flower garden that's at the foot of a venerable white pine in our backyard. Beyond, there's a barn built circa 1770, a pond, and eight acres of rough grass and wild flowers. This was an unlikely setting for an argument that started about one thing and eventually ended up about something entirely different, which in this case was about which one of us was the older soul. According to Donna this was my first time around. She told me that I'm a new soul—green, raw, and unwise. I'm bright, but compromised.

"And what's that supposed to mean?" I asked, somewhat sarcastically. It's irksome to me that she's somehow assumed a position as a registrar of souls.

"Oh, you know, having to do with wisdom, inner peace, the power of tranquility. That sort of thing."

"As compared to whom?"

Donna named several internationally prominent figures as old souls, those having experienced this mortal coil more than once, even myriad times. It's tough enough being married to a psychoanalyst, no less a reincarnated Mahatma Gandhi. But what I found galling was that she considered several friends in her circle as old souls, but not me.

"How many times do you think I've been around?" I asked.

"The fact that you're turning spiritual understanding and wisdom into a competition speaks for itself. This," she says, cutting down some tulips for a bouquet, "is your first try. You're an even newer soul than I had imagined! Getting jealous because you don't make my old souls list."

"I'm curious—how many times have you been around?"

"Who's counting? But since you ask, I think I've been around several times. I tolerate your nonsense. That takes patience. And the deal breaker for you entering any circle of wisdom is your anger. It's your default position, a no-win, no wisdom position. I'd say you need to straighten that out this time around."

She really knows how to piss me off.

"Do you want to be right, or do you want to be happy?" Donna asks.

If I've heard that once, I've heard it a hundred times. It's supposed to be a rhetorical question, but I see beyond the binary options.

"Why not right *and* happy?" I ask. After she expels a dramatic sigh, I continue, "I mean, that's pretty much your state of being, why shouldn't it be mine? You might step back to self-reflect and consider *that* possibility."

After another heartfelt sigh, she turns her back and continues to work the soil. Pushing her buttons is temporarily satisfying, but there's no enduring happiness in it. Still, I've got to say not making her old soul's team really galls me—treating me like I was an *untermensch*, when I've overcome so much. Born in far-away Nippon, a child that was a stranger in a strange land wherever he went, abandoned by Mom, neglected by Dad, growing up as a so-called banana, yellow on the outside, white on the inside, quasi-high-functioning alcoholic and compulsive gambler, I've 12-stepped my way into sobriety, howled through years of psychotherapy, *et cetera, et cetera, et cetera*. Also, I'm the one who's read Herman Hesse's *Siddhartha*. Yeah, and I'm a VP of a university for Christ's sake! Sounds like the profile of a soul who's back for a third or fourth helping, don't you think?

Okay. I acknowledge I've got anger issues. It usually works against me. In the aftermath of my anger, I become the remorseful beast that ushers itself down the ramp and through the gate to my own personal slaughterhouse. Or something like that. Still, all things considered, I've listened to Donna when it counts. Although on impulse, I'm impelled to resist and disagree, but usually come around to her point of view.

There's that trope about the Zen master who says that a snowflake never falls in the wrong place. It's a comfort to see intentionality in what some say is the random universe, governed by chaos. I look at Donna in our garden. She is all hat, hands, and knees, working the earth as if in praise, supplication, or both. The birds and insects are busy. The sun and clouds preside over our industry. How can my breath and heart be so still and so full? I look at my wife and think of my son. We three have landed in the right place. This is how Here and Now looks and feels, my first time around.

THE END

Epilogue

EPILOGUE

On this summer day, I sit by my pond atop a sloping meadow. I watch wisps of clouds drift across the sky, and they are reflected in the pond, as are the barn swallows skimming its surface.

The scene is quite beautiful and tranquil, but there are disturbances from within.

I need to reckon with the unavoidable calculus that there's far less time ahead for me than there is behind. Time rules. It thrashes forward as we pursue our worldly ambitions. But when we remember, time loses its grip on us. When that happens, it's memory that rules, free to dictate its own terms, shoving time back and forth or freezing it. I'm hooked on remembering. Livestreaming and multi-channeled, memory assays the past from its perch in the ever-moving Here and Now. The question is, what do you want from it?

I've read that the universe not only holds all information that ever was or will be but is the physical record of matter, energy, and all activity across an infinite expanse and eternity. Memory resides both inside and outside of us. Surely, we invoke it – memory is our guide, counselor, and interpreter. It can be the kindest mother, reminding us of our shared humanity or it can come at us, an unwelcome guest, gate crasher, judge, betrayer. For some, it is the unrelenting pulse of the eternal grudge.

I believe we are obliged to seek witnesses to confirm our remembering. It is to these witnesses that we blurt out our so-called truths, our promises, appeals, and lies. We call out to our confidantes in our dreams, murmur in an ear in our lovemaking, and perhaps, in the end, stare upward at our last gasp from our death beds.

In memory's twilight, we may feel less than who we hoped to be. I say, look again. There's more to see than what meets your eye.

Do I invoke memory, or does it call me? I gaze up at the cirrus clouds, forming, evaporating, and reforming. Memory kidnaps me to elsewhere. On this summer's day I see my father, the ruins of him, the ribs of the Colossus as I once imagined him. Looking up at the clouds, I wish to remember more than I am able, to reach back, and touch the cheek of the woman I lost as a boy. Back then, I could not grasp why she left and why I stayed. Did she abandon me, or did I abandon her? Some would call it unfinished business. The kind that ghosts come back for.

ACKNOWLEDGMENTS

I was fortunate to be the beneficiary of extraordinary support from friends and family as I wrote *Sayonara Cowboy*, a story made infinitely better by a committed posse who saddled up at different points in its development. For keeping my literary aim steady and true, I will be forever grateful to Dianne Maccario, Lisa Weiss, Gray Basnight, Janice Meyerson, and Ray Scheindlin.

Thank you, Ramona Jan, for the happy trails you blazed with Yarnslingers, the memoir writers group you founded. I rode with Ramona, slinging our yarns from one town to another in the far west—the western Catskills, that is. It was an experience, without which, the Sayonara Cowboy may never have left the ranch.

Speaking of another posse, I wish to tip my hat to Cathy Ara and her Stoneridge Writers group for sharing their insights and critiques during monthly roundups. I became a better writer because of the two years I met with the group.

For this manuscript to become a book required a publisher who takes and gives chances to new writers. I thank Robert Canipe of Redhawk Publications for giving my book a chance, and I'm deeply grateful to Redhawk's wonderful staff for turning *Sayonara Cowboy*'s chance into a sure thing. Thank you, Patty Thompson, Melanie Zimmermann, Tim Peeler, and Katherine Hickman!

Thank you, Greg Triggs, for busting doors open for me and wrangling my doubts when they were after me. The friendship and encouragement of this writer whom I respect and admire made a huge difference.

Thank you, Donna Lynn Fellenberg, for making sure that the only shooting I'll do is straight from the heart, and that we stay steady on the trail. You are my True North.

Finally, I remember John P. Roberts, professor of English at Montclair State College. He saw something special in me and encouraged me to write. That's where it all began for me, and I wish he were here to receive my thanks.

ABOUT WILLIAM YUKIKAZU FELLENBERG

Born in Yokohama, Japan, Bill immigrated to America when he was four. He resided in New Jersey most of his life. After enjoying a career in marketing and communications, primarily in the arts and in higher education, Bill pursued his long-held dream to write full-time. *Sayonara Cowboy* is his memoir about his childhood in Post-War Japan and transition to life in the USA.

Bill frequently presents his work with Yarnslingers, the writers cooperative of memoirists in the Upper Delaware River Valley. He has also been featured at readings with the Hudson River Poets of Upstate New York. His poems and short stories have appeared in *Clementine Unbound*, *The Tower Journal*, *The Narrowsburg Literary Gazette*, and other literary magazines.

He retired as vice president of university advancement at New Jersey City University in 2014, where he headed a division responsible for fundraising, alumni relations, marketing and advertising, and public relations. Before joining NJCU, Bill was executive director of the International Institute of New Jersey, a service and advocacy organization for refugees and immigrants. His career in the arts and cultural institutions was highlighted by appointments as director of membership at the Museum of Modern Art; deputy director of The Montclair Art Museum; and director of communications at the American Society of Interior Designers. He has an MBA from Rutgers University and a BA in English from Montclair State College.

Bill lives in Pennsylvania—near a lake, deep in the woods—under the collective spell of his wife, Donna, a retired psychoanalyst, and his two tuxedo cats, Bella and Carmine. When he hears music in those woods, it comes from his son Miles, and daughter-in-law Alice, playing four hands on the piano —the music of Ravel and many other magicians.

Made in the USA
Columbia, SC
24 April 2024